OFFICIAL

Netscape
JavaScript
BOOK

Netscape
JavaScript
BOOK

The Nonprogrammer's
Guide to Interactive
Web Pages

An imprint of
Ventana Communications
Group

PETER KENT
JOHN KENT

Official Netscape JavaScript Book: The Nonprogrammer's Guide to Interactive Web Pages
Copyright © 1996 by Peter Kent

First Edition 9 8 7 6 5 4 3 2 1
Printed in the United States of America

Published and distributed to the trade by Ventana Communications Group, Inc., P.O. Box 13964, Research Triangle Park, NC 27709-3964
919/544-9404   FAX 919/544-9472

Limits of Liability and Disclaimer of Warranty

The authors and publisher of this book have used their best efforts in preparing the book and the programs contained in it. These efforts include the development, research, and testing of the theories and programs to determine their effectiveness. The authors and publisher make no warranty of any kind, expressed or implied, with regard to these programs or the documentation contained in this book.

The authors and publisher shall not be liable in the event of incidental or consequential damages in connection with, or arising out of, the furnishing, performance or use of the programs, associated instructions and/or claims of productivity gains.

Trademarks
Trademarked names appear throughout this book. Rather than list the names and entities that own the trademarks or insert a trademark symbol with each mention of the trademarked name, the publisher states that it is using the names only for editorial purposes and to the benefit of the trademark owner with no intention of infringing upon that trademark.

ABOUT THE AUTHORS

John Kent of London, England, owns CISS Ltd., a software development company. He programs in most of the popular languages, including SQL, Visual Basic, and C++ on mainframes, PCs, and UNIX systems.

Peter Kent of Lakewood, Colorado, is a freelance writer and consultant with 15 years experience in technical writing and software-interface design. Among his 25 book credits is *PGP Companion for Windows* (Ventana).

Acknowledgments

Thanks John, couldn't have done it without you! Thanks also to my wife and kids, who can now go on vacation.
—Peter Kent

I'd like to thank my wife, Jayne for everything. I'd also like to thank my brother and coauthor, Peter. It was tough but we got there in the end.
—John Kent

DEDICATION

Dedicated to our mother, Muriel Kent (1920-1995), the family's first author.

Contents

Chapter 14 Controlling Windows & Documents With JavaScript 277

Chapter 15 Using JavaScript With Frames 315

Introduction

Welcome to the *Official Netscape JavaScript Book*, the introduction to JavaScript. This book has been written for the non-programmer, for the hundreds of thousands of Web developers who know how to create Web pages, who've heard so much about JavaScript, and who want to see what it's all about.

You may never have programmed anything before, but that needn't stop you from getting involved in JavaScript. While JavaScript can get quite complicated—and the most sophisticated of JavaScript applets require a programmer's skills—there are many things you can do without wearing pocket protectors, drinking Jolt, and eating nothing but donuts. You don't have to turn into a programmer to use JavaScript.

We've structured this book in such a way that programming concepts are introduced slowly, in a way designed to teach non-programmers what they need to know to get started in JavaScript. We've also provided many scripts that you can take and drop straight into your own Web pages—modify them slightly and you'll have little JavaScripts that you can use right away. You can type these scripts from the page, or you can go to the book's Online Companion (at http://www.vmedia.com/support/javascript) and copy the scripts off our example Web pages (each example in the book has an Online Companion reference number to help you find the correct page). You can even download the sample pages off the Online Companion and onto your hard disk (we've provided these pages in .ZIP, .SEA, and .TAR so you can grab them all at once).

WHAT DO YOU NEED?

In order to use this book, you need several things. First, you must have a JavaScript-compatible browser—that is, a World Wide Web browser with the capability of executing JavaScripts. At the time of this writing, Netscape Navigator 2.0 or later (always get the most recent available, as it will include bug fixes and enhancements) was available. You can download that from http://www.netscape.com/ and http://www.netscape.home.com//. By the time you read this, other JavaScript-compatible browsers may be available; but note that this book is based on Netscape. In the same way that different browsers display HTML pages in slightly different ways, different JavaScript browsers will almost certainly act in slightly different ways. It's inevitable that different development teams will introduce different bugs and features.

You also need at least *some* knowledge of HTML; this is not a book about HTML. We have assumed that you understand how to create Web pages—when we talk about HTML forms, for instance, or paragraph formats, we don't describe them in detail. When we show you how to use JavaScript to carry out an action when the user clicks on a button, we're not going to explain everything there is to know about forms. We have enough ground to cover without worrying about these basics. We'll explain just the HTML information required to do the job. If you need more information, you'll have to refer to a book on HTML (such as *HTML Publishing on the Internet* by Brent Heslop and Larry Budnick, Ventana) or HTML online documentation.

You'll almost certainly have a connection to the Internet, too, though it's not absolutely essential. Once you have the browser and this book, you can do everything on your hard disk if you wish. But if you have an Internet connection, you'll be able to go to the

Online Companion, as well as view JavaScript examples through-out the Web.

What about a JavaScript Developers Kit? In many programming languages, in order to create programs, you need a special kit that includes a variety of tools to help you work with the system. But there is no such thing for JavaScript. JavaScript is ASCII text—it is not compiled into an executable program file. You can create JavaScripts in any text editor or word processor (assuming, of course, that you save them in ASCII text). Actually, you'll want to create your JavaScripts in the same application you use to create source documents for your Web pages—Windows Notepad, HotDog, HTML Assistant, or whatever—JavaScripts are simply additional instructions written into the HTML documents. (Note, however, that some authoring tools simply don't let you enter tags that the program doesn't recognize; you won't be able to use such tools to create Web pages that contain JavaScripts.)

WHAT'S INSIDE?

Chapter 1, "What Is JavaScript?" is an introduction to JavaScript. We explain what it is and how it's different from Java, and we show you some of the things that people have done with JavaScript.

Chapter 2, "A Few Quick JavaScript Tricks," gets you working with JavaScript right away. You'll learn a few simple things you can do with JavaScript, such as adding a document-modified date to your Web pages, or displaying messages in the status bar. We won't spend a lot of time explaining exactly *how* these things work, though they are so simple you'll probably figure it out. The pur-pose of this chapter is to show how doing some basic things in JavaScript can be quite simple—before we move on to the more complicated stuff.

Chapter 3, "First Steps—Scripts, Functions & Comments," begins your real JavaScript education. In this chapter, you'll learn how to enter scripts into your Web pages, what functions are and how to use them, and how to enter comments.

Chapter 4, "Variables & Literals—Storing Data," continues your education. In this chapter you'll learn about how JavaScript stores data—in *variables*. You'll also learn about how you can enter data into these variables using *literals*.

Chapter 5, "Expressions & Operators—Manipulating Values," teaches you how to manipulate values using a variety of techniques.

Chapter 6, "Loops & Conditionals—Making Decisions & Controlling Scripts," explains the real power of programming—how you can use loops and conditional expressions to get your scripts to actually make decisions.

Chapter 7, "More on Functions," revisits functions, explaining how to work with them in more detail. For instance, you'll learn how information can be passed to a function when you call it.

Chapter 8, "Troubleshooting & Avoiding Trouble," talks about what you can do to fix the problems in your scripts. . . yes, you will have problems. It also discusses ways to avoid trouble in the first place, and how you can write your scripts so they are easy to read and understand.

Chapter 9, "Building Arrays," explains how to create *arrays*, which are variables that can hold multiple values. You'll see how you can match arrays, so that you can pull information from one array dependent on the value held in another array—search for a last name, for instance, and pull a matching address from another array.

Chapter 10, "Objects, Properties & Methods," is an easy lesson in object-oriented programming. JavaScript contains objects—*things*. Each thing has its own properties, and its associated functions (called *methods*) are used to "do things."

Chapter 11, "More About Built-in Objects," explains JavaScript's objects in more detail, and covers several important objects.

Chapter 12, "JavaScript Events—When Are Actions Carried Out?," looks at how *event handlers* are used to control your scripts; you can make your scripts "do things" when you click on a button, point at a link, press the Tab key, and so on.

Chapter 13, "Advanced Topics," goes into darkest JavaScript—the sorts of topics that are quite advanced and which many JavaScript programmers may never want to touch. You'll get an overview of what else JavaScript can do.

Chapter 14, "Controlling Windows & Documents With JavaScript," shows you how you can use scripts to open secondary windows, to write text or load html files into those windows, how to add confirmation boxes to links, how to let a user choose from a range of destinations, and much more.

Chapter 15, "Using JavaScript With Frames," describes how you can use JavaScript to control frames within a window—for instance, how an action in one frame can write to another.

Chapter 16, "Forms & JavaScript," describes how to write scripts that work with forms—for instance, grabbing information from a form and passing it to a function, and how to validate data within a form to make sure that the user is entering good data.

Chapter 17, "Communicating With the User," introduces you to the different methods of communicating through messages with a user.

Chapter 18, "The Area Code Application," puts it all together. We've created a working application that you can use to search for area codes within the North American Numbering Plan (which covers the United States, Canada, and much of the Caribbean). You can enter an area code, city, state/province/island nation, and the program will search for the associated information. We'll show you *exactly* how this program is put together, leading you through the script line by line.

Chapter 19, "Ready-to-Use Scripts," shows you the easy way to add scripts to your Web pages—borrow them! There are script libraries you can visit, from which you can take scripts and incorporate them into your documents.

We have included several appendices. In order to use JavaScript, there are a lot of technical details to know—or, rather, you have to know where to find the details when you need them.

Appendix A, "About the Online Companion" is detailed on page xxvii.

Appendix B, "The JavaScript Objects & Arrays," is an overview of JavaScript objects. This appendix lists all the objects, and describes which properties each object has, which methods and event handlers can be used with each object, and, in some cases, states the "parent" object—that is, the object of which the object being described is a property.

Appendix C, "JavaScript Properties," is an overview of all of JavaScript's properties. We describe each one's purpose, and we state which objects each can be used with.

Appendix D, "JavaScript Event Handlers," describes the JavaScript event handlers and explains in what conditions they can be used.

Appendix E, "Reserved Words," is a quick list of the reserved words—words that you must not use when declaring variables, defining functions, or creating objects.

Appendix F, "Symbol Reference," contains a list of all the symbols that you'll run across in JavaScript, with a quick summary of what each one does.

Appendix G, "JavaScript Colors," is a list of all the colors you can use in JavaScript, and their corresponding hexadecimal codes (though you rarely, if ever, need to use the codes—you can just use the names).

Appendix H, "Finding More Information," is your source for advanced information about JavaScript. Work your way through this book, then continue on with your education in the JavaScript newsgroups, Web pages, mailing lists, and so on.

Appendix I, "The Scripts We Used" is a list of all the scripts in the book, listed by purpose. You can look up a technique—*navigation buttons*, *status-bar messages*, and so on—and you'll find the page on which the script can be found, along with the Online Companion's reference number, so you can copy the script off our Web documents.

ABOUT THE ONLINE COMPANION

This book has an associated *Online Companion*. That's a special collection of Web pages at the Ventana Web site. These Web pages contain information to help you work with this book, and to continue learning about JavaScript after you've finished this book. You'll find all the examples in this book in the Online Companion—you can read about them in the book, then try the actual scripts in the Online Companion. You can also download all the Web pages and save them on your computer's hard disk, so you can work with the scripts even when you are offline.

In addition to sample scripts, you'll also find links to other useful JavaScript sites; there you'll find many more samples, news releases, tutorials, and the latest information about JavaScript. We've included a bookmark file, so you can quickly copy all the links from Appendix H, "Finding More Information," to your bookmark system. There's also a color chart that shows you all the colors you can use—just click on a color, and the page's background changes to show you that color. Also provided is an Object Hierarchy page, which will help you understand and learn the JavaScript object hierarchy.

You can get to the Online Companion by pointing your Web browser to http://www.netscapepress.com/support/javascript.

IT'S ALIVE!

Unlike most programming languages, JavaScript is changing very fast. Most languages are fixed when they are "released," and you don't have to worry about changes until the next release. But JavaScript is almost a living thing. Once you've written a script, the way that script operates is not written in stone. Different browsers may interpret the script slightly differently, and even different versions of the same browser will work differently. We've used the Netscape Navigator 2.01 family of browsers, though we've included Navigator 3.0 beta 3 as well as beta 4. Beta 4 was the most recent browser available at the time of this writing. There are some important differences between these two versions, which we've pointed out in the text.

> **TIP**
>
> *When you create JavaScripts, don't get on the cutting edge. You want to be a step—or two or three steps—behind. If you write JavaScripts that use the most recent JavaScript features, most of the people viewing your Web sites won't be able to use those features, and may even run into problems with them.*

We recommend that you use the very latest version of Netscape to ensure you get the "best" version of JavaScript. Subsequent versions of Netscape Navigator will undoubtedly work with JavaScript in a slightly different manner.

You may find things that we've covered in our book that operate slightly different. If so, please let us know. You can contact us at

71601.1266@compuserve.com (Peter Kent) and
100553.1346@compuserve.com (John Kent).

We'll keep the Online Companion updated with any changes we find.

So let's get started. We're going to start slowly, explaining what JavaScript is, showing a few sophisticated uses of JavaScript, and then demonstrating how you can quickly use JavaScript to add a few simple things to your Web pages. Turn to Chapter 1 and we'll begin.

Peter Kent
John Kent

CHAPTER 1

What Is JavaScript?

If you've been working on the Web for more than a week or two, you almost certainly have run across the terms *JavaScript* and *Java*. What are they, and what can you do with them? If you've bought this book, you already know that they enable you to create little programs that are run from your Web browser. Before we get started working with JavaScript, however, let's spend a few moments taking a look at what it is, how it compares to Java, and what you can do with it.

FIRST THERE WAS OAK...

It all began with *Oak*. The story begins in 1990—before the World Wide Web had even begun—when a special team was set up at Sun Microsystems. The team was intended to create a new product using the sort of inspiration and initiative that had originally inspired companies such as Apple and NeXT Computer, Inc.—the qualities that many felt were lacking at Sun. The team decided—they had a remarkable amount of autonomy, and operated to some degree in secrecy, cut off from the rest of the company—that they would create a new operating system that could run on anything, even things that people couldn't yet imagine requiring software: refrigerators, televisions, radios, toasters, door locks, anything. This team saw the next computing revolution as an extension of consumer electronics. Software would find its way into every electronic product, and their new operating system would be there first. Furthermore, the operating system had to be reliable—as reliable as the electronic devices that would use it. The high level of bugs accepted as the norm in most PC software would be unacceptable in consumer electronics.

If all these devices used the same software—and if the software was smart enough to make all these devices easy to use—life could be a lot simpler. Instead of being confronted by a multitude of different ways to use different devices, they'd all be familiar. The language the team began work on was known as *Oak*. They also created a cannibalized electronic device as the first piece of equipment to be run by Oak: an LCD screen from a minitelevision, speakers from Nintendo's Game Boy, a touch screen on the front, the guts of a Sun workstation squeezed into a tiny case, and so on.

Oak was much more than an operating system for consumer electronics, though. It would link everything. All electronic devices could be networked, and Oak could be the electronic glue sticking it all together. Everything electronic, everything digital, could be run by Oak. Sun Microsystems got so excited about Oak that it set up a new company, FirstPerson, Inc., to develop and push the system.

But Oak never quite found a home. Companies that expressed an interest in using it—France Telecom for its Minitel data system, Mitsubishi for its electronic devices, Time Warner for its interactive TV controllers, and so on—never quite came through. The devices were too expensive, or the potential clients ended up buying products from other companies.

Eventually, FirstPerson went back to basics. They decided to forget consumer electronics, but rather to focus on personal computers. However, they were unable to come up with a way to create demand for Sun's workstations, so FirstPerson was eventually scrapped in early 1994.

Oak was revived a few months later, though, by Bill Joy, one of the founders of Sun. He realized that Oak could be useful on the Internet, and he decided that Sun should develop it and give it away. "Let's create a franchise," he said. In other words, give it away, get enough people to use it, and eventually Sun would "own" that particular market. Oak was modified for use on the Internet and, early in 1995, was renamed *Java*.

A special program was developed, *HotJava*, which could actually run programs that were created using Java. Later, of course, a Java interpreter would be incorporated into Netscape Navigator; in other words, Navigator itself could run Java applications—Java *applets*, as they became known—making HotJava unnecessary for Navigator users.

So What Exactly Is Java?

Java is a programming language, similar in some ways to C++, but intended to be more reliable. Remember, Java was originally designed for the consumer electronics market, which is far less tolerant of unreliability than the consumer software business.

So Java allows you to create programs, but you need an operating system to run a program. Generally speaking, if you want to create a word processor that runs in DOS and Windows, on the Macintosh computer, and on Sun workstations, you'll have to create four different versions (at least four, maybe more: one for Windows 3.1, one for Windows 95, and so on). But Java is different. The idea behind Java is that a programmer can create a single version of the program, which then runs inside a Java "interpreter," a program such as HotJava or Netscape Navigator. There are different interpreters for different computers and operating systems— there's a Netscape Navigator that runs on the Macintosh, one that runs in Windows 3.1, one for Windows 95, and so on. So a single Java program can run on a number of different operating systems, as long as the user has an interpreter that will run on his computer.

These Java interpreters are not true operating systems, though the principle is the same to some degree. An *operating system* is the interface between a computer's hardware and a program. Rather than writing a program that "talks" directly to the computer's hardware—to the keyboard, to the video screen, and so on—a programmer simply has to write a program that talks to the operating system, and can enable the operating system to do the routine hardware stuff. A Java interpreter works in a similar way. It sits between the operating system and the Java program. Instead of writing several versions of the program—each of which talks to a different operating system—the programmer writes a single program, that can talk to any Java interpreter on any computer system. The Java interpreter then liaises between the Java program and the operating system, in effect translating what each says into something the other can understand.

This is a breakthrough technology, Java proponents claim, because it smashes constraints forced on software by operating systems. "Interpreted" languages have been around for a while, but they haven't been as sophisticated as Java. Java provides a powerful programming language with which very sophisticated programs can be created and then run on a variety of different computers. No longer is a program only a Macintosh program, only a Windows program, or only a UNIX program. Now it's a Java program, and it can run on anything that has an available Java interpreter.

WHERE WILL IT TAKE US?

It's been predicted by many that Java is the beginning of the end for "shrink-wrapped" software. Eventually, we'll all use programs created using Java, JavaScript, and similar languages. Instead of buying a word processor or spreadsheet and loading it onto our hard disks, we'll log on to an Internet site and run the program from there, paying a per-minute or per-use fee.

There are many problems with this idea, of course. It remains to be seen whether this will come to pass—and if it does, don't expect it to be soon. It will take years before the really fast connections required for such a scenario are cheaply and easily available, and before connecting to the Internet is as reliable as "connecting" to your hard disk. (We admit to more than a little skepticism about this scenario, but who knows what the future will bring. As nuclear physicist Niels Bohr said, "making predictions is very difficult, especially about the future.") Still, Java does seem to be the Internet programming language of the moment—even if we never throw our hard-disk applications away; and Java still provides a mechanism for Web site developers to add life to their pages.

THEN CAME JAVASCRIPT

A system like Java is only useful if it's ubiquitous, or close to being so. It has to be everywhere. Here's a classic example of a system that failed because it *wasn't* ubiquitous: OS/2. Many OS/2 users will complain loudly that this IBM operating system is far superior to any version of Microsoft Windows. Maybe, maybe not (we don't want to get into that argument!). But one thing we can be sure of is that relatively few PC users actually use OS/2. Consequently, very few programs are written for OS/2—so few that if OS/2 couldn't run Windows programs, it probably would have died years ago. It's a vicious cycle: few people use OS/2, so few programmers write programs for it, so OS/2's "user base" remains relatively stagnant, so programmers continue to ignore it.

Sun realizes this little software fact of life, and wants to make sure that Java becomes *the* system on the Internet—"the DOS of the Internet," as Sun engineer Arthur van Hoff has put it. And they know that Microsoft is hard on their heels, with products such as *VBScript* and *ActiveX*. But there's a problem: Java is a programming language. It's not easy to sit down and create a Java application, unless you happen to be a programmer who understands how to write Java. So Sun says that it will provide ways to make it easier for people to create these Java applications. They plan to provide special toolkits that will allow any nonprogrammer—any Web-site developer, writer, artist, businessperson—to create Java programs.

There's no toolkit in sight yet, but the first step to simplifying Java is *JavaScript*. Think of JavaScript as Java's little brother. Although Netscape began development of JavaScript independently (it was originally called LiveScript), they soon joined in a partnership with Sun, agreeing to make JavaScript a sort of subset of Java. JavaScript is similar in some ways to Java, but is much simpler to use. You don't need a Java development kit, and you don't need to compile Java applications. All you need to do is add a script to your Web pages and, when a JavaScript-enabled browser (currently only the Netscape browser) opens the Web page, it reads the script and follows the instructions.

WHAT DOES COMPILED MEAN?

Compiled is the term given to the process of taking code (ASCII text) written by a programmer and converting it into something that a computer can read and very quickly understand, often in the form of an executable (.EXE or .COM) file. JavaScripts are additional statements in HTML files and are never compiled—they remain ASCII text along with the remainder of the file.

JAVA VS. JAVASCRIPT

There are some important differences between Java and JavaScript. Table 1-1 compares the two systems:

Java	JavaScript
Complicated to use.	Relatively easy to use.
You'll need the JDK (Java Developer's Kit), free from Sun Microsystems.	You don't need a developer's kit. All you need is information about how to write scripts (this book is your introduction to that information) and a JavaScript-compatible browser such as Netscape Navigator.
Programs are compiled into executable files. These files are embedded into Web pages using the <APPLET> tag. When a browser opens the Web page and sees the <APPLET> tag, it retrieves and runs the Java applet.	"Programs" are built into the Web page in the form of a script. There is no separate JavaScript program file, so there's no need to compile, download, and interpret a separate file.

Java	JavaScript
On today's Internet, Java applications tend to be a little slow. The compiled file has to be transferred to a user's computer before it can run.	JavaScript tends to run very quickly. The script is built into the Web page—it's just text—and JavaScripts tend to be smaller than Java applets anyway.
Java is more powerful. It's a full-blown programming language.	JavaScript is more appropriate for relatively simple uses. You won't build a word processor using JavaScript!
Java is *object-oriented*. Java applets, to quote the Netscape documentation, "consist of object classes with inheritance." What does that mean? It means that Java uses a fairly complicated system that we don't need to know about in this book. (We don't want to introduce any more programming-speak than we need to.)	JavaScript is *object-based*. "Code uses built-in, extensible objects, but no classes or inheritance." And that means, you'll be pleased to know, that JavaScript is simpler than Java. JavaScript is not a true object-oriented programming language, though you can still work with objects. (Don't worry about the distinction, it doesn't really matter for the nonprogrammer.)
Java has strict rules about how to use *variables*. They must be declared before using them. You'll learn more about variables in Chapter 4, "Variables & Literals—Storing Data."	JavaScript has what's known as loose typing. That is, it's less restrictive about how you create and use variables.
Java uses *static binding*. More programming jargon, meaning that references to objects must exist when the program is compiled.	JavaScript uses *dynamic binding*. References to objects are checked when the script is run. You'll learn more about objects in Chapter 10, "Objects, Properties & Methods," but you don't need to worry about these binding terms right now.

Table 1-1: *The Differences Between Java and JavaScript.*

> **TIP**
>
> *There's an important limitation in both Java and JavaScript that you ought to understand right away. For security reasons, when used with a browser for displaying Web pages, neither Java nor JavaScript can write to the hard disk (except in a very limited way; see the information on cookies in Chapter 13, "Advanced Topics"). This limitation makes them safer, though. Web users can't download a rogue Java or JavaScript applet that can trash their hard disks. However, this limitation is significant, because it restricts what a Java or JavaScript applet can do.*

JavaScript is similar to Java, but it's simpler. It's easier to write using JavaScript, and it's easier to incorporate JavaScript applications into your Web sites. There's no need to compile your applications—you simply write the scripts directly into your Web pages, and the browser interprets them along with the other HTML codes.

Programmers love to argue about semantics, and some would argue that JavaScript is not quite a programming language. You see, the program is already written—your JavaScript-compatible browser already has the JavaScript interpreter built into it. JavaScript is simply a way of creating instructions that tell the browser what to do. You, the Web-page developer, write a series of JavaScript instructions in your HTML documents. The browser reads those instructions and "interprets" them—that is, it carries out your instructions (assuming of course, you've written something that the browser can understand).

In a sense, then, you are not writing a program when you write JavaScript. The script you write is not *compiled* as a real program must be, and it cannot work alone. This sort of "programming" is often called *scripting;* and there's a common belief that because JavaScript is a form of scripting, it's not quite the same as programming. Rather, it's simply a set of instructions and it requires a browser to run. Not just any browser, but a browser that has the JavaScript interpreter built in. However, in another sense you most certainly *are* writing a program. While some JavaScripts are very simple and easy to put together (as you'll see in Chapter 2, "A Few Quick JavaScript Tricks"), JavaScript can be very complicated. Just take a look at the Netscape JavaScript documentation. If you're not a programmer, you'll come away dazed and confused by terms such as *objects*, *methods*, *functions*, *expressions*, *values*, *literals*, *statements*, *event handlers*, and so forth.

The Penguin Dictionary of Computers defines *program* as a set of instructions composed for solving a given problem by a computer, and that is most certainly what JavaScript is and does. It is, however, easier to use than some programming languages (though much harder than others). In fact, JavaScript (and this book) is a really good first step into programming. If you then move on to Java (and C and C++), you will find that much of the code you write looks very similar to JavaScript.

WHERE CAN YOU GET JAVASCRIPT?

If you want to create C++ or Visual Basic programs, you need a software development "environment," and you need a compiler. But there is no JavaScript software development environment; and you never have to compile your scripts, so the only thing you need is the knowledge—which is what this book is all about, of course. The only other thing you'll need is a JavaScript-compatible browser. That is, a World Wide Web browser that can read, interpret, and run the JavaScripts you create. At the time of this writing, the only JavaScript-compatible browsers available are the Netscape Navigator family of browsers. JavaScript was introduced in the 2.0 browsers. However, at the time of this writing, the latest available browser was the Netscape Atlas Preview Release 2 browser (which is also known as Netscape Navigator 3.0 beta 3). If you are using an earlier version of Netscape (1.x or one of the 2.0 betas), you should upgrade to the latest Netscape. In fact, even if you are running one of the 2.x versions, check to see that you have the very latest version, as it will contain bug fixes and perhaps new JavaScript features. At the time of this writing, if you are using any other browser, you'll need to switch to Netscape to work with JavaScript. However, JavaScript will start turning up in other browsers soon. By the time you read this, you may find that other JavaScript-compatible browsers are available.

Note, however, that it's not a good idea to write JavaScripts that use features only available in the very latest browser—those features won't work in the browsers that most users are working with. So stay a step or two behind. (Give the browser programmers a chance to sort out bugs, too.)

TIP

> *You can get the latest version of Netscape Navigator from http://www.netscape.com/ or http://home.netscape.com/.*

So WHAT'S IT GOOD FOR?

What, then, can you get JavaScript to do? Well, you can make JavaScript carry out procedures automatically—that is, when a Web page opens or closes (or rather, when the user loads a different page). Or you can make JavaScript carry out procedures at a particular event; for example, when the user clicks on a button or link, simply points at a button or link, moves focus from one component of a form to another component of the form, and so on.

These procedures may be simple—the script may write the date that the document was last updated into the Web page, or display a message in a dialog box, or in the status bar at the bottom of the browser window. Scripts may open new browser windows and display particular HTML files, or display a page selected from the browser's history list. Or they may be complicated—a script may check the contents of a form that the user wants to submit, and then warn the user if the information is not valid. A script may search for information in a "mini-database" built into the Web page, or perform complicated financial calculations.

JAVASCRIPT EXAMPLES

You'll find loads of JavaScript examples scattered across the Web. Right now you'll rarely run into them by chance—JavaScript is still too young to be found in a majority of sites. But visit some of the Web sites listed in Appendix H, "Finding More Information," or visit our Online Companion (http://www.netscapepress.com/ support/javascript/), and you'll find your way to examples galore.

So rather than us telling you what *can* be done with JavaScript, why don't we take a quick look at what *has* been done with JavaScript already—with the understanding, of course, that JavaScript is still young, still developing, and few people are currently writing JavaScript applications.

TAKEAWAYS & REMOTES

Here's a nice idea you might think about for your own Web pages, if there's something useful in the pages that people might want to take with them: Use JavaScript to create a small secondary window containing something they can use after they've left your site.

For instance, the @republic search page (http://www.republic.se /search/search.html) lets you take away a small WebCrawler window. (WebCrawler is a popular Web-search service.) You can then continue on your Web journey. If at any time you need to quickly search for something, you can enter a search word into this "takeaway," then click on the Search button—a request is sent to WebCrawler, and the response is displayed in a new window.

Yahoo has a similar capability. Go to http://www.yahoo.com, and click on the Yahoo Remote button to create a small Yahoo search window that you can "take with you." You can see both of these takeaways in Figure 1-1.

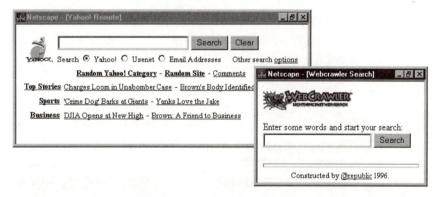

Figure 1-1: *Yahoo Remote and the WebCrawler takeaway.*

ORDER FORMS

You'll find lots of order forms created using JavaScript. There's a simple example at http://www.csiro.au:8000/steve/javascript/marketing/order.html, for instance. This particular form, which you can see in Figure 1-2, lets a customer select from a list, enter the quantity number and total value, and the form keeps a running total at the bottom.

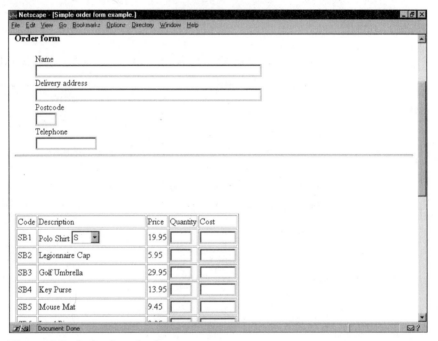

Figure 1-2: *A simple order form.*

AN INTERACTIVE TEXT GAME

Go to http://vanbc.wimsey.com/~grantm/tertius/ to help write *Tertius the Scribe*, a multi-writer story (see Figure 1-3). You read the beginning and then add your own text to the story, or read what others have added. This is not pure JavaScript, though. It's using

JavaScript to display and collect information, along with a CGI (Common Gateway Interface) script that receives the new text that has been submitted and incorporates it into the HTML documents.

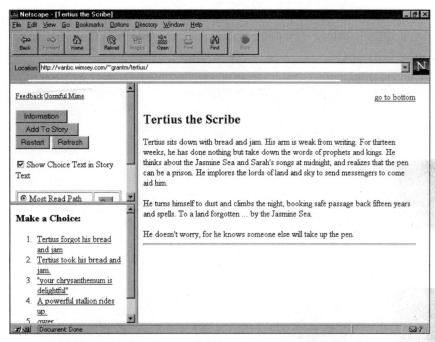

Figure 1-3: *Tertius the Scribe.*

THE 1040EZ TAX FORM

The tax form at http://www.homepages.com/fun/1040EZ.html is not provided by the Internal Revenue Service, though it was created from the IRS's rules and information by a Web and JavaScript consulting company. It shows how JavaScript can be used to create forms that carry out calculations. You enter information into the text boxes and when you Tab out of the box or click elsewhere, the form recalculates (see Figure 1-4). When you click on option buttons, the appropriate values are entered into the text boxes, too.

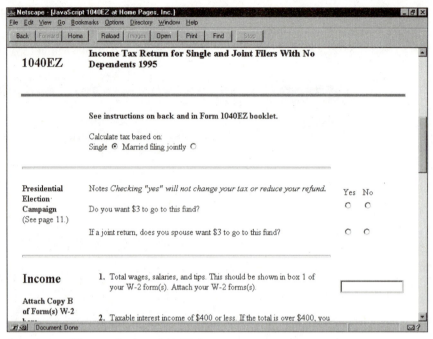

Figure 1-4: *The JavaScript 1040EZ form.*

THE BOZO FILTER

Want to block access to your Web page from certain other Web pages? Perhaps a "disreputable" Web site has a link to you and you don't want to be associated with it. Using Alistair Fraser's *Bozo Filter*, you can block access to JavaScript-enabled browsers that come from a specific URL. Or you can display a specific page of information for those users coming from that particular URL. You can find more information about this site at http://www.ems.psu.edu/~fraser/Bozo/Bozo.html. (Sounds like this guy has a feud with Mirsky's Worst of the Web. Something to do with an anti-bagpipe bias.)

NAVIGATION BARS

It's fairly easy to create navigation bars using JavaScript. Of course, you can create them in HTML, too, but JavaScript provides a few extras—such as the ability to include Back and Forward. You can see an example of a floating navigation bar in Figure 1-5, which is found at http://www.grolier.fr/~grange/javascript/. This one even has a Show URL command that will open a dialog box and show the URL of the current document.

Figure 1-5: *A floating navigation bar.*

WEBPAGE PERSONALIZER   *TRAVELLING ROAN*

Here's another takeaway. This is a little utility for changing window colors. When you visit the http://www.geocities.com/SiliconValley/3555/starter.html Web page, a special window opens (see Figure 1-6) that contains color controls. You can now travel around the Web and, in theory, use this window to modify the colors of the Web pages you view.

Figure 1-6: *The Webpage Personalizer.*

Selecting Where You Want to Go

You can use JavaScript to allow the reader to select from a list of items. For example, when the reader clicks on a button, the information that the reader has selected will be displayed. That information may be another Web page, a picture, a sound, or whatever.

You'll find a good example of this is at http://www.tripnet.se/ home/brodd/preview.html (see Figure 1-7). This is a picture viewer; the user can select an entry from a drop-down list box, then click on the Preview Image button. Up pops another window containing the selected picture and a Close button.

Figure 1-7: *A picture viewer.*

You can find another example of this sort of selection system at work at http://websys.com/javascript/leapto_samp.html (the Site Tree). At this site, you select from a list of documents; and when you click on the button, you jump to the selected page.

THE HiREX DIRECTORY

The Health Information Resource EXecutive is a nice example of how an organization or company might keep a directory on the Web, so that its members can access it from anywhere in the world. You can try this out at http://hiru.mcmaster.ca/cgi/ hirexs.exe?START. At the time of this writing, though, it had a few bug problems.

METRIC CALCULATOR

There is a variety of different specialized calculators and converters popping up on the Web—from relocation estimators to runner's calculators to mortgage calculators—and one way to create them is by using JavaScript. You can find a handy little distance-measurement converter at http://www.seercom.com/vothcom/convert.html, for instance. Select the metric unit, select the unit into which you want to convert, and then use the keypad to type in the metric value. The equivalent "English" value appears in the Convert to text box, as you can see in Figure 1-8.

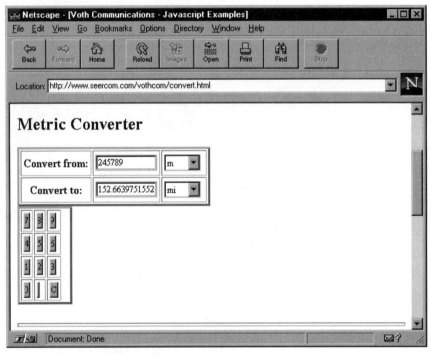

Figure 1-8. *A metric converter.*

If you find neat little utilities that you want to keep, you can simply save the page on your hard disk. You can open the page later, when you need to use the utility. Of course, it's more complicated if these utilities span more than one HTML page, as some of the more sophisticated ones do.

YEAR TO ERA CONVERTER

Here's another handy utility found at http://www2.gol.com/users/furu/js.html. Enter the year, click on Convert, and you'll see the Japanese Imperial Era (Gengou) along with the animal symbol for that era (see Figure 1-9). You can go the other way, too—entering the era and the year within that era, and converting to the year.

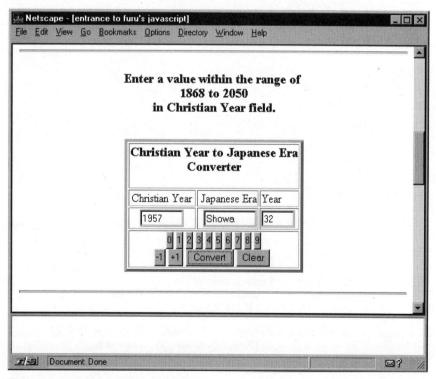

Figure 1-9: *A Year to Era converter.*

GAMES, GAMES, GAMES

True to the spirit of the Internet, much of the energy going into creating JavaScript apps is going into goofing off—you'll find loads of JavaScript games. For instance, there's a JavaScript Maze at http://www.tisny.com/js_demo.html, which you can see in Figure 1-10. You use buttons to move an asterisk around in a maze created using the hatch symbol (#). You will also find card games (Blackjack and Five Card Stud, for instance); Rock, Paper, Scissors; a variety of strategy and adventure games; and so on.

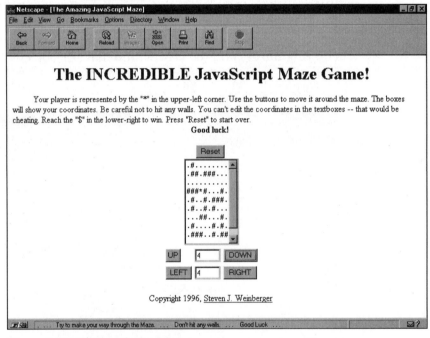

Figure 1-10: *The JavaScript Maze.*

AN HTML EDITOR—HTMLJIVE

More sophisticated programs can be created using JavaScript. An example is HTMLjive (a program that may be used in conjunction with a CGI script), which allows people to create Web pages online and immediately post them. For instance, a professional organization could use such a system to allow its members to post job leads and resumes to its Web site. You can find more information about HTMLjive at http://www.cris.com/~raydaly/hjdemo.shtml. You can see an example there (see Figure 1-11) and links to the sites that are using the program.

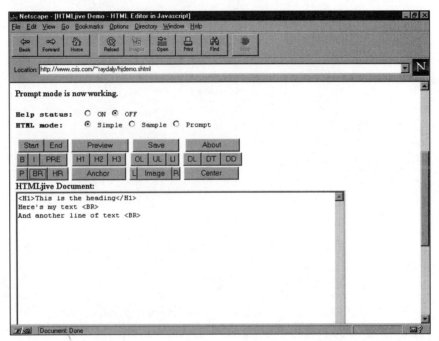

Figure 1-11: *HTMLjive.*

Remember, though, that JavaScript doesn't let you save anything directly, which is why this editor must be used with a CGI. JavaScript can send the information to the CGI, which can then save it in the correct place. Of course, the completed HTML text can also be highlighted and copied to the clipboard.

INTERACTIVE TABLES OF CONTENTS

JavaScript can be used to manage browser frames. One method is to use JavaScript to create interactive tables of contents. For instance, at http://www.cuesys.com/ you'll find the document shown in Figure 1-12. In the left pane is a table of contents with a small icon before the name of each entry. Click on the icon to "open" a list of subcategories below the name, or to close that list.

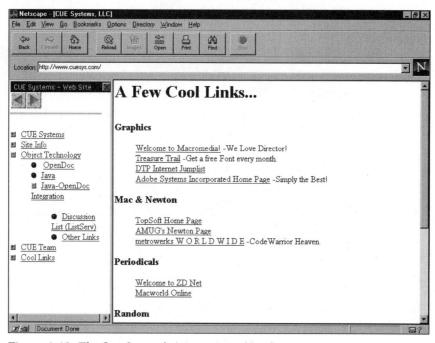

Figure 1-12: *The Cue System's interactive table of contents.*

LIKE WHAT YOU SEE?

If you like what other people have done, you can often take their scripts. Many of these scripts have been made publicly available by their authors. (We'll be explaining how to do some of these things later—see Chapter 19, "Ready-to-Use Scripts.") You can find loads of useful scripts that can be copied from the Internet using Netscape. Simply choose View|Document Source to open the document-source window; then copy the text of the Web page (including the script) from the open document-source window, or use File| Save to save it to a new file. (Whether you can do that depends on the type of viewer you are using. The viewer that opens is defined in the Preferences menu. Select Options| General Preferences, click on the Apps tab, and look in the View Source text box.) Remember two things, though. First, many scripts are *not* intended for public use. If a script author hasn't specifically stated that you can use the script, then you'd better not use the script in a public Web page or even in a private Web page on a corporate "intranet."—And even if an author says that you can take the script, it doesn't necessarily make it yours. You may not be able to use it commercially—for instance, selling it to other Web developers. However, you can always borrow scripts (any scripts), for your own personal use or to see how the author has done something. Then you can take what you've learned and create your own.

OFF THE SHELF JAVA

JavaScript will soon provide a way to use Java applets in your documents. Creating Java applets is a time-consuming and skilled job—it's a programmer's job—and if you aren't a programmer, you won't be able to create Java applets. But you *will* be able to take a public domain, shareware, or commercial Java applet, and use JavaScript to "connect it" to your Web pages. The JavaScript will send information from the page to the Java applet, and the Java applet can then return something to the Web page. JavaScript will work as a sort of interface between your documents and the Java applet.

However, at the time of this writing, this feature was not working (it was introduced in Netscape Navigator 3.0 beta 3—but in a very preliminary form, and not yet "ready for prime time").

WHAT IS THE <APPLET> TAG?

You'll run across the <APPLET> tag now and again in HTML documents. This is used by Java, not JavaScript. It's the tag used to
embed Java applets into Web pages.

IS YOUR JAVASCRIPT BROWSER TURNED ON?

You have a JavaScript browser, but will it work? The only JavaScript-
enabled browsers at the time of this writing were the Netscape Navigator browsers. These browsers provide a way for the user to turn
Java and JavaScript on and off. (The other JavaScript browsers that
will appear on the Web soon will probably also provide this capability.) This is for security reasons; although both Java and JavaScript
are designed to be safe, some users may want to be completely sure
of their security, and disable Java or JavaScript apps from running.
(Netscape provides the ability to turn off Java and JavaScript independently.) Many users don't like the idea of a program running
automatically when they enter a Web page, regardless of how safe
it's supposed to be. And, in March 1996, a bug was found that introduced a potential security risk; to quote the Netscape press release,
"Through a sophisticated attack, an experienced programmer could
potentially write a malicious applet that might exploit this bug and
cause a file to be deleted or cause other damage on a user's machine." By the time you read this, the bug will almost certainly be
fixed—that is, more recent versions of Netscape Navigator will not
contain the bug. Other security bugs exist, though, and new ones are
found every now and then.

So before we start, make sure that JavaScript is turned on in your
browser; if it's not, you won't be able to test our example scripts. In
Netscape, choose Options | Security Preferences, then click on the
General tab. You'll see the dialog box shown in Figure 1-13.

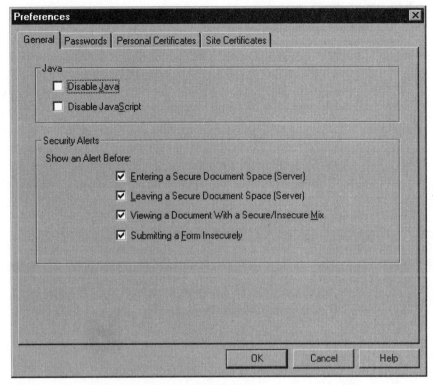

Figure 1-13: *The Security Preferences dialog box.*

Also make sure that the Disable JavaScript check box has been *cleared*. If there's a checkmark in this box, any JavaScripts that you try *will not work*.

TIP

In Netscape Navigator 3.0 beta 3, the check boxes had been moved. Try Options | Network Preferences, then click on the Languages tab. Also, in that version note that a checkmark means that JavaScript is enabled, not disabled.

MOVING ON

We've learned what JavaScript is and a little of what can be done with it. Now it's time to do some work. Some of the examples you've seen are quite complicated, but there are things that can be done very quickly and easily—things that you can do to your Web pages to add features with a few keystrokes. For instance, you can add a "modified date" to a Web page in about 10 seconds. Many other JavaScript tools are very simple to use, too.

So, as a practical introduction to the quick and easy things you can do with JavaScript, we're going to move on to Chapter 2, "A Few Quick JavaScript Tricks."

A Few Quick JavaScript Tricks

Now that you've seen what JavaScript can do, wouldn't it be nice to do something straight away? Well, you can. No, you won't be able to create a sophisticated JavaScript application, but there are a number of simple things you can do immediately.

You may have heard that JavaScript is a simple-to-use scripting language that anyone can use to bring life to Web pages. Well, that's only half true. It's easy when compared to Java. It's not easy when compared to writing a simple word-processing macro, though. It's easy for a programmer—not so easy for a nonprogrammer. Nonprogrammers who want to completely understand JavaScript will have to spend quite a bit of time and effort learning new concepts.

However, having said all that, there *are* a number of things you can do with JavaScript quickly and easily—without really understanding what you are doing! We're going to look at a few of these examples in this chapter. By the time you've finished the chapter—having seen that JavaScript isn't *always* complicated—we're sure you'll have the courage to move on to the trickier stuff.

Remember, we're assuming you understand HTML—at least the basics. We're going to show you how to drop a few simple JavaScript tools into your Web documents. Don't worry about exactly how and why everything works in this chapter; you'll understand more after we examine the detailed explanations later. So, let's start with a simple technique to put a date in your document.

> **TIP**
>
> *All of the examples in this book are in our Online Companion at http:// www.netscapepress.com/support/javascript. (Notice the Online Companion icons in the margins next to the examples—these show you the example number.) You can go to the Online Companion and try each example. Then you can copy the script directly from the Web page (no need to open the source; we've put a script sample in each document so you can copy straight from the Web page) and paste them into your own Web pages. By the way, you can also copy the entire Online Companion examples—stored in an archive file—back to your hard disk.*
>
> *If you decide to type these scripts for yourself, make sure you type these examples exactly as they appear. If you type anything incorrectly, even typing an uppercase letter where there should be a lowercase letter or vice versa, the script may not work.*

PLACING A MODIFIED DATE IN YOUR WEB PAGES

It's often useful to show a date in your Web page indicating the last time that the source document was saved. Readers can quickly see just how old the information is. Well, JavaScript gives you a quick and easy way to do this. Here's what you must do.

> **TIP**
>
> *Writing JavaScript is similar in some ways to writing HTML. It's convenient to have both your HTML editor and Netscape Navigator open at the same time; you can then make changes to your HTML document and script, and quickly view the changes in your browser.*

1. Open one of your Web pages in the HTML editor you use, and place the cursor exactly where you want to see the Last Modified date.

Example 2.1

2. Now type the following:

```
<SCRIPT LANGUAGE="JAVASCRIPT">
document.write("This document last modified on: ")
document.write(document.lastModified)
</SCRIPT>
```

3. Save your page. Now take a look at it in any JavaScript-compatible browser. (At the time of this writing, Netscape is the only JavaScript-compatible browser; though by the time you read this, others may work with JavaScript, too.) You'll see something like Figure 2-1.

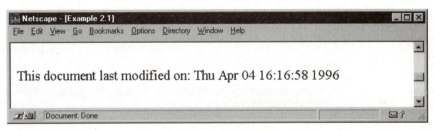

Figure 2-1: *Adding a modified date to a document.*

Note that you can modify the text if you choose. You may want to see *Last Modified* instead of *This document last modified on*. If so, simply replace the text with the text you prefer.

So here you have a JavaScript that you can start using right away, even if you don't really understand what it all means.

TIP

If you've been viewing a document in your browser and have just made a change to the JavaScript, remember to save the change in your HTML editor and then click on the browser's Reload button to get the updated JavaScript.

> ### TIP
>
> ***Important:*** *Some versions of Netscape Navigator have a cache bug. Using the Reload command often does* not *reload the document. This is a particular problem when creating HTML tags and scripts that incorporate forms; reloading often doesn't properly re-create the form. There are several things you can do to get around the problem. Try pressing the Shift key (or the Option key on the Mac) while clicking on the Reload button—this is supposed to throw out the cached copy and grab a fresh copy of the Web page, even if the page hasn't changed. You can also try using the File\Open File command and opening the page again, or creating a bookmark to the page and using the bookmark to open it. If all else fails, you'll have to close the browser.*

HIDING SCRIPTS

There's a problem with the script we've just written, though. Take a look at Figure 2-2. This is Internet Explorer 2.0, which cannot work with JavaScripts. It treats it just like text, so it ends up looking a little funky—like you've screwed something up in your source document.

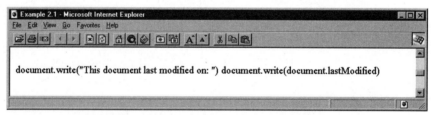

Figure 2-2: *The modified date, shown in a non-JavaScript browser.*

Example 2.2

You can fix that problem, however, by telling old, non-JavaScript browsers to ignore the script. Modify your previously created script as follows:

```
<SCRIPT LANGUAGE="JAVASCRIPT">
<!--
document.write("This document last modified on: ")
```

```
document.write(document.lastModified)
// -->
</SCRIPT>
```

Notice that we've added two lines, `<!--` and `// -->`. These are, of course, the comment tags used in HTML; browsers ignore everything between the comment tags. Well, not all browsers—JavaScript-compatible browsers know that there's a script between the tags, so they look there and read the script.

Once you've added these tags in the correct places (they must be on the line below the `<SCRIPT LANGUAGE="JAVASCRIPT">` tag and the line above the `<SCRIPT>` tag), the script becomes invisible to browsers that don't know what to do with the JavaScript. Take a look at the document with Internet Explorer 2.0, for instance, and you won't see anything there. Use Netscape Navigator, though, and you'll see the *This document last modified on* line.

WHAT PAGE HAS THE READER COME FROM?

If you've moved your Web site recently, you may have left a document at the previous site informing people of the change. You've seen these messages: "Our Web site has moved, please change your bookmarks and inform the owner of the document you've just come from," or something similar. You can add a simple JavaScript to one of these documents to enter the URL of the document from which you've just come. For instance, enter this:

Example 2.3

```
The URL of the document you are seeking has changed. Please
inform the owner of the document you've just come from
<SCRIPT LANGUAGE="JAVASCRIPT">
<!--
document.write(" (" + document.referrer + ")")
// -->
<SCRIPT>
that this link has changed.
```

Figure 2-3 shows what the user will see when arriving at this document. (Well, something like what the user will see, depending on where he or she has come from. As you can see, the URL in this example is a file:///URL.)

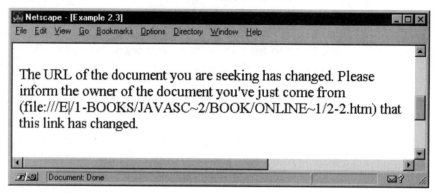

Figure 2-3: *Using the URL of the document the user has come from.*

As you can see, the document is showing the text as well as, in parentheses, the URL of the document from which the user has just come. What would the user of a non-JavaScript browser see? Because most of the text is outside the comment lines, and because only the document.referrer instruction is inside (referrer is a *property* of the document object, but don't worry about that right now—you'll learn about objects and properties in Chapter 10, "Objects, Properties & Methods"), the reader will see everything but the parenthetical information (the URL of the document). The reader will see something like this:

```
The URL of the document you are seeking has changed. Please
inform the owner of the document you've just come from that
this link has changed.
```

OPENING SECONDARY WINDOWS

When the Web first came on the Internet scene, it was a relatively simple hypertext system. Other hypertext systems—such as Windows Help, for instance—had a feature that the Web sorely lacked:

secondary windows. That is, clicking on a link could open another window, leaving the original window open, too. Well, you can use JavaScript to do all sorts of tricks with secondary (or, in Netscape-speak, *targeted*) windows. Here's a simple one you can try. If you want to open another window and place the contents of a particular HTML document in that window, here's how you can do it.

Example 2.4

First, add this information in the head of your HTML document:

```
<head>
<SCRIPT LANGUAGE="JAVASCRIPT"><!--
function WinOpen() {
    open("window.htm","Window1","toolbar=yes");
}
//-->
</SCRIPT>
</head>
```

> **TIP**
>
> *It's a sad truth that JavaScript is not the same on all browsers. A script that runs in one browser may not run in another. The preceding script, for instance, would not run on one Solaris version of Netscape. JavaScript is still young, and the wrinkles have not all been ironed out yet.*

This was a bit more complicated, but nothing too bad. You have just declared a *function.* A function is like a little program that you create and store for later use. We've named the function WinOpen—when you *call* the function (we'll look at how you call it in a moment), certain things happen, and those things are defined within the squiggly brackets { and }. What will happen? Well, the open instruction will run, opening a window. (open is actually a special function already built into JavaScript.) Inside the parentheses you'll see information about that window. First, it's going to load the window.htm file. Next, you'll see the name of the window—in this case Window1, but you can call it whatever you like (Fred, if you are so inclined). This is simply a name that can be used later in HTML tags to target this particular window.

Next, you'll see some more information about the window. You can see that in this case the window will have a toolbar. If we had put `"toolbar=no"`, or left this information out (by simply leaving `""` in its place), we would not have the toolbar. If we had simply ended with `"Window1"`) we would get the toolbar, along with the Location bar and the Directory bar—but that's another story; you can specify other window characteristics, which you will learn about in Chapter 14, "Controlling Windows & Documents With JavaScript."

Okay, now let's run this function. Somewhere in your document you can insert the following:

```
<form>
<input type="button" name="WindowButton" value="Secondary
Window--Click on me" onclick="WinOpen()">
</form>
```

If you've created forms in your HTML documents, you'll know that this is HTML, not JavaScript—at least, most of it is. We start with the `<form>` tag, which tells the browser that we are going to create a form; then we use the `<input type=` tag, which tells the browser what sort of form component we want.

We're creating a button (`type="button"`—this is an INPUT element that has been introduced with Netscape Navigator 2.0 and JavaScript), and we're calling the button `WindowButton`. Then we are defining the text that will appear on the button: in this case, *Secondary Window--Click on me*.

You then see something a little different: the `onclick=` attribute. This is JavaScript, not HTML; it's one of the JavaScript *event handlers*. We'll look at them in more detail in Chapter 12, "JavaScript Events." All you need to know right now is that `onclick` means *when* the user clicks on the item, of course. And what will happen when the user clicks on the item? The `WinOpen` function will run! And what does the `WinOpen` function do? It opens `Window1` and displays the `window.htm` document. Easy. Figure 2-4 shows what you will see after clicking on this button. This window is a bit big, though, for that little text. You will learn about positioning these windows in Chapter 14, "Controlling Windows & Documents With JavaScript."

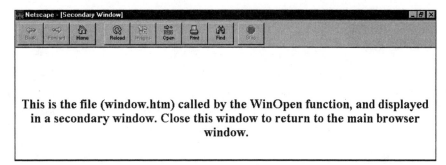

Figure 2-4: *We've opened this secondary window by clicking on a button.*

NAVIGATION BUTTONS

JavaScript provides a variety of navigation controls. For instance, you could add Back and Forward buttons to your documents; these buttons would carry out the same function as the Back and Forward buttons found on the toolbar. Try this:

Example 2.5

```
<form>
<input type="button" value=" <-- 2 Pages "
onclick="history.go(-2)">
<input type="button" value="Previous Page"
onclick="history.go(-1)">
<input type="button" value="  Next Page  "
onclick="history.go(1)">
<input type="button" value=" 2 Pages --> "
onclick="history.go(2)">
</form>
```

The onclick event handlers tell the browser what to do when the user clicks on the button—the browser has to run the history.go instruction. This simply takes the user through the browser's history list. You can specify how far, and in which directions, using numbers: –2 means back two pages, 2 means forward two pages, and so on.

WELCOME MESSAGES

How about welcoming readers to your site? You can make their JavaScript-enabled browsers open a dialog box with a special message from you when they arrive at your site. Perhaps a message of the day, important news, or information that changes frequently. Here's what you need to do. Just before the </HEAD> tag, enter this text:

Example 2.6

```
<SCRIPT LANGUAGE="JAVASCRIPT">
<!--
alert("Welcome to the World Wide Web\'s Premier slug-farming→
page. Unfortunately we have some bad news. Uncle Albert
slipped while walking across the pasture last night, and will→
be unable to maintain this site for a few days. Don\'t worry→
though, he\'ll be back just as soon as we can get the slime→
off.")
//-->
</SCRIPT>
```

Unfortunately, there's a bug present in some browsers related to long lines like this—if a line of JavaScript code is 255 characters or more, the browser may "choke" on it. Here's another way to create a message, though:

```
<SCRIPT LANGUAGE="JAVASCRIPT">
<!--
var msg1="Welcome to the World Wide Web\'s Premier slug-→
farming page. Unfortunately we have some bad news. Uncle→
Albert slipped while "
var msg2="walking across the pasture last night, and will be→
unable to maintain this "
var msg3="site for a few days. Don\'t worry though, he\'ll be→
back just as soon as we can get the slime off."
alert(msg1 + msg2 + msg3)
//-->
</SCRIPT>
```

LINE BREAKS AND THE → SYMBOL

Notice the little arrows we've shown in Example 2.6's code? These are *continuation characters*. They simply show you where we've moved the text down a line, even though *you* can't do so when typing your code. There are many cases in which you cannot break lines. For instance, when you are entering the alert text you cannot simply press Enter at any point; you should keep all this on one line, even though it's a very long line.

Of course we can't show this as one line in this book, so we have to move parts of the line down. And we've placed these little arrow continuation symbols to show that you can't break the line there.

Where, then, can't you break a line? Avoid breaking a statement. When assigning a value to a variable, do it all on one line. Whenever you are entering text between quotation marks, don't break the line. When using a document.write statement, don't break the line. As you can see, we indent text to the right to make the code easier to read (we'll discuss this more in Chapter 8, "Troubleshooting & Avoiding Trouble"). That means that sometimes even short lines are pushed way off to the right, so you may be tempted to press Enter and break the line into two; don't do it.

Later in this book we'll be talking about *event handlers*, which are placed in HTML tags. These also should not be broken between lines, except when you are using multiple statements in an event handler (in which case you can end a statement with ; then press Enter and type the next one).

How do you deal with this problem of very long lines while you are typing your text? Turn on your text editor's word wrap feature. The text will be wrapped down to the next line where necessary, even though you haven't entered a line break, making it easier to read and work with.

We've created three variables (msg1, msg2, and msg3), then placed the message (in three parts) into those variables. Then we placed those variables into the alert function. (This is more advanced than we really want to get right now!)

TIP

If you include an apostrophe or quotation marks in your message text, precede the characters with a forward slash (\ ). For instance, in the above example we used Web\'s, Don\'t, and he\'ll. For double-quotation marks you'd do the same: \"special\", for instance. Actually, in some cases you can get away without using the forward slash—in others you can't. It's better to get into the habit of using them all the time.

Okay, so you don't have to enter this exact message—replace everything between the quotation marks with whatever message you want. We've used a built-in JavaScript function—alert—to display our text in a dialog box. As soon as the browser starts loading the document and sees this script, it will run it and display the dialog box. So, what happens when people arrive at your Web page? Before the page even opens, they'll see the dialog box in Figure 2-5. When they click on the OK button, the page will continue loading.

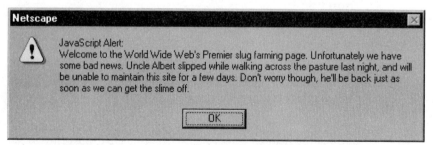

Figure 2-5: *Creating Alert messages is very easy.*

TIP

This is a very long message. If you were placing a message of this length in an HTML Web document, you would normally break up the lines with carriage returns in your editor—to make it easier to work with. The browser reading the document will ignore the breaks. Don't *add breaks in this case, though, when using the built-in alert function, or your readers will see error messages instead of the dialog box.*

If you prefer to show the message *after* the document has loaded, there's another way to display it: you can use the `onload` event handler. This is placed inside an HTML tag (the `<BODY>` or `<FRAMESET>` tag) and tells the browser to carry out an action as soon as it's finished loading the HTML document, or the contents of the last frame. Use this `<BODY>` tag:

Example 2.7

```
<BODY onload="alert('Welcome to the World Wide Web\'s Premier→
slug-farming page. Unfortunately we have some bad news. Uncle→
Albert slipped while walking across the pasture last night,→
and will be unable to maintain this site for a few days.→
Don\'t worry though, he\'ll be back just as soon as we can→
get the slime off.')">
```

This time, the Web document loads, and *then* the message box appears.

DEPARTURE MESSAGES

You can also display messages when the reader *leaves* a page. Of course, you should be careful how you create these messages, because if the reader moves from the current page to another page, he'll see the message, even though he's not actually leaving your site.

Here's how to create a departure message. Instead of using `onload`, this time we use `onunload`:

Example 2.8

```
<BODY onunload="alert('Wait, don\'t go! There\'s lots more!→
Have you seen our slug cuisine section, yet?')">
```

TIP

If you see the words donbt *and* therebs *in the message, you should upgrade your browser. This was a bug in earlier versions of Netscape Navigator 2.0—the browser didn't recognize \ ' as an apostrophe.*

STATUS BAR MESSAGES

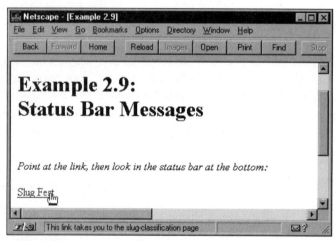

Figure 2-6: *Status Bar Message.*

Another thing you'll see a lot of—because it's very easy to do—is status bar messages. You'll see messages appear in the status bar when you click on a link, and even messages in the status bar that appear automatically when you open the document, or even scroll across the status bar. Be careful with these messages, though.

They're the sort of thing that lots of people will use, because they are so easy. But many users will find them irritating. Users who like to glance at the status bar to see the URL of the links they're pointing at won't thank you for making it harder for them to do so. Still, if you want to try it, here's how. Create a link anywhere in your document, like this (link to whatever page you want—it's the onmouseover bit that we're interested in):

Example 2.9

```
<a href="slug.htm" onmouseover="window.status='This link→
takes you to the slug-classification page';return true">Slug
Fest</a>
```

Simple, eh? We've used another of JavaScript's event handlers—this time, the onmouseover event handler, which, not surprisingly, does something when the mouse pointer moves over the link. Make sure that you include the ;return true part, or it won't work. This is not part of the message, it's part of the window.status instruction. You can replace the text between the single quotation marks with anything you want, of course. Note that they must be single quotation marks, however. When you "nest" quotation marks within other quotation marks (notice the double quotation marks before window.status and after return true), you must use singles inside.

Notice, also, that when you move away from the link, the message remains in the status bar. Point at another link, though, and the message will be replaced by the URL of that link. However, when you move the mouse pointer away from that link, the message reappears. If you pointed at another link that places a message into the status bar, then the new message is used. (There's a way to use a command to clear the status bar, too. You will see that in Chapter 17, "Communicating With the User.")

ADD MESSAGES TO YOUR FORMS

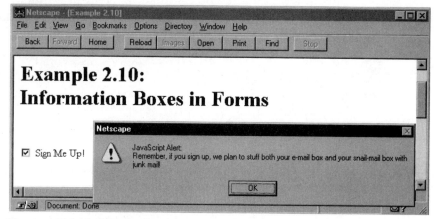

Figure 2-7: *Information Box.*

Would you like to add messages to the forms inside your Web pages? You can use these messages to make the forms easier to use. When the reader clicks on an element, for instance, or even moves from one element to another, you can display a message providing information about that particular form element. Here's an example. First, in the HEAD of your document, place this script:

Example 2.10

```
<SCRIPT LANGUAGE="JAVASCRIPT">
<!--
function AlertBox1(){
        alert("Remember, if you sign up, we plan to stuff→
both your e-mail box and your snail-mail box with junk mail!")
}
//-->
</SCRIPT>
```

Next, create your form and use the function in the form. We're going to create a check box, like this:

```
<FORM>
<INPUT TYPE="CHECKBOX" NAME="check1" onclick=AlertBox1()>
Sign Me Up!
</FORM>
```

In this check box, we've used the `onclick` event handler; so when the user clicks on the check box, something happens. What? The `AlertBox1()` function—which we defined in the HEAD—is called, which in turn calls the built-in `alert` function, which displays our message.

It also would be nice if we could create a message that appeared when someone moved to or "focused" on an element in any manner—by tabbing into a text box, for instance. Unfortunately, JavaScript makes that difficult. There are some other events you can use. `onBlur`, for example, which runs when the focus moves from an element to another, could display a message when the user tabs from one element to the next; it would also display when the user did just about anything, such as moving to another application, using the Back or Forward button, and so on. Then there's the `onfocus` event handler, which runs when focus moves to an element. It's not very helpful, however, because the browser gets stuck in a loop: focus moves to the element, so the message appears, so you close the message box, so the focus moves to the element, so the message appears. This is not a problem exclusive to JavaScript; the same thing would happen in Visual Basic, for example. But JavaScript has only a small number of events to choose from, so there are fewer ways around the problem. We'll revisit this issue later, in Chapter 12, "JavaScript Events."

AUTOMATICALLY FORWARDING READERS

Would you like to automatically forward readers from one page to another? For instance, if you've set up a page that uses JavaScript, you can forward people with JavaScript browsers from your plain old home page to a fancy JavaScript page. Or if you move locations, you can automatically forward JavaScript-browser users to your new page. Here's an example:

Example 2.11

```
<SCRIPT LANGUAGE="JAVASCRIPT">
<!--
alert("Our URL has changed. Please bookmark the new one when→
we forward you to the new page. And please inform the owner→
of the page you have come from of the change. Thank you.")
//-->
</SCRIPT>
</HEAD>
<BODY onload="location='2-12A.htm'">
```

First, we put an alert message at the top of the page. This runs as soon as the browser begins reading the HTML document, so the JavaScript Alert message box opens first. Then, when the user clicks on the message box's OK button, the browser continues reading the HTML until it comes across the `<BODY>` tag. When it sees the `onload` event handler, it continues loading the page; then, when it's finished, it runs the `onload` instruction. That instruction tells the browser the location of a document that it should load; in this case, the 2-12A.HTM document. So the browser automatically loads the next document.

There's a problem with using this technique, though: it messes up the user's History lists to some degree. If someone uses the Back button to go back through the history list, he'll arrive at your document, which will then push him forward again. (He can still use the history list itself, selecting an entry that appears *before* your automatically forwarding document.) There is yet another way to forward people, however—we could use a Confirm dialog box.

AUTOMATIC FORWARDING—WITH A CONFIRM DIALOG BOX

You can get around this problem by adding a Confirm dialog box. The user will see the message, but will have both the OK and Cancel buttons to choose from. When the user first sees the message, he'll click on OK and will be transferred to your new page. But when he uses the Back button, moving back through the history list, he can simply click on the Cancel button, then on the Back button again. This time he won't be pushed forward again. Here's how to do this:

Example 2.12

```
<SCRIPT LANGUAGE="JAVASCRIPT">
<!--
function redirect() {
        if (confirm ("The Web page has been moved. Please book-→
mark the new page, and ask the owner of the page you've come→
from to change the link. Click on OK to continue to the new →
page."))     {
                location='2-12A.htm'

        }
}
<!--End-->
</SCRIPT>
</HEAD>
<BODY onload="redirect()">
```

This is a little more complicated. We've created a function called `redirect`, which contains an `if` statement. The `if` statement uses a built-in function called `confirm`, which is very similar to the `alert` function that you have used already—except that it creates a JavaScript Confirm message box, one with an OK and a Cancel button. At the end of the `if` statement is the `location='2-12A.htm'` instruction. This means, "if the user clicks on OK, display Web document 2-12A.htm."

If this isn't completely clear right now, that's okay—you don't need to understand it to use it; simply type this script into your page, replacing the filename `2-12A.htm` with the correct filename or URL.

YOU CAN'T HIDE EVERYTHING!

JavaScript presents you with a dilemma: it makes it more difficult to create documents that work in a variety of different browsers. Of course, there's already a similar problem on the Web—some browsers won't work with many of the HTML tags you want to use. Many Web-site designers have simply decided they don't care, that they will use all the advanced tags they want (and recommend that users get Netscape so that all the tags work). Others have created two sets of documents: one for the advanced browsers, and one for the not-so-advanced browsers. And others have done their best to develop sites that work reasonably well with both types of browsers. With JavaScript it's more difficult to do that, though. Create one of these special buttons or links, and a non-JavaScript browser won't be able to use it—it may not even display the button correctly. There's not a lot you can do about that. You can hide these components using the <!-- and --> tags, but it may get complicated trying to provide two ways to access material in the same page, one for JavaScript and one for non-JavaScript browsers. With some of the simple things we've looked at, there's no problem. For instance, you can create Welcome messages that will display if the browser can work with JavaScript, but will be completely invisible to the users of non-JavaScript browsers.

Once you get heavily into JavaScript, you'll probably assume that anyone viewing your site *must* be using a JavaScript browser. That's not too much of a problem. By the time you read this, most Web users will be using JavaScript browsers (the Netscape 2.0 family of browsers), and other browsers will become JavaScript-compatible soon.

MOVING ON

Okay, that's the easy stuff—now it's time for work. As you've seen, JavaScript allows you to do a number of very easy tasks quickly. But you'll only be able to use the real power of JavaScript if you learn more—a lot more—about how to really program with JavaScript. In the next few chapters, we're going to take JavaScript apart, breaking it down component by component and learning what each piece does.

So, move on to Chapter 3, and we'll begin by taking a look at the different places you can put JavaScripts, and how to use functions.

CHAPTER 3

First Steps— Scripts, Functions & Comments

Y ou've seen how easy JavaScript can be, but we cheated a little. We didn't fully explain what we were doing (though the samples were so simple that in most cases you could probably figure out what was going on). Before we can go any further, you need to understand the basic structure of JavaScript—the various elements of this programming language.

First, we need to explain a little problem in programming. Programmers use all sorts of strange terms to describe their code, and these terms are often imprecise. (Get a group of programmers together and ask exactly what they mean by the term *object*, for example, and you may be forced to listen to a long and confusing argument.)

We're going to use the programming terms as best as we can, but we're not going to delve too deep into the semantics of programming. Some terms we've ignored, as they are ambiguous and imprecise. We've given simple, down-to-earth descriptions of all the programming terms we are using. It's more important to know how to use each component of this programming language than to get an education in programming terminology.

There's a lot to learn about JavaScript, so we're going to begin with the very basics. Remember, we are assuming that you understand HTML. This is not a book about creating Web pages—it's a book about adding JavaScript to those Web pages; so you'd better understand HTML authoring first. We will explain a little about the HTML tags that we are working with, and you may be able to follow along with limited HTML knowledge; but if you get stumped by the HTML, take a look at an HTML reference for more information about the particular tags or procedures we are using.

 ## TWO WAYS TO RUN JAVASCRIPT

There are two occasions on which your browser carries out instructions it finds in a JavaScript:

1) Some parts of your JavaScript run as soon as the browser has loaded the Web page.

2) Some parts of your JavaScript run as a result of the user initiating an action.

There are two types of things you may want to do when the browser loads the page. First, you may want to do something that the user can see immediately. For example, you may want to display a Welcome message to the user in a dialog box that pops up over the browser. (You've seen how to do that already, in Chapter 2, "A Few Quick JavaScript Tricks.") Second, you may also want to do something that will not be visible to the user—something that is really preparing things for later. For example, you may want to define *functions* that you plan to use later—when the user clicks on a button, say. When the browser loads the page, it will read the script, see that you want to define a function, and will define the function for you—basically, placing a little bit of information into memory. The user won't notice anything happening. (We'll come back to functions in a few moments.)

As we have two occasions on which scripts are run, we have two ways to write scripts. We can put them between <SCRIPT> and </SCRIPT> tags, or we can place them inside HTML tags.

THE <SCRIPT> TAGS

In order to get the browser to carry out a script's instructions automatically, without any input from the user, you must place the script between <SCRIPT LANGUAGE="JAVASCRIPT"> and </SCRIPT> tags, like this:

```
<SCRIPT LANGUAGE="JAVASCRIPT">
The JavaScript goes here
</SCRIPT>
```

<SCRIPT> Tags

Throughout this book we've used the <SCRIPT LANGUAGE="JAVASCRIPT"> opening tag. However, the LANGUAGE="JAVASCRIPT" piece is actually optional. The scripts will still work if you do this:

```
<SCRIPT>
The JavaScript goes here
<SCRIPT>
```

It's generally a good idea, though, to use LANGUAGE="JAVASCRIPT". Eventually, this tag attribute may be essential very soon—at the time of this writing, JavaScript was the only scripting language in wide use; but other languages are in the works, notably Microsoft's VBScript. This language also uses the <SCRIPT> tag (LANGUAGE="VBS"), so it will soon be important to identify the type of script being used. It's good programming practice to create scripts that need minimum maintenance. If you prefer, though, you can use <SCRIPT> now. When it becomes essential to add the LANGUAGE="JAVASCRIPT" piece, you can always do a search and replace. (There are a number of tools that allow you to automatically replace selected tags in a collection of Web pages.)

Also note that now and again you'll see "LIVESCRIPT" instead of "JAVASCRIPT". LiveScript was the original, pre-release name for JavaScript; JavaScript-enabled browsers assume that LIVESCRIPT means the same as JAVASCRIPT. Other attributes are likely to be added to the <SCRIPT> tag in the future, too. In fact, we'll look at the SRC= attribute in a moment.

Where can you put a script? Anywhere in the HEAD or BODY of your HTML document. (You'll learn as we progress that there are preferred locations for certain scripts, depending on what they are trying to accomplish.) Also, note that you can put multiple scripts in your pages. You don't necessarily need to shove everything into one big script. Rather, you might have a script in the HEAD and a couple of scripts in the BODY.

INSIDE HTML TAGS—USING EVENT HANDLERS

Another method for placing JavaScripts into your Web pages is to place the script within an HTML tag. This provides a way that the script can respond to things that users do on a page. These scripts are executed only when a user does something like click a button or point at a link. In other words, the scripts are executed in response to *events*, and they rely on special *event handlers*. This is where the real power of JavaScript comes in. You can make your JavaScript respond to an action the user takes, without communication between the Web server and the user's browser. All the processing is done in the browser.

What events are we talking about? There are currently onblur (when the focus moves away from a form element), onchange (when the focus moves away from a form element after the element has been changed by the user), onclick (when the user clicks on something), onfocus (when focus moves to a form element), onload (when the Web page is loaded into the browser), onmouseover (when the user points at a link), onselect (when the user selects text in a text box or text area), onsubmit (when the user clicks on a

Submit button), and `onunload` (when the user does something that causes another Web document to load, removing the current one). We've already used some of these event handlers in Chapter 2, and we'll look at them in more detail in Chapter 12, "JavaScript Events."

TWO SIMPLE SCRIPTS

Let's see an example of what we have just discussed. (Remember, you can find all these examples and see exactly how they work in the Online Companion at http://www.netscapepress.com/support/javascript/) We've created a simple HTML document with two scripts inside it. These scripts display the date that the source document was saved, and they display a message box when the user clicks on a button.

First, we placed this script into the BODY of the document, below the <H1> header.

Example 3.1

```
<SCRIPT LANGUAGE="JAVASCRIPT")
<!--
document.write("This document last modified on: ")
document.write(document.lastModified)
//-->
</SCRIPT>
```

Then we created a button in the Web page, like this:

```
<FORM>
<INPUT TYPE="button" NAME="AlertButton" VALUE="Click here"→
onclick="alert('You just clicked the button')">
</FORM>
</BODY>
</HTML>
```

What does this look like? You can see both the Web page and the message box that appears when you click on the button in Figure 3-1. Just click on the OK button to remove the box.

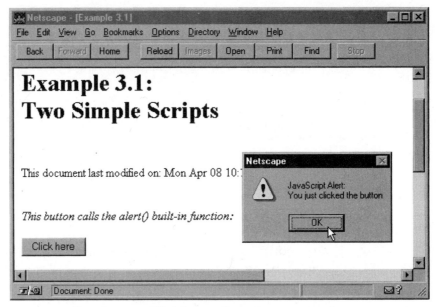

Figure 3-1: *Entering a modified date, and creating a message box.*

Let's take a look at the first script:

```
<SCRIPT LANGUAGE="JAVASCRIPT")
<!--
document.write("This document last modified on: ")
document.write(document.lastModified)
//-->
</SCRIPT>
```

This piece runs as soon as the browser reads it. As you can see from the illustration, it displays the words *This document last modified on:* in the Web page, followed by the date.

The second script is as follows:

```
<INPUT TYPE="button" NAME="AlertButton" VALUE="Click here"→
onclick="alert('You just clicked the button')">
```

In this case, the script is inside an <INPUT> tag. We are creating a button, and we're using the onclick JavaScript event handler. When the user clicks on the button, the script that appears after onclick, the alert function, runs. (In this case, the command is a *built-in function*. This is a function that is already available to you, but which you don't need to define—in this case a function that is associated with an *object*. We'll learn more about these later, in Chapter 10, "Objects, Properties & Methods."

TIP

The TYPE="button" is not a standard <INPUT> attribute, and many browsers currently can't recognize it. It's a new attribute, introduced with Netscape Navigator 2.0 and JavaScript.

USING SCRIPT SOURCE FILES

There's another way to manage scripts for your Web pages—or at least, there will be soon. Place them in a file separate from the HTML documents. Then link to the script file (a text file containing the script) using a SRC=source attribute in the <SCRIPT> tag. When the browser reads the Web page, it will see the attribute and read the script file as if it were actually written into the HTML document itself. This is particularly useful if you want to create complicated JavaScripts and use them in multiple Web pages. Rather than trying to keep all the scripts in all the HTML files up to date and the same, you only need to maintain one script file, then refer to the file from your source documents.

At the time of this writing, this function was not yet working in Netscape Navigator. By the time you read this, however, a later version of Navigator—one that does use this feature—may have been released. So here's how to use it. As a simple example, let's look at how to embed the script we've just seen. First, create a text file with the following information:

```
<!--
document.write("This document last modified on: ")
document.write(document.lastModified)
//-->
```

Name this file something that ends with .js; insert.js, for instance. Now, in your Web page, enter the following <SCRIPT> tags:

```
<SCRIPT LANGUAGE="JAVASCRIPT" SRC="insert.js"></SCRIPT>
```

If you prefer, you can drop the LANGUAGE="JAVASCRIPT" piece, like this:

```
<SCRIPT SRC="insert.js"></SCRIPT>
```

This tells the browser to go find insert.js and follow the script in that file.

A QUICK LOOK AT FUNCTIONS

The next example shows a JavaScript that is read by the browser as soon as the page is loaded, but which causes no actions that the user can see. Try putting the following in the BODY of your document:

Example 3.2

```
<SCRIPT LANGUAGE="JAVASCRIPT")
<!--
function AlertBox(){
     alert("This is the alert box" )
}
document.write("This document last modified on: ")
document.write(document.lastModified)
//-->
</SCRIPT>
```

This time, you'll see that all you get is the *This document last modified on:* line (along with the actual date), but you don't get a button or anything else. Why? What does the part of the script starting with function and ending with } do? Well, this bit of script *defines* a *function*. We will discuss functions in detail in Chapter 7, "More on Functions"; but for now, you can think of a function as a block of script that can be used many times by other scripts within the HTML document. The browser reads the function, loads the function into memory, and then uses the function later, when something *calls* the function. The function then carries out some kind of action—for example, writing some text in a Web page, calling another Web page, carrying out a calculation, or whatever. So this is how a browser can read a script and carry out instructions. It defines the function so it can be used later, even though the action is transparent to the user.

Calling the Function

Of course, in the previous example we haven't called the function, so it won't do anything. So before we move on, let's quickly look at how we can call the function. In the example below we've taken the HTML document from Example 3.2 and added a button that, when clicked, executes the script in the function. That is, it *calls* the function. In the body of the document, we added the following button:

Example 3.3

```
<FORM>
<INPUT TYPE="button" NAME="AlertButton" VALUE="Click here→
to call the function" onclick="AlertBox()">
</FORM>
```

When the user clicks on the button, the `onclick` event handler calls the `AlertBox()` function.

The `<!--` and `//-->` Comment Tags

In some cases, you may want to hide the JavaScript from other browsers. You can do that by adding HTML comment tags. (In other cases, you may have so much JavaScript in your HTML document that it doesn't really matter—the document will be unusable by any non-JavaScript browser.) Anything between the comment tags will be ignored by the non-JavaScript browsers. Make sure that you place the tags *between* the `<SCRIPT>` and `</SCRIPT>` tags, like this:

Example 3.4

```
<SCRIPT LANGUAGE="JAVASCRIPT")
<!--
The JavaScript goes here
//-->
</SCRIPT>
```

Notice the // at the beginning of the line containing the -->. This is not normally used within comment tags; but it is required in this case, as it tells the browser that what follows is not part of the script. Some people create comment tags like this:

```
<SCRIPT LANGUAGE="JAVASCRIPT")
<!--  hide script from old browsers
The JavaScript goes here
// end hiding from old browsers -->
</SCRIPT>
```

There's absolutely no need to do this. The practice has probably arisen from the fact that Netscape engineers who created the original public JavaScript documents wanted to show what they were up to. We prefer not to do this—it just adds to the clutter.

JAVASCRIPT COMMENTS

As you can see, the HTML comment tags have a limited affect on JavaScript browsers. If the HTML comment tags appear between <SCRIPT> and </SCRIPT> tags, the JavaScript browser ignores them—it doesn't really treat them as true comment tags, it simply pretends they're not there. So how can you put real comments into your scripts, notes to yourself and others, that the browser will ignore? Use the following characters:

Example 3.4

```
// This is a comment line

/* This is the beginning of a multi-line comment
this is the second line
this is the third line
This is the last line of the multi-line comment */
```

If you want to place a single comment line into your script, start the line with //. In fact, you'll notice that's what we did when entering the last line of the HTML comment: we put // -->, so the // would tell the browser that the --> is not part of the script.

If you want to enter several lines of comments, you can either start each line with // (you'll notice that many JavaScript authors do that), or you can start the first line with /* and finish the last line with */. You can also use // to put comments at the end of script lines, as follows:

```
<SCRIPT LANGUAGE="JAVASCRIPT")
<!--
function AlertBox(){      //I've defined a function here
     alert("This is the alert box" ) //the function→
runs alert
}
document.write("This document last modified on: ")   //now→
I'm writing text
document.write(document.lastModified) //grabbing the→
document's modified date

//-->
</SCRIPT>

<FORM>
<INPUT TYPE="button" NAME="AlertButton" VALUE="Click here to→
call the function" onclick="AlertBox()">    //this button calls→
the AlertBox function
</FORM>
```

A browser reading this will run the script as normal; but when it gets to the // on each line, it will ignore the text after the //, skipping to the next line. By the way, it's also popular for programmers to add a line like this:

//

to set off a block of comment lines, so that they are easy to see while scanning the program. Such lines are also used to split up parts of a script, so you can quickly find your way through it (you might put a line like this above each function you define, for example).

Finally, here's another way to use comments. Some programmers like to do this for multi-line comments:

```
/* This is the beginning of a multi-line comment
 * this is the second line
 * this is the third line
 * This is the last line of the multi-line comment
 */
```

This makes it easier to see the number of lines the comment spans. It's also a method that can be read by an automatic document generator that's provided with the Java Development Kit, so many Java programmers use this method.

These comments are very handy. Often you may want to enter comments to yourself, to remind you what you did in a particular script. In fact, comments are essential, especially for inexperienced programmers, because they help you figure out what a script is doing. Right now, as you write a script, you may think you'll remember the script; but come back in six months and try to figure it out, and you'll appreciate having comments to lead the way. Also, remember that if you have colleagues who may need to work with your scripts at some time, they'll be very grateful for any help you can put into your scripts.

Bug Alert—Use HEIGHT & WIDTH Attributes

Many people are reporting problems with their JavaScripts related to inline images. They've found that they run into problems if they don't include the HEIGHT and WIDTH attributes in the <IMG> tag. Of course, the fix is simple: simply use the HEIGHT and WIDTH attributes in any documents containing JavaScript. You can also try placing an empty script (<SCRIPT> </SCRIPT>) after the last image tag, though using the HEIGHT and WIDTH attributes is probably better.

MOVING ON

You've seen where to put your JavaScript scripts, and you've learned how to define functions and use comments. If you tried the examples, you've actually created some JavaScripts—albeit very simple ones. Before you can do anything more complicated, there is plenty more to learn. We're going to move on now to learn about *variables* (little "boxes" that store information for your scripts) and *literals* (the data that you put into those variables).

CHAPTER 4

Variables & Literals— Storing Data

This chapter will explore *variables*. Variables can be thought of as boxes to keep things in that you'll need while running your JavaScript. Perhaps you want to add two numbers together (say, 5 and 7), and you plan to use the result later in your script. Where are you going to store the result? You could put it into a variable in your script:

```
sumresult = 5+7
```

After this piece of code has finished, `sumresult` will contain the number 12 (the result of 5 + 7). This number is now stored in your document, and you can use the stored number whenever you need it by referring to `sumresult`. You can also put a number directly into the variable. For instance, instead of making a calculation and placing the result in the variable, you could simply state that the variable is equal to something, as follows:

```
thisnumber = 2
```

Look, for example, at these scripts:

Example 4.1

```
<SCRIPT LANGUAGE="JAVASCRIPT")
var sumresult = 5+7
```

```
var thisnumber = 2
document.write("Here's what's in the sumresult variable:  " →
+ sumresult + "<P>")
document.write("Here's what's in the thisnumber variable:  " →
+ thisnumber)
</SCRIPT>
```

We've created the two variables, `sumresult` and `thisnumber`. We then used the `document.write` command to write the contents of the variables to the Web page. What will you see? The following:

```
Here's what's in the sumresult variable: 12
Here's what's in the thisnumber variable: 2
```

Notice that when we used the `document.write` instruction, we were able to write three different things: text that we wanted displayed in the page (we enclosed this text with the " and " quotation marks), the variable values (`sumresult` and `thisnumber`, which don't need to be enclosed in quotation marks), and an HTML tag, `<P>`, the tag that starts a new paragraph. (The HTML tag, like the text, must be enclosed in quotation marks.) We joined all these items together using + signs.

TIP

We put spaces before and after the + sign. You don't have to use spaces (the script still will work), it just makes reading it a little easier.

It is usual in most programming languages to *declare* variables. This means that before you use a variable, you give it a name. This tells whatever is running the program to put aside appropriate memory for the contents of your variable.

In JavaScript, you declare variables using the `var` keyword:

```
var firstname
```

This declares a variable called `firstname`. You can also put some data into the variable when you declare it. This is called *initializing* a variable. For instance:

```
var state = "Colorado"
var salary1 = 50000
```

We've created two variables here: `state` and `salary1`. In each case, we've also placed something into the variable (the "box" that stores the contents of the variable). In the first case, we've stored the word `Colorado`; while in the second case, we've stored a number, 5000.

TIP

When you place text into a variable, you enclose the text in quotation marks: "and". We'll discuss this more later in this chapter.

Actually, what we've done here is not *entirely* necessary—though it's advisable. We've used a somewhat formal method for declaring a variable; but JavaScript allows you to declare one in an informal manner, by simply naming the variable without using the `var` keyword first. We could have done this, for instance:

```
state = "Colorado"
salary1 = 50000
```

In this case, we didn't use the `var` keyword; we simply provided a variable name and the contents of the variable. This, in effect, automatically declares the variable. However, it's good programming practice to declare all variables formally, by preceding the name with `var`. Unfortunately, the fact that JavaScript allows variables to be declared informally means that mistakes can be introduced quite easily by simply mistyping. For instance, let's say you have declared a variable somewhere, like this:

```
var month
```

and then, later, placed a value into the variable like this:

```
months = "June"
```

You mistyped the second name (`months`). What does JavaScript do? Because it allows informal variable declarations, when it sees `months` it assumes that it's a new variable—it declares the `months` variable. Some programming languages won't allow informal declarations, or they provide a way that the programmer can restrict informal declarations if he wishes. In a programming language that doesn't allow informal declarations, `months = "June"` would be regarded as an error, not simply taken as another variable.

Still, JavaScript does allow informal declarations, but there are two things you can do about that: be very careful when you type variable names, and use the formal method when you intentionally declare variables. It's tidier, and it also helps you find variables in your scripts—you can quickly search on the var keyword.

There's another problem with not using var, one associated with the *scope* of variables (where the variables are available). As you'll see later in this chapter, there are both *global* and *local* variables; and if you don't use var, these may get mixed up. We'll look at that problem later in this chapter, under "Variable Scope—Where is This Variable Available?"

NAMING VARIABLES

You can call a variable almost anything you want, as long as you follow a few simple rules.

1. The first character in the name must be a letter (a–z or A–Z) or an underscore (_).

2. The rest of the name can be made up of letters (a–z or A–Z), numbers (0–9), or underscores (_).

3. Don't use spaces inside names. For instance, you could use FirstName but not First Name.

4. Avoid the "reserved" words, words that are used for other purposes in JavaScript. For instance, you couldn't call a variable *with* or *transient*. You can find a list of reserved words in Appendix E, "Reserved Words."

TIP

It's a good idea also to avoid the names of JavaScript's objects, methods, built-in functions, and so on. In some cases you may be able to use these names and get away with it, in other cases you won't—you'll create a bug in your script. Avoid them—your scripts will be less confusing and less likely to malfunction. You can find lists of these names in the appendices.

5. You must use the same case for your variables whenever you refer to them. If you declare a variable called state, don't refer to the variable as State or STATE.

Here, for instance, are some valid variable names:

year1999

First_Name

_people

Here are some invalid names:

$1000

1000

&Me

Date&Time

TIP

You may come across the term identifier; *this is programming-speak for* name. *Variables and functions have* identifiers.

VARIABLE NAMES ARE CASE-SENSITIVE

It's very important to remember that variable names are case-sensitive. In other words, you can't use the variable by typing its name using the opposite letter case than the way that you originally declared the variable. Take a look at this little script:

Example 4.2

```
<SCRIPT LANGUAGE="JAVASCRIPT")
<!--
var thetext = "The year is "
var TheText = thetext +  "1996"
//-->
</SCRIPT>
```

What does this script do? Well, it begins by defining two variables. First, there's thetext. This variable contains the text, The year is. The following line declares TheText. This variable contains two things: the contents of the thetext variable, plus the text 1996.

You can see this example at work in the Online Companion. You'll see that we added two buttons. Each button uses the `onclick` event handler to use the built-in `alert` function to display the contents of the variables, like this:

```
<I>Clicking on this button shows you the contents of the
thetext variable:</I><BR>
<form>
<input type="button" value="thetext" onclick="alert→
(thetext)"><BR>
<input type="button" value="TheText" onclick="alert(TheText)">
</form>
```

What happens when you click on the first button? You'll see a dialog box that contains the words *JavaScript Alert: The year is*. It *doesn't* include the text *1996*, though. Why? Because the `thetext` variable only contains the words *The year is;* it doesn't include the year. The year is in the `TheText` variable—the contents of which can be seen when you click on the second button. As you can see, case matters—type the variable in the wrong case, and your script won't work. (By the way, we're not suggesting that it's a good idea to have two variables of the same name, distinguished only by case. You'll only confuse yourself!)

TYPES OF VARIABLES

In most programming languages, you can have different *types* of variables for the different types of data you use. You can have *numeric* variables—that is, variables that hold numbers with which you can then do math. You could also have variables that hold text (text stored in a variable is known as a *string* in programmer babble). You can't use a string variable in math calculations, because the data is held in its own *type* of variable. For example, look at these variables:

```
var number1 = 5
var firstname = "Chuck"
```

The variables have been given types by putting some data into them. The variable `number1` above is a numeric variable, because it has been *initialized* with the number 5. The variable `firstname` is a string variable, as it contains a string—we know that it's a string, because it's between quotation marks.

JavaScript actually has three types of variables:

string variables—these contain text (the text appears between quotation marks). For instance: `var firstname = "Joe"`

numeric variables—these contain numbers. For instance: `numberofpeople = 9`

boolean variables—these contain "logical" statements (`true` or `false`). For instance: `Member = true`

TIP

Also, there's a special keyword, `null`, that is treated as an "empty" variable.

Unlike some programming languages, though, in JavaScript you don't need to specify the type of data that will be held by the variable when you declare it. If you declare a variable without specifying the data type, that variable is classified as *uninitialized*. In fact, if you try to display a variable that has never had data assigned to it, you will get *<undefined>* in your output. For instance, take a look at the following script:

Example 4.3

```
<SCRIPT LANGUAGE="JAVASCRIPT")
<!--
var text2
//-->
</SCRIPT>
```

This time we've declared only the `text2` variable, and we haven't placed any data into it. So `text2` is an *undefined* variable. Later in the script we create the following button:

```
<form>
<input type="button" value="Undefined variable, text2"
onclick=alert(text2)>
</form>
```

The built-in function `alert` calls the `text2` variable. What do we see? We see a message box that says *JavaScript Alert: <undefined>*. (It shouldn't really say *undefined*—it should say *uninitialized*, which is a more accurate term.) This, at least, is how Netscape 2.0 currently deals with this situation. Remember, though, that each browser may act—*will* act—a little differently when working with JavaScript, just as different browsers display HTML slightly differently.

TIP

There are two types of "faulty" variables. First, there's the uninitialized variable, which is one that has been declared but has no data; the JavaScript Alert message box will open, as we've just seen. Or, if you try to use the variable somewhere—in a calculation, for example—you'll get an error message. Second, there's the undeclared variable. This is a variable that you have used in a script somewhere— perhaps you refer to it in a button—but you have never declared it. In this case, you'll see an Error message box. (You can see an example of this message box later in this chapter, in Figure 4-1. Note, however, that in Netscape 2.0 the message box says that it's an "undefined" variable; really it should say "undeclared.")

As soon as you put some data into a variable, it becomes one of the three types we mentioned: string, numeric, or boolean. The very act of placing data into a variable defines the variable's type.

TYPES CAN CHANGE

JavaScript is said to be a *loosely typed* language. That is programmer-speak, meaning that you don't have to be too fussy about how you use your variables. You don't have to specify the type of data that will be held by the variable when you declare it, and a variable type can actually change. For instance, you may have this variable at some point in a script:

```
var Member = 5
```

Then, later in the script you may have this:

```
var Member = False
```

The variable started life as a numeric variable, holding the number 5. Later, it became a boolean variable, holding `False`. You can think of JavaScript's variables as boxes that can hold different things. They can only hold one type of information at a time: numbers, text, or logical statements. But you can change the content type at any time by replacing one content type with another. In our example, we've replaced a number with a boolean value; so the variable changed from a numeric to a boolean variable.

In many programming languages you would have to actually declare what the variable would hold; you would actually state what type of variable you were declaring using a special keyword. In JavaScript you don't need to worry about this—the act of giving the variable data gives the variable its type.

You have to be very careful with changing a variable from one type to another, because you can mess up your scripts if you do something wrong. Look at the following, for example:

```
var text1 = 19
var numb1 = 96
var variable1 = text1 + numb1
```

This gives the result of 115—19 plus 96 equals 115. But now look at this:

```
var text1 = "19"
var numb1 = 96
var variable1 = text1 + numb1
```

In this case you are taking a variable containing a string (`"19"`) and adding a number to it (`96`). Instead of getting 115, you get `1996`. The number in `numb1` is converted to a string, because `text1` is a string, and the value is tacked onto the end of the `text1` value. Thus, 19 "plus" 96 equals 1996.

> **TIP**
>
> *Don't change variable types! Yes, you can do it if you really want to; but it's a good idea, especially for new programmers, to avoid changing types. Changing types can get you into trouble, so save yourself some headaches and don't do it. However, there's also something called* type conversion, *which refers to the way in which variable types can be mixed in expressions, and how the program will automatically change types for you in some circumstances. We've covered that in Chapter 5, "Expressions & Operators" under "Type Conversion."*

STRING VARIABLES HOLD TEXT

A string variable is one that holds text. What is text? Well, it can be letters and numbers, and any other characters, such as !"^%$$*4654654*&. A variable may contain a number and still be a string variable (but not a numeric variable). For example:

```
NumberOfPages = 95
NumberOfPeople = "95"
```

The variables above are treated in very different ways by the computer. The variable `NumberOfPages` is numeric, because it has been initialized with the number 95. This number can be used in calculation. However, `NumberOfPeople` is a string variable, because the number 95 is enclosed in double quotes. You can use this to print the number *95* at some point, but you cannot use it in a calculation. We will see later how strings and numeric variables are treated differently.

If a JavaScript browser looks at a variable in a script and sees that the data after the = sign is enclosed in quotation marks, it creates a string variable—regardless of what is inside the quotation marks.

NUMERIC VARIABLES HOLD NUMBERS

Numeric variables hold nothing but numbers. They may hold integers (4 or 156, for example) or floating-point numbers (3.1459, for example). Integers are whole numbers, and floating-point numbers have a decimal point. In many computer languages you'd need two different types of variables to hold these two different types of numbers. However, in JavaScript there's only one form of numeric variable and it can contain either of these number types. You can also use scientific notation: 5.1245e21, for instance, or 1.235E-26.

If a JavaScript browser looks at a variable in a script and sees that the data after the = sign is *not* enclosed in quotation marks, and if it is not the word `true` or `false`, it creates a numeric variable. Actually, it looks a little closer than that, because there are three types of numbers you can use: decimal (base 10, the numbers we are all used to), octal (base 8), and hexadecimal (base 16). If it finds a number with no leading zero, it assumes that it's decimal; if it finds a number with a leading zero, it assumes that it's octal; and if it finds a number with a leading zero followed by x, it assumes that it's hexadecimal. However, having said all that, you probably won't need to use octal or hexadecimal often.

By the way, if you try to assign non-numeric data to a variable without putting that text in quotation marks, Netscape won't like it. You'll probably get a *"xxx* is not defined" error message (where *xxx* is the data you were trying to place into the variable).

BOOLEAN VARIABLES HOLD TRUE OR FALSE

Boolean variables get their name from boolean algebra, which is a mathematical representation of logical operations. Computers use logic to perform all of their operations, and computer languages use it as well. It's really quite straightforward. A Boolean variable can only contain one of two values: `true` or `false`. Computers operate using 1s and 0s—these can also be represented as `true` or `false`.

Boolean variables are provided in a computer language so that you can write instructions such as:

```
If something is true
    (then do this)
otherwise
    (do this)
```

This is known as a *conditional expression*. It's one of the most powerful instructions you can have in a computer language, because it allows you to put decisions into your program or script—and these decisions are dependent upon boolean variables. We'll learn more about these conditional expressions in Chapter 6, "Conditionals & Loops—Making Decisions & Controlling Scripts."

VARIABLE SCOPE—WHERE IS THIS VARIABLE AVAILABLE?

Scope is programmer-speak for "where can I get at the contents of this variable." Variables can be declared either outside or inside a function, and where they are declared has an effect on the scope:

- **Inside a function.** In the examples that we've just seen, the variables were declared inside functions. The variables are said to be *local* to the function. If you declare a variable inside a function, you can only use it inside the function. Try to use it in some other way—in another function, for example—and it won't work. By the way, this means that you can have a variable declared inside a function and then can use another variable of the same name outside that function, as JavaScript regards the variables as two separate things.

- **Outside a function.** If you declare a variable outside a function, it is said to be *global*. This means that it is available anywhere in the script—inside or outside functions.

Let's take a quick look at the way scope affects variables. In the Online Companion, you'll find a page using this script:

Example 4.4

```
<SCRIPT LANGUAGE="JAVASCRIPT")
<!--
var variable1 = "Contents of variable1 OUTSIDE the functions"

function funcExmpl1() {
    alert(variable1)
}
function funcExmpl2() {
var variable1 = "Contents of variable1 INSIDE the function"
    alert(variable1)
}
function funcExmpl3() {
    alert(variable2)
}
//-->
</SCRIPT>
```

What does this script do? It starts by declaring a variable named `variable1`, and it then places the string `Contents of variable1 OUTSIDE the functions` into that variable. This is a global variable, because we declared it outside a function. Next, it defines a function named `funcExmpl1`, which uses the built-in function `alert` to display the value of `variable1`.

Then we define another function, this time `funcExmpl2`. In this function, though, we've started by declaring a variable called `variable1`. This time we put the following text into the variable: `Contents of variable1 INSIDE the function`. This is a *local* variable, because it's *inside* the function. Finally, the function uses `alert` to display the contents of `variable1`.

Then we define another function, `funcExmpl3`. This simply uses `alert` to display the contents of `variable2`, which hasn't been declared anywhere.

Later in this Web page we've created a few buttons, like this:

```
<FORM>
<INPUT TYPE="button" NAME="ButtonA" VALUE="
Show the global variable1 outside the functions         "
onclick="alert(variable1)">
<P>
```

This button uses the `onclick` event handler to call `alert` directly—it's not calling a function that we've created. The `alert` object displays the contents of `variable1`, because it has been "passed" to it inside the brackets (more on this later). Go to the Online Companion and try this; when you click on the button, you see a message box showing this: *JavaScript Alert: Contents of variable1 OUTSIDE the functions.*

As you can see, we're viewing the contents of the global variable named `variable1`. We don't see the contents of the local variable named `variable1`, because it's only available to the function in which it is declared. Now, here's the second button:

```
<INPUT TYPE="button" NAME="ButtonB" VALUE="      Show the→
global variable1 as seen from function funcExmpl1     "
onclick="funcExmpl1()">
<P>
```

This button uses the `onclick` event handler to call the function named `funcExmpl1`. Refer back to the earlier scripts, and you'll see that `funcExmpl1` uses `alert` to display the contents of the *global* variable `variable1`. So this time we see this: *JavaScript Alert: Contents of variable1 OUTSIDE the functions.*

```
<INPUT TYPE="button" NAME="ButtonC" VALUE="        Show the→
local variable1 as seen from function funcExmpl2        "
onclick="funcExmpl2()">
<P>
```

> **TIP**
>
> *The button* INPUT TYPE *currently doesn't allow size control, so we added spaces to make all the buttons more or less the same size.*

This button uses the `onclick` event handler to call function `funcExmpl2`, which, as we saw earlier, used `alert` to display the contents of `variable1`. This time, though, we are seeing the *local* `variable1`, because we declared a variable with that name *inside* the function. The local variable overrides the global variable in this case. (By the way, the global variable has not been reset in any way; use the previous buttons and you'll still see the contents of the global variable. It's just that when using this particular function, the global variable is overridden—though see the problem we cover in the next section, "Why You Should Use Var.") We see the following message: *JavaScript Alert: Contents of variable1 INSIDE the functions.*

```
<INPUT TYPE="button" NAME="ButtonD" VALUE="Using a variable→
in a function where the variable not been declared"
onclick="funcExmpl3()">
</FORM>
```

Finally, this button uses the `onclick` event handler to call function `funcExmpl3`, which in turn uses the `alert` object to display the contents of `variable2`—a variable that has not been declared anywhere. This time we see what's shown in Figure 4-1. As we mentioned earlier, if you try to use an undeclared variable, you'll get an error message.

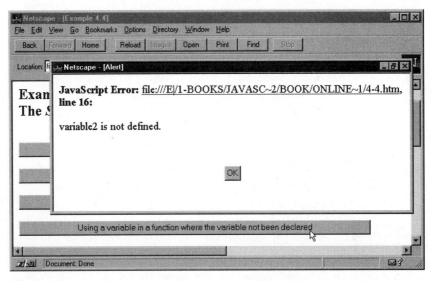

Figure 4-1: *Referring to the contents of a variable that hasn't been declared displays an error message.*

WHY YOU SHOULD USE VAR

Earlier in this chapter, you learned why you should use the var keyword when you declare your variables. Well, here's another reason: if you don't, things can get awfully mixed up. For example, take a look at this script:

Example 4.5

```
<SCRIPT LANGUAGE="JAVASCRIPT")
<!--
var func1 = "This is the global variable named func1"
function Display1() {
    alert(func1)
}

function Display2() {
func1 = "This is local variable named func1"
alert(func1)
}
```

```
//-->
</SCRIPT>
```

We started by declaring a variable called func1. This is a global variable, because it's not inside a function. Next we defined a function, Display1, which uses the built-in alert function to display the contents of the func1 variable.

Then we defined another function, Display2. This time we declared a variable within the function, a *local* variable, again called func1. Notice, though, that we didn't use the var keyword this time. Next we used alert again to display the contents of the func1 variable.

After this, in the BODY of the Web document, we created a couple of buttons:

```
<FORM>
<INPUT TYPE="button" NAME="ButtonDisplay1" VALUE="Display1"
onclick="Display1()"><BR>
<INPUT TYPE="button" NAME="ButtonDisplay2" VALUE="Display2"
onclick="Display2()">
<FORM>
```

The first button calls the Display1 function, and the second button calls the Display2 function. Each function displays the contents of the func1 variable, remember; but which func1 variable, the local or the global?

Well, if you go to the Online Companion and try this, make sure that you click on the Display1 button first. You'll see a message box that says this: *JavaScript Alert: this is the global variable named func1.*

Now click on the second button, Display2, and you see: *JavaScript Alert: this is the local variable named func1.*

Okay so far; everything is working correctly. But now click on the Display1 button again. This time you'll see this: *JavaScript Alert: this is the local variable named func1.*

Now we are seeing the contents of the *local* variable, even though we thought we'd be calling the global variable. It doesn't matter which buttons you click on now or in what order—the local variable has taken over. Until you reload the document, you won't see the contents of the global variable.

Example 4.6

What happens if we modify the script, though. In the Online Companion's Example 4.6, we added the word `var` when declaring the local variable. Instead of this:

```
func1 = "This is local variable named func1"
```

we now have this:

```
var func1 = "This is local variable named func1"
```

in the `Display2` function.

Everything else about this example is exactly the same. Try Example 4.6 and you'll find that the buttons now work correctly. The local variable remains local, and the global variable remains global—regardless of whether you've used the Display2 button or not.

So, *use* `var` *and save yourself some confusion!* (Of course, you may come across an event in which you want to change the value of a global variable in a function, but be careful not to confuse yourself.)

TIP

Here's another case of something you can do, but should avoid. You can, if you wish, use a name for a variable inside a function that you've already used for a global function—but save yourself trouble and don't do it.

WHAT IS A LITERAL?

Let's discuss *literals* for a moment. You've already used them, and you don't really need to know much more than you've already learned. *Literal* is simply a fancy term for the data that you place into your script—actual numbers and text, rather than calculated values.

A variable may contain a calculated value, or it may contain a number *32*, or a word *John* that we have *literally* typed into the script. Literals are things that *you* have put into the script, rather than things calculated by the script. For example, look at this variable:

```
numberofpeople = 27
```

Here, `numberofpeople` is the variable and 27 is a literal. The number 27 cannot vary. It is literally 27. In this case, we are using a *numeric literal*. As we've already seen, a literal can also be a string or piece of text:

```
firstname = "Derek"
```

Here, `firstname` is the variable, and its contents are "set to the literal" `Derek`. This is a string, of course, as it's enclosed in quotation marks. So this is known as a *string literal*. Just because you put a literal into a variable, though, doesn't mean that the variable is stuck with it; you can do something later in the script that will modify the variable, of course. Remember, literal is just a fancy way for saying, "the stuff you entered (when writing the script) rather than the stuff that's calculated."

SPECIAL CHARACTERS IN STRING LITERALS

You can use special "codes" in string literals to represent special characters. For example, let's say you want to include quotation marks in the text that you are placing into a string literal. This presents a problem, because quotation marks are characters used by the script itself to identify different parts of the script. As we've seen, they are used (among other things) to identify string literals! Adding more quotation marks will just confuse the script.

So if you want to include quotation marks in a script, you do it like this: `\"`.

> **TIP**
>
> *Don't get these slashes mixed up; remember, we're using the backslash here (\\), not the normal forward slash (/) used in HTML tags.*

If you wanted to add a backslash in a script, you'd do it like this: `\\`.

The backslash (\\) says, in effect, "the following character (the quotation mark or forward slash or whatever) is part of my text, not part of the script." There are other things that you can do, too. You can use `\n` to move the text to a new line, for instance. You can use `\t` to enter a Tab character. And you can also include HTML tags; for instance, you can include `<BR>` to place a line break in the text.

SPECIAL CHARACTERS

There are a few more special characters (\r, \f, and \b), although you are not likely to use them. Here's the current full list of special characters:

Backslash:	\\
Single quotation mark:	\'
Double quotation mark:	\"
Tab:	\t
Carriage return:	\r
Backspace:	\b
Form feed:	\f
New line:	\n

By the way, \r is a little ambiguous. This is old terminal-computing stuff. Traditionally, \r means carriage return, not line feed (\l). The two (return and line feed) can be replaced by \n, which is equivalent to \r\l. (In other words, "move the text to the left and down a line.") But in JavaScript, \r means carriage return and line feed. If you work in other programming languages or plan to move onto other languages, such as C or C++, you may want to use \n instead of \r for compatibility. However, there are also a few idiosyncracies in the way that JavaScript handles line breaks. For instance, when writing text to a text area form element, you must use \r\n if the browser is running in a Microsoft Windows operating system. However, you only use \n if the browser is running in Unix. We've discussed this problem further in Chapter 11, "More About Built-in Objects," under "Using String Methods With Object Properties."

The characters you use will depend on what you intend to do with the text, because they don't work in all situations. You can include quotation marks in text written to the Web page (using `document.write`, for example) and to Alert boxes. However, you'll find that HTML tags won't work in Alert boxes (though they *will* work when written to the Web page, of course); and most \ characters won't work when written to the Web page (but *will* work in the Alert box!).

Take a look at the following example. We started by declaring these variables:

Example 4.7

```
<SCRIPT LANGUAGE="JAVASCRIPT")
<!--
var twainA = "\"I never write \'metropolis\' for seven cents,→
because I can get the same price for \'city.\' \" Mark→
Twain."
var twainB = "\"I never write \'metropolis\' for seven cents,→
\rbecause I can get the same price for \'city.\' \" Mark→
Twain."
var twainC = "\"I never write \'metropolis\' for seven cents,→
<BR>because I can get the same price for \'city.\' \" Mark→
Twain."
var twainD = "\"I never write \'metropolis\' for seven cents,→
\tbecause I can get the same price for \'city.\' \" Mark→
Twain."
//-->
</SCRIPT>
```

You can see that they all have \" and \' to place double and single quotation marks into the text. We then used \r, <BR>, and \t, to show the effect of these different codes (carriage return, HTML line-break tag, and Tab).

In our Online Companion example (Example 4.7), we used the document.write instruction to write the contents of each variable to the page. And we created four buttons that write the contents to Alert boxes. You can see an example in Figure 4-2. You'll find that in all cases the quotation marks appear, while the <BR> tag works in the document.write instruction but not in the Alert box. The \r and \t codes work in the Alert box, but not in the document.write instruction.

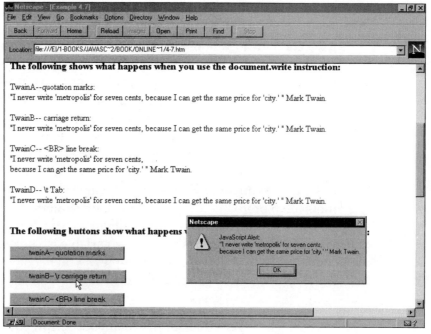

Figure 4-2: *Using special characters in string literals.*

THE 255-CHARACTER BUG

There's a bug in a number of Netscape browsers (in the 2.0 series, and even—in some cases—in the 3.0 beta series) that limits the number of characters you can put on a single line—no more than 255. So it's a good idea never to exceed this limit, even if the browser you are working with does not have this problem; many of the browsers already in use *do*, so if you use long lines, many of your Web site's users may run into problems.

For example, if you want to write a very long message into a variable, don't do it all at once. Instead, write a small portion into several variables, then join them together and place them into the final variable (you'll see how to do that in Chapter 5, "Expressions & Operators").

MAKE VARIABLE NAMES IDENTIFY THE VARIABLES

It's a good idea to choose descriptive names for your variables. Using a variable called X may have the advantage of being easy to type; but when you need to make a change to your code in six months, you will have to spend time trying to figure out what X is. If you had called it Salary, then what it represents will be much easier to discern. You will also find it easier to read your programs if you capitalize the first letters in words (FirstName, for example).

Because it is easy to forget what type of variable (string, numeric, or boolean) you are referring to and where it is defined, programmers often prefix the variable name with something that tells them what kind of variable it is and what its scope is. In JavaScript this is easy. Use the s prefix to show that a variable is a string, n for numeric, and b for boolean. For example, if you had a variable called Month, you would prefix the name with s for a string variable:

```
var sMonth = "April"
```

Now whenever you use sMonth in your script, you will know that it is a string. There is no way that you will get it confused with a variable containing the number of the month as in:

```
var nMonth = 4
```

You can also use the prefix g to denote a global variable. This can help avoid the errors that we talked about earlier. For example, a variable gsMonth is a global string variable. If you change the type of a variable in your program, it may be best not to prefix it with a type. In general, using the prefix notation will make things clearer.

MOVING ON

You've got a good grounding in variables now. The concept of variables is really quite simple: they are little places in which you or the script store information, that the script can then use later. We'll learn more about using variables later.

For now, we'll move on to expressions, conditional expressions, and loops—the most powerful part of programming, really. This is often called *program control* or *control flow*, and is all about how you get your programs to do things—how programs make decisions and repeat actions. In effect, you are showing your programs how to interact with the user and the browser.

CHAPTER 5

Expressions & Operators— Manipulating Values

You may not realize it, but you already have used *expressions* in the example scripts. An expression is a piece of script that uses variables, literals, and *operators*. An expression takes the values of variables and literals and derives other values from them. Without expressions your programs are nothing more than one-trick ponies; click on this button and the dialog box opens, open this document and a welcome message starts, and so on. To do more, you need to make your programs do some computation and data processing work. Programmers do that by manipulating values in expressions.

So what's an operator? Not surprisingly, an operator is an action of some kind—doing arithmetic on numbers, adding variables together, and checking to see what a variable contains, for example. The operation produces a result—a value that can then be used elsewhere in the script. As we'll see, the result can be *assigned* to another variable. So let's begin looking at the operators you can use in JavaScript.

USING OPERATORS IN EXPRESSIONS

Take a look at this simple expression:

```
nSum = 4 + 5
```

We are using two operators in this expression. The + is an operator that adds together two literal values and the = puts the result into something, in this case into a variable called nSum. Here is another expression:

```
nTax = nCost * nTaxRate
```

This expression is only slightly more complicated. This time we've used the multiplication operator * to multiply the values held by two variables (nCost and nTaxRate). Again we've used the = operator to take the result and place it into another variable, this time nTax.

TIP

Remember, we're using an identification system for our variables. In this case the n in front of the names means that the variables are numeric variables. See Chapter 4, "Variables & Literals—Storing Data" for more information.

Expressions do their work on the right side and *assign* values to the variable on the left. The = symbol is known as an assignment operator, because it assigns values to variables.

The result of an expression is always a single value. You will now be able to clearly see the difference between a variable and a literal in the following:

```
7  =  6 + 7
```

This is gobbledygook. You cannot assign a new value to the number 7. That's a *literal*. As we will discuss in Chapter 14, "Controlling Windows & Documents in JavaScript," you can't change the value of a literal. (You can use it to create another value, but a literal is a literal, and cannot itself be changed.) The above expression is just plain wrong. You cannot assign new values to literals, you can only assign values to variables. There is, however, nothing wrong with this:

```
nSum = 6 + 7
```

We've carried out the same calculation; we've used the + operator to add two literals together, but this time we've assigned the result to the variable nSum.

Expressions, then, take this form:

```
variable = (operators working on variables and literals)
```

In other words, on the left you have a variable to which you'll assign the result of the operation carried out on the right. The operation uses variables, literals, or both variables and literals together to create the result. So this expression is also wrong:

```
nSum = nValue = 6 + 7
```

This is incorrect because it doesn't follow the form we just looked at above; we tried to assign a result to two variables at the same time, and you simply can't do that. Of course you *could* do the following, if you really wanted the same value in both variables for some reason:

```
nValue = 6 + 7
nSum = nValue
```

You have a valid expression on the first line because you've assigned the result to just one variable. Then, on the second line, you've assigned the new value in that variable to the other variable.

ARITHMETIC OPERATORS

Now, let's look at the operators that JavaScript uses for doing mathematics. This table lists JavaScript operators and describes their uses:

=	As we've seen, this is used to assign values to variables.
+	Adds two values together.
–	Subtracts one value from another, or changes a value to a negative value (this is known as a *unarynegation*—for example, nValue = –nCost— in this example we changed the value in nCost to a negative value, and then assigned the result to nValue).
*	Multiplies two values together.
/	Divides one value by another.
%	The Modulus operator divides one number by another, discards the remainder, and gives the result as an integer.
++	Increments a value (adds 1 to it) in a variable.
--	Decrements a value (subtracts 1 from it) in a variable.

There are also some other assignment operators (other than =) which we'll discuss later.

Let's look at a few examples of how you can work with these operators.

ADDING & SUBTRACTING

Example 5.1

```
var nSum = 0
var nCost = 57
nSum = 25 + nCost + 33
```

This simple script declares two variables and assigns initial values to each. It then adds 25 (the value in nCost), and 33 together, and assigns the result (115) to the nSum variable. If you click on the button we've placed in the Example 5.1 page in the Online Companion, you'll see the value of nSum in a message box.

Example 5.2

```
var nProfit = 0
var nPrice = 99
var nCosts = 47
nProfit = nPrice - nCosts
```

This time we've declared three variables, used the subtraction operator to subtract one value from another, and then assigned the result to the nProfit variable; 99 minus 47 equals 52.

MULTIPLYING

Example 5.3

```
var nArea = 0
var nWidth = 100
var nLength = 33
nArea = nWidth * nLength
```

In this example, we are using the multiplication operator to multiply a width (the value in nWidth), by a length (nLength) and then assign the result to the nArea variable; 100 x 33 = 3300.

DIVIDING

Example 5.4

```
var nPricePerPerson = 0
var nTotalCost = 1500
var nPeople = 40
nPricePerPerson = nTotalCost / nPeople
```

This time we use the division operator to divide the value in nTotalCost by the value in nPeople; 1500/40 = 37.5.

MODULUS—DIVIDING & DISCARDING

Example 5.5

```
var nRoughPrice = 0
var nTotalCost = 1500
var nPeople = 40
nRoughPrice = nTotalCost % nPeople
```

The Modulus operation is, in effect, a type of "rounding" operation; when you don't need total accuracy, you can carry out a calculation and then drop everything to the right of the decimal point. This example is almost the same as the previous one. We divide the value in nTotalCost by the value in nPeople; 1500/40 = 37.5. But this time we use the % symbol instead of the / symbol; so after dividing the values, the .5 is dropped and the number 37 is assigned to the nRoughPrice variable.

> **TIP**
>
> *Bug Alert: If you are using any of the Netscape browsers up to and including Netscape Navigator Version 3.0 beta 4, then the Modulus operation probably doesn't work. You'll get a completely incorrect number. This will be fixed in later releases of these products.*

INCREMENTING & DECREMENTING VARIABLE VALUES

The increment and decrement operators are a little different from the others we've looked at. When you add, subtract, divide, or divide and discard, the original value in the variable remains unchanged. For instance, in the last example, the value originally placed in nTotalCost is 1500. What is the value held by nTotalCost after the calculation is made? It's still 1500. We're using the variable as a place to store a value that we can use in a calculation. When we need to make the calculation, the script takes a look in the variable to see what it holds—in this case 1500—and then uses that value. But it doesn't change what's held by the variable.

The increment and decrement operators *do* modify what's in the variable, though. Take a look at this:

Example 5.6

```
var nY = 6
nY++
```

This uses the increment operator to add 1 to nY; we start by declaring nY and placing the value of 6 inside; then we use the increment operator to add one, so we end up with 7. The variable nY (as you'll see if you click on the button in our Online Companion), contains the number 7; so the operator has actually modified the variable itself. We haven't even assigned the value to any other variable in this case.

Using the increment operator like this is, in effect, equivalent to this:

```
var nY = 6
nY = nY + 1
```

The third line may look a bit funny, but it is perfectly okay as far as an expression is concerned. This is like taking the value in nY and adding 1 to it, and then assigning the value back to nY.

++?

++ sound familiar? You may recognize the increment operator, ++ from somewhere else. You may have heard of the C and C++ programming languages. The name C++ is a pun on the increment operator, as it implies that C++ is an increment (or development) of the C programming language.

Example 5.7

```
var nY = 6
nY--
```

Uses the decrement -- operator to make nY equal 5. The decrement operator is like the increment operator, except that you take 1 away from the variable. This expression is equivalent to this:

```
var nY = 6
nY = nY - 1
```

STRING OPERATORS

The addition operator + also can be used to put strings together and is called the *concatenation operator* when used this way. (*Concatenate* is a word, little used by nonprogrammers, that means to string or chain together in series.) We've used this operation in earlier examples, but let's take another look:

Example 5.8

```
var sFirstName = "Derek"
var sLastName = "Halfabee"
var sFullName = sFirstName + " " + sLastName
```

The + operator here *concatenates* the strings—that is, it connects them together so the result in variable sFullName will equal Derek Halfabee. The expression begins by taking the sFirstName variable. Then it adds a space. It has performed this operation because we used the + symbol (the concatenation symbol in this case), then enclosed a space between quotation marks: " ". The quotation marks indicate that the space is part of the text. (If you *don't* include this, you'll end up with DerekHalfabee, of course.) It then used another + symbol followed by sLastName. The result of the operation is assigned to sFullName. Remember that sFirstName and sLastName will not change because the result is assigned to the left side of the expression. (We'll talk more about manipulating strings later.)

LOGICAL OPERATORS

Logical or *boolean* operators are used often in programming. They are used to get programs to make decisions about what to do next. JavaScript, along with most other programming languages, has two boolean literals: *true* or *false*. Logical operators are used to create expressions that involve these true or false values. In effect you are creating logical "calculations." Instead of working with numbers, though, you work with states: true or false.

The operators are:

!	Not (tells you what value the variable *doesn't* contain)
&&	And ("adds" two variables together)
||	Or (this is the "pipe" symbol, usually the shifted \ key. This operator also "adds" variables, but treats the result slightly differently)

These operators are used to make these logical "calculations" by manipulating the contents of a boolean variable in various ways. The *Not* operator (!) takes a boolean value and changes it to its opposite value:

```
!true evaluates to false

!false evaluates to true
```

Let's see what this means. Take a look at this example:

Example 5.9

```
var bFirstValue = false
var bCheck = !bFirstValue
```

We've declared a boolean variable called bFirstValue. We've initialized that variable with the boolean value of false. But on the next line we modified that value. We used the *Not* operator by placing it in front of the variable name. This means, in effect, "get the value that is *not* in the !bFirstValue variable. bFirstValue contains false. As there are only two possible boolean values, the value that is *not* in the bFirstValue variable is, of course, true. We then used the = assignment operator to place the returned value into the bCheck variable. So if you click on the button in this example in our Online Companion, you'll see a dialog box that displays the contents of the bCheck variable: true.

The *And* (&&) and *Or* (\|\|) operators are used to combine two boolean values. The *And* operator combines two values in the following ways:

```
true && true evaluates to true
true && false evaluates to false
false && false evaluates to false
```

We've put these into the following example.

Example 5.10

```
var bFirstValue = true
var bSecondValue = false
var bThirdValue = true
var bFourthValue = false
var bCheck1 = bFirstValue && bSecondValue
var bCheck2 = bFirstValue && bThirdValue
var bCheck3 = bSecondValue && bFourthValue
```

As you can see, in this example we carried out three operations. In the first, in which the result is assigned to bCheck1, we added the values of two variables that contain true and false. In the next case, we added true and true. And in the last case we added false and false. In the Online Companion, we added three buttons to the page to display the contents of bCheck1, bCheck2, and bCheck3. You'll see that the first variable contains false, the second variable contains true, and the third variable contains false.

> **TIP**
>
> *Here's a quick way to remember this. When you use And you'll get* **true** *returned only if all the variables contain true. In all other cases, you'll get* **false***. Which, of course, makes perfect sense. Or think of it like this: "both* this one *and* that one *must be true in order for the expression to be* **true***." So if only one value is* **true***, it's not enough.*

The *Or* operator combines values in a different way. You might think of it like this: "*either* this one *or* that one must be true in order for the expression to be **true**." So even if only one value is true, it's enough. :

```
true || true evaluates to true
true || false evaluates to true
false || false evaluates to false
```

As you can see, the difference is in what happens when you have two values that are not the same. If you are using And, you'll always get `false`. If you are using Or, you'll always get `true`. In the two other cases, you'll get the same result. For instance:

Example 5.11

```
var bFirstValue = true
   var bSecondValue = false
   var bCheck = bFirstValue || bSecondValue
```

In this case, as you'll see in the Online Companion, the `bCheck` variable contains `true`, not `false`.

We will go into the use of these operators in more detail in the section on conditional expressions.

OTHER ASSIGNMENT OPERATORS

The = symbol isn't the only operator that assigns values to variables. There are also other operators that allow you to include the value from the variable to the left of the operator and include it in the operation. Here's what we mean:

=	As we've seen, this takes the result of the operation on the right and places it in the variable to the left of the symbol. For instance, nPricePerPerson = nTotalCost / nPeople.
+=	This takes the value in the variable on the left and adds it into the operation on the right, then replaces the original value with the new one from the operation. For instance: x += y means add x to y, then place the new number in x. This is equivalent to x = x + y.
-=	This time the original value is decremented. For instance: x -= y means subtract x from y, then place the new number in x. This is equivalent to x = x - y.
*=	This time we are multiplying. For instance: x *= y means multiply x times y, then place the new number in x. This is equivalent to x = x * y.
/=	This divides. For instance: x /= y means divide x by y, then place the new number in x. This is equivalent to x = x /y.

| %= | This is modulus; it performs division and throws away anything to the right of the decimal point. For instance: x %= y means divide x by y, remove anything to the right of the decimal place, then place the new number in x. This is equivalent to x = x % y. |

These operators, along with ++ and −, are known as *shorthand operators* because they provide an abbreviated way to write expressions. If you are just starting to learn programming, you may prefer the long form for these operators. When you feel more confident with the language, you may want to start incorporating them into your scripts.

BITWISE OPERATORS

There are some other JavaScript operators called *bitwise operators* that you may encounter—in the Netscape documentation, for instance. These perform operations on numbers as strings of bits. Computers, of course, think in terms of bits. Although we may write programs using numbers, letters, and a variety of typographical characters, at some point all this must to be translated into binary units—*bits*. Bitwise operators allow a programmer to manipulate these bits for a variety of purposes (which we're *not* going to discuss in this book!). These are advanced operators and are way beyond the scope of this book. In fact, bitwise operations are rather geeky things that are rarely used in programming and *very* rarely used in JavaScript. However, just so that you can recognize bitwise operators if you run across them somewhere, here they are:

shift (various kinds)	<< >> >>> <<= >>= >>>=
and	& &=
xor	^ ^=
or	| |=

CONDITIONAL OPERATORS

We haven't looked at all the available operators yet. There are the *conditional operators*, symbols that are used when creating *conditional expressions*. A conditional expression is one in which you are getting your script to make a decision. For example, you can ask it to compare two variables, and carry out a particular operation if the values match, or another operation if the values *don't* match. Conditional expressions are discussed in the next chapter, so we'll cover conditional operators there.

OPERATOR PRECEDENCE

When an expression is evaluated, there is a certain order to how it is done. This is known as *operator precedence*. As you will see, this precedence is important to understand, though the details are not so important to remember. Take a look at this expression:

Example 5.12

```
var nCostPerItem  = 100
var nNumItems = 5
var nTaxPerItem = 10
var nTotal1 = nCostPerItem * nNumItems + nTaxPerItem * →
nNumItems
var nTotal2 = nCostPerItem * (nNumItems + nTaxPerItem * →
nNumItems)
```

Notice that we have two different calculations, one assigning the return to nTotal1, the other assigning the return to nTotal2. You'll also see that both calculations use the same values, and in the same order. Yet when you click on the buttons in the Online Companion, you'll find that you get *very* different values; nTotal1 contains 550, while nTotal2 contains 5500.

Let's examine the first expression:

```
var nTotal1 = nCostPerItem * nNumItems + nTaxPerItem * →
nNumItems
```

The value returned by this expression is dependent upon the order in which it is evaluated. If it is evaluated simply by going left to right, it will give this:

```
nCostPerItem * nNumItems    (100 times 5 = 500)
+ nTaxPerItem               (500 plus 10 = 510)
* nNumItems                 (510 times 5 = 2550)
```

But this is *not* the result we get, as you can see in the Online Companion. This is what actually happens when this expression is evaluated:

```
nCostPerItem * nNumItems    (100 times 5 = 500)
nTaxPerItem * nNumItems     (10 times 5 = 50)
Add the two results         (500 plus 50 = 550)
```

Expressions are not simply evaluated from left to right, because certain parts are evaluated before others. Higher precedence operators are applied before lower order ones. You can see from the above example that the multiplication operators are applied before the addition operator.

You can force an expression to be evaluated in a particular way using parentheses. For example, look at the last line of the previous example:

```
var nTotal2 = nCostPerItem * (nNumItems + nTaxPerItem * →
nNumItems)
```

This time the expression has to start by working on the items within the parentheses first. After all, until it calculates a result from within the expression, it has nothing to multiply by nCostPerItem. However, note that within the parentheses the order of precedence still holds. In other words, in this case the multiplication operator will be carried out first, then the addition. Finally the result from within the parentheses will be multiplied by the value held by nCostPerItem. Here's how it works this time:

```
nTaxPerItem * nNumItems     (10 times 5 = 50)
nNumItems + 50              (50 plus 5 = 55)
nCostPerItem * 55           (100 times 55 = 5500)
```

This now evaluates to 5500 (remember within the parentheses the multiplication operator is evaluated first).

Multiplication and division take a higher precedence than addition and subtraction, and that is about all you need to know, really. If you are in any doubt about the order in which an expression is to be evaluated, then use parentheses; clearly the calculations within parentheses must be carried out first, before the result of the parentheses can be used. Programmers often can't remember operator precedence because, well, life is just too short to be wasted learning it. Instead they use parentheses to force calculations to work the way in which they want them to.

If you are in any doubt about how your expression is evaluated it is best to use parentheses. Using parentheses makes it easier to read the program and will save you time because it reduces confusion, especially if you don't know who will be reading your program and what level of knowledge they have. And finally the biggest bonus is that you won't need to remember a long and uninteresting list of operator precedences.

You can see all the operators in the following table. At the top of the table you'll find the operators that are given the highest precedence (the ones that are used first). At the bottom you'll find the operators with the lowest precedence (the ones carried out last). It looks complicated, but you should understand that few programmers remember all the details of the precedence table used in the language in which they program. Instead, they use parentheses to keep everything straight. Of course we haven't covered all these operators yet, either, so the table will make more sense as we progress. You can see a quick definition of all the symbols in Appendix F, "Symbol Reference."

call (calling a function), member	() [] .
negation/increment	! ~ – ++ ––
multiply/divide/modulus	* / %
addition/subtraction	+ –
bitwise shift	<< >> >>>
relational	< <= > >=
equality	== !=
bitwise-and	&
bitwise-xor	^
bitwise-or	|
logical-and	&&
logical-or	||
ternary or "shorthand if" operator	?:
assignment	= += –= *= /= %= <<= >>= >>>= &= ^= |=
comma (separates parameters)	,

TYPE CONVERSION

Type conversion occurs in expressions in which you use variables of different types. In other words, the program decides what to do with a particular variable, and modifies the data in the variable so that it can be used with the other variables. The result, after all, can only be of one type. For example:

Example 5.13

```
var sMonth = "August"
var nYear = 1996
var nDay = 15
var sDate = sMonth + " " + nDay + ", " + nYear
```

The + operator here concatenates the variables and literals into one string and puts it into sDate, which is a string variable. Why is it a string variable? Because one of the variables providing data to be concatenated is a string variable; sMonth contains the word *August*. And because there's no real way to convert a string to a number, one of JavaScript's type-conversion rules is that if you add a numeric variable to a string variable, the numbers must be converted to strings and the result is a string.

TIP

Using the concatenation operator (+) to "add" strings to numbers, or numbers to strings, will always *result in numeric values being converted to strings—even if the strings are numbers. For instance, adding* "8" + 1996 + 15 *results in 8199615, not 2019.*

Because the values in nYear and nDay are numbers, they are converted to string values before they are concatenated with the other strings. The number 1996 in nYear becomes the string *1996*, and the number 15 in nDay becomes the string *15*. As we have said earlier, numbers and strings are held by the computer in different ways and during type conversion the way this data is represented internally to the computer changes. You can see that adding the s and n prefixes to your variable names is important, as it helps you keep all this straight.

At the time of writing the type-conversion rules were not clearly documented, but we can identify a basic rule: If a calculation doesn't make sense, you'll get an error. JavaScript is what's known as *loosely typed*. Other programming languages have much stricter rules about how you can assign a datatype to a variable, and how you can convert one type to another. JavaScript, on the other hand, is more tolerant and lets you change types quickly and easily—but you may run into problems when you do so.

For instance, if you use an expression that mixes both numeric and string values, JavaScript will convert the numeric value to a string *if it makes sense to do so*. We've just seen an example of how

JavaScript converts a number to text when you are using the addition/concatenation operator (+). Whether you add a string to a number, or a number to a string, you'll end up with a string value. This makes sense, and it works.

But this *doesn't* work when you use the subtraction operator (–). Subtract one from another and you'll end up with a numeric value:

Example 5.14

```
var sVariable1 = "555"
var sVariable2 = sVariable1 + 10
var sVariable3 = sVariable1 - 10
```

Here we started with a string variable, with the string value of *555*. Then we added 10 to the string and assigned the result to sVariable2. This is the same sort of thing we did in the previous example—click on the first button on this page in the Online Companion and you'll see the value held by sVariable2: *55510*. The value is a string, not a number.

Then we *subtracted* 10 from sVariable1, and assigned the result to sVariable3. This time, when you click on the associated button, you'll see the number 545. The result, then, is a numeric value (555 - 10 = 545). This makes sense. Why? Because you can't "subtract" a piece of text from another piece of text, so there's no point trying. Instead JavaScript assumes that you want to do a mathematical calculation, so it converts the text to a number.

The problem arises when you use the subtraction operator between a numeric value and a string value that isn't a number. For instance, take a look at this Online Companion example:

Example 5.15

```
var sVariable1 = "Fred"
var sVariable2 = sVariable1 + 10
```

This is fine; adding sVariable1 and 10 gives a string value (we'll end up with *Fred10*). But we also created a button that uses the subtraction operator:

```
<input type="button" name="VariableButton" value="sVariable1→
 - 10:String with Text - Numeric" onclick="alert(sVariable1→
 --10)">
```

You can see that we used `sVariable1 - 10` in the alert instruction. Now, when you click on this button, you'll see two things: an error message saying *sVariable1 is not a numeric variable*, and the JavaScript message box, which contains the value *0*. (We put this calculation directly into a button rather than up in the HTML HEAD along with the other stuff, because we didn't want the error message to appear as soon as you opened the Web page, which it would if the variable had been declared in the HEAD.)

But that's okay. The expression is meaningless; what does *Fred* minus *10* mean, after all? Here's another example. What happens when we try to multiply text by a number?

Example 5.16

First, we have the following in the HEAD:

```
var sVariable1 = "Fred"
var sVariable2 = "15"
var nVariable3 = sVariable2 * 2
```

The variable named `nVariable3` has been created by multiplying the contents of `sVariable2` (15) by the number 2. When you click on the associated button, you'll see that we end up with *30*. The script converts the value in the variable to a numeric value and then multiplies it by 2. It does this because it *can*, and because it doesn't make sense to do it any other way.

On the other hand, we also have this button in the page:

```
<form>
<input type="button" name="VariableButton" value="sVariable1→
* 10: String with Text * Numeric" onclick="alert(sVariable1→
* 10)">
</form>
```

This button displays the result of multiplying `sVariable1` (Fred) by 10. How can this be done? We don't know, and neither does JavaScript, so it gives us an error message.

Type conversion takes place in a fairly logical manner. If your expression does not make sense, it will probably produce an error. If you are unsure of what may happen, test it by modifying one of the scripts from the Online Companion, or try your own.

MOVING ON

You've now seen how computers can use expressions and operators to take values and derive other values from them. This is a great start, but there's still something missing. How can a computer take these values and make decisions based on them? That's done with what are known as *conditionals*, special statements that can be used to examine data and carry out operations depending on the value held by the data. Conditionals allow a computer to say, for instance, "if this variable contains such and such a value, I'll do this; if it doesn't, I'll do something different."

This is where the real power of programming lies, and that's what we'll be looking at next.

CHAPTER 6

Conditionals & Loops— Making Decisions & Controlling Scripts

Now, let's move on to the ways in which you can get your program to make decisions and to do things repetitively. Let's look into decision-making first. You can do this by using *conditional* expressions. We all use conditional expressions in everyday speech. For instance:

"If your report card is good, I will give you $10."

The first part of this sentence, "If your report card is good," is a conditional expression. It is either true or false. If it is *true*, the second part of the statement will be performed, and the cash will be handed over. If it's *false*—if the report card is bad—the second part of the statement is *not* carried out. Actually, the statement could be a little more complicated:

"If your report card is good, I will give you $10. Otherwise, you'll have to go to summer school."

In this case, something *does* happen if the condition is false. If the report card is not good, then you'll have to go to summer school.

A conditional statement can evaluate to true or false—that is, there are two possible results, true or false. Computers are pretty stupid and cannot handle partly true values, so this expression cannot cope with a situation in which your report card was barely acceptable, but not absolutely awful—you didn't get the $10, but you didn't have to go to summer school either. JavaScript's conditional expression must evaluate to either true or false, and there is no in-between position.

TIP

That doesn't mean that you can't get a script or program to figure out "shades of gray"; you can do so by using a series of conditional expressions. But each single conditional expression can only have two possible outcomes.

THE 'IF' STATEMENT

One way of writing conditional statements in JavaScript (and in many other programming languages for that matter) is by using `if` statements. If statements follow this form:

```
if(conditional expression) {
    do something
}
```

The conditional expression goes in between the parentheses—( ). If the conditional expression evaluates to true, the expression between the braces {} is performed. If the condition is not true, then the expression between the braces is *not* performed. Let's take a look at an actual example:

Example 6.1

```
var sButton
function function1() {
    if (sButton == "A") {
        alert("You pressed button \'A\'")
    }
}
```

TIP

Important: You must write if, *not* IF *or* If. *These last two forms will not work.*

This creates a function (`function1()`) that uses an `if` statement to decide what to do. Look at the first line of the `if` statement. Inside the parentheses you see this: `sButton == "A"`. This means, "Look at variable `sButton` and see if it is equal to A"(that is, if the variable contains the character A). If the variable *does* contain A, then the expression evaluates to true. (As we'll see in a moment, `sButton` will contain A if you click on Button A. It *won't* contain A if you click on Button B.) It's important to note that the expression within the parentheses after `if` *must be true.* If it's not true, the instructions within the braces—{ }—*will not run.*

> **TIP**
>
> *You'll notice that there are two sets of {} symbols. The first set belongs to the function and encloses its statements, in this case the `if` statement that the function carries out. The second set, which is "nested" within the first, encloses the instructions that the `if` statement carries out if the condition is true.*

Note that the operator used here is not = but ==, two equals symbols together. There is a difference in meaning between the conditional equals == and the assignment equals =. When you use the assignment symbol (which we talked about in Chapter 5, "Expressions & Operators"), the variable to the left of the = is assigned the value of the expression to the right of the =. However, you don't want to do that in a conditional expression. All we're trying to do is see what is inside the variable to the right of the symbol; we're not trying to actually change anything. In a conditional expression there is no assignment of values—a comparison is done, but variables are not given any new values.

Now, remember that in the case where the expression is *true*, the line (or lines) of script between the braces is performed. In this case, we have this line: `alert("You pressed button \'A\'")`. In other words, if the condition is true (if the variable contains A), then the script will display the Alert message box with the text *You pressed button 'A'*. (As you saw in Chapter 4, "Variables & Literals—Storing Data," we have to precede the quotation marks with a \.)

There are two buttons in this example, Button A and Button B:

```
<form>
<input type="button" value=" Button A " onclick="sButton = 'A';
                                    function1()">
<input type="button" value=" Button B " onclick="sButton = 'B';
                                    function1()">
</form>
```

> **TIP**
>
> *You can see that the* onclick *instruction carries out two tasks: first it sets* sButton, *then it calls function1(). Notice that we've moved the second event down one line and indented it. This is simply to make it easier to read. And there's a semi-colon at the end of the first line; this must be there.*

We're using the onclick event here. When the user clicks on Button A, the sButton variable is assigned the character A. If the user clicks on Button B, the sButton variable is assigned the character B. In both cases, immediately after assigning the value the onclick event handler calls function1( ), which, as we've just seen, takes a look at what's inside the sButton variable.

> **TIP**
>
> *Remember to use single quotes for* 'A' *and* 'B' *when used in the* onclick *events, because the instruction after* onclick *is within double quotes.*

DON'T MISTAKE = FOR ==

What happens if you forget the difference between = and ==, and use = in your if statement? Take a look:

Example 6.2

```
function function1() {
    if (sButton = "A")       {
        alert("You pressed button \'A\'")
    }
}
```

Example 6.2 is the same as 6.1, except that the equality conditional operator (==) has been replaced with the assignment operator (=). When the page loads, you will get the following message (this is using Netscape Navigator—other JavaScript browsers may display a different message):

test for equality (==) mistyped as assignment(=)? Assuming equality test.

The function will load, but Navigator is smart enough to assume that you really wanted to put the conditional ==; and the function will behave in exactly the same way as the previous example. Click on Button A to see the message box.

IF STATEMENTS WITH BOOLEAN VARIABLES

Look at the if line from Example 6.1 again:

```
if (sButton == "A")   {
```

As you've seen, this means "if the stuff inside the parentheses is true, then carry out the instructions beginning after the { symbol." In this case it means "if sButton *does* contain A, then carry out the instructions."

Note, however, that the contents inside the parentheses may be a single word. For instance:

Example 6.3

```
var bStatus = true
function CheckStatus()     {
    if (bStatus) {
        alert("The value in bStatus is true")
    }
    else {
        alert("The value in bStatus is false")
    }
}
```

In this script we've declared a boolean variable named bStatus and initialized its value to true. Then we've created a function called CheckStatus(), which uses an if statement to see what value is held by the variable and to display the appropriate Alert box. Notice that the parentheses after if contain nothing but the name of the variable. In effect, this means "if the value held by bStatus is true."

To complete the page, we have two buttons:

```
<form>
<input type="button" value="True" onclick="bStatus = true;
                                          CheckStatus()">
<input type="button" value="False" onclick="bStatus = false;
                                          CheckStatus()">
</form>
```

The first button sets the value of bStatus to true, then calls the CheckStatus() function. The second button sets the value of bStatus to false, then calls CheckStatus().

THE 'ELSE' CLAUSE

As you saw in our report-card analogy, you can create conditional expressions that do something if the condition is false. If you didn't get a good report card (a false condition), you'd have to go to summer school. This is done by using an else clause with the if statement, like this:

Example 6.4

```
function function1() {
    if (sButton == "A")      {
        alert("You pressed button \'A\'")
    }
    else {
        alert("You pressed button \'B\'")
    }
}
```

We've created function1() in the same way as before, but added three more lines, starting at "else {." Again, the instructions that are to be carried out in the false or else condition are enclosed within { and }. In this case we display the Alert message box, but with a different message. If the condition is false, sButton doesn't contain the value A, so we display a message saying *You pressed button 'B'.*

THE USE OF BRACES

In the examples so far, you've used the braces { } to enclose the instructions that are carried out in the true and false conditions. You don't *have* to do this, though we believe it's a good idea to do so. If you don't, only the first expression after the if is conditionally executed. In the next example, the braces have been dropped; but the program is not as easy to read:

Example 6.5

```
var sButton
function function1() {
    if (sButton == "A")
        alert("You pressed button \'A\'")
        alert("This is the line after the if statement")
}
```

(Note that the if statement itself is still enclosed within { }, which belong to the function; it's just the true instructions that are not enclosed.) Try this example and you'll find that if you click on Button A, you'll get *two* Alert message boxes—one after the other. Click on Button B, and you'll just see the second Alert box, which says *This is the line after the* if *statement*. So you *can* do this. You may even be able to think of some uses for this situation; but in general it's a good idea to always use the braces—it is too easy to get confused otherwise.

CONDITIONAL OPERATORS

There are other conditional operators. If you could only check to see if a value equaled something, you would be rather limited. So we have operators that let us see if a value *doesn't* equal something, if it's greater or less than something, and so on. Here are the conditional operators:

==	Equal to (you have just seen this one in action).
!=	Not equal to; checks to see if the value is *not* something.
>	Greater than; checks to see if something is greater than something else. x > y means "check to see if x is greater than y."
<	Less than; checks to see if something is less than something else. x < y means "check to see if x is less than y."
>=	Greater than or equal to; checks to see if something is the same as or greater than something else. x >= y means "check to see if x is the same as or greater than y."
<=	Less than or equal to; checks to see if something is the same as or less than something else. x <= y means "check to see if x is the same as or less than y."
?	Shorthand if operator, often known as the *ternary operator*. It checks a conditional expression to see if it's true, then assigns a value to a variable depending on whether the expression is true or not. x = (condition) ? y : z means "check to see if the condition is true; if so, place the value of y in x; if not, place the value of z in x."

Not Equal (!=)

Our next example shows the "not equal" operator in use. This `if` statement evaluates to true when the variable sButton does *not* contain the value A. This example now has three buttons: A, B, and C. Try it.

Example 6.6

```
function function1() {
    if (sButton != "A")      {
        alert("The variable is not equal to \'A\' \n→
    It is \'" + sButton + "\'")
    }
}
```

The `if` statement conditional evaluates to true when the variable nButton is not equal to A. There are three buttons in this example now; the third button assigns the value C to sButton. When you try this example, you'll see that if you click on Button A, nothing happens. Remember, this `if` statement only does something if sButton is *not* equal to A. If you click on Button B or C, though, you'll see the Alert message box. This box displays *The variable is not equal to 'A'*; then, on the next line (remember, \n means new line), it displays *It is '* followed by the value held by sButton (B or C), followed by a space and '.

Greater Than (>)

The greater than operator (>) is used, not surprisingly, to see if a value is greater than something else. For instance:

```
x > y
```

This means, "see if the value of x is greater than the value of y." The next example shows the greater than operator in use. This `if` statement conditional evaluates to true when the variable sButton is not A. This example now has three buttons: A, B, and C. Try it.

Example 6.7

```
function function1() {
var dToday = new Date()
var nSeconds = dToday.getSeconds()
    if (nSeconds > 30) {
       alert("We are MORE than halfway through this minute. →
       Seconds=" + nSeconds )
    }
    else {
       alert("We are LESS than halfway through this minute. →
       Seconds=" + nSeconds )
    }
}
```

What's going on here? Well, we began by defining the function function1() again. This time, though, we've created an *object* called dToday. This object contains the current date and time, and makes use of the built-in object called Date. (Don't worry too much about this right now—all you need to know is that the dToday object gets the date and time from the built-in Date object.)

On the next line we've declared a variable called nSeconds. This gets the seconds from our dToday variable. (Again, don't worry about the dToday.getSeconds() instruction; we'll be looking at these built-in objects and how they work in Chapter 11, "More About Built-in Objects." For now all you need to know is that nSeconds contains the number of seconds past the current minute.)

TIP

These date and time objects derive the date and time from the computer on which the script is running—that is, on the computer on which the browser is running.

Now, what does the if statement do? It takes a look at the value in the nSeconds variable—the number of seconds past the current minute. We are using the greater than operator, so we're not looking for an exact value; we just want to know if the value is more than 30. If it *is*, we display the first Alert message box. If it *isn't*, we display the second Alert message box (after else).

GREATER THAN OR EQUAL TO (>=)

You can get even more precise by using the "greater than or equal to" operator. In the last example, you told the if statement to determine if the nSeconds value was greater than 30. So what would happen if it was right on 30 seconds when you click on the button? Well, 30 isn't greater than 30, so the condition would be false, and the else Alert box would appear.

That's okay in many situations, but it's possible to be a little more accurate by getting the if statement to check for a value that is the same or more than another. Here's an example:

Example 6.8

```
Welcome to this Web page, and
<SCRIPT LANGUAGE="JavaScript">
<!--
var dToday = new Date()
var nHours = dToday.getHours()
    if (nHours >= 12) {
        document.write("Good Afternoon.")
    }
    else {
        document.write("Good Morning.")
    }
//-->
</SCRIPT>
```

We've actually embedded this little script into the Web page text. As you can see, the text says *Welcome to this Web page, and*. The script determines what appears next, though. Again, we've grabbed the time from the Date object. This time, though, we've grabbed the hours (instead of the seconds) and placed the value into the variable named nHours. Then we used an if statement to see if the value is more than—or the same as—12. If it is, it's the afternoon; so we use the document.write instruction to write Good Afternoon. to the Web page. If it *isn't* (that is, if it's anything less than 12), we use the document.write instruction after else, and write Good Morning. to the Web page.

NESTED "IF" STATEMENTS

In some cases if statements may be *nested*. That means that one if statement is placed within another. You'll remember from earlier in this chapter that conditional statements only allow two choices, so it can't choose from a range of possible decisions. Well, nesting if statements provides one way for you to do this. While one if statement cannot choose from a range, if you nest a few if statements together, the script *can* choose. Your first if statement has two options: a final decision or another if statement, or maybe two if statements. It's the same for the second if statement. It may have a final decision and an if statement, or two more if statements. You can continue down a *cascade* of if statements, each one leading to another.

This is more like the way that people make decisions, isn't it? Rather than saying, "Either we'll go to eat tonight or we'll go to the movies," you make a series of decisions. If you decide to eat, what sort of food do you want to eat? If you decide to eat Indian food, which Indian restaurant will you visit? Will you eat from the buffet or from the menu? If from the menu, what will you choose? Each decision leads to another.

Take a look at this simple example:

Example 6.9

```
<SCRIPT LANGUAGE="JavaScript">
<!--
function function1() {
var dToday = new Date()
var nDay = dToday.getDay()
   if (nDay == 0) {
   alert("It's Sunday")
   }
   else {
        if (nDay <= 5) {
            alert("It's a week day")
        }
            else {
                alert("Hey, it's Saturday")
            }
```

```
      }
   }
   //-->
   </SCRIPT>
```

We're using the Date object again; this time we're grabbing the actual day, which is a number representing the day of the week, from day 0 (Sunday) to day 6 (Saturday).

TIP

When JavaScript uses a range of numbers, it starts at 0, not 1. So the last day of the week is 6, not 7. Sorry, but that's a geek convention.

The processing cascades down these if statements. If nDay is equal to 0 (it's Sunday), the first alert line is executed—*It's Sunday*. If it's any other number, though, the else part of the statement is executed. Inside the else braces is another nested if statement. In this if statement, we check to see if the day is equal to or less than 5. (In other words, it must be 1, 2, 3, 4, or 5—it can't be 0. If it was 0, the script would have executed the first part of the previous if statement.) If it is, then the first alert line is executed; you'll see the message *It's a week day*. If it isn't, then there's only one thing it can be—it must be Saturday—so the else line is executed.

Unfortunately, nesting if statements can get a little complicated. You end up with lots of { } symbols; and you must make sure that you get them paired correctly, or you'll get errors. Remember, for every opening {, you must have a closing } in the correct position. Very deep nesting can look very cluttered, but it's simply a matter of practice to read them and keep it all straight.

TIP

Notice that we've indented the { } symbols to the right, and placed the closing } on its own line. You can also use blank lines in places, to help break up each section. This makes it easier to read the scripts. We'll talk a little more about this in Chapter 8, "Troubleshooting & Avoiding Trouble."

BOOLEAN (LOGICAL) OPERATORS IN CONDITIONAL EXPRESSIONS

There is a class of operators that we haven't discussed much yet, the *boolean* operators. Boolean algebra is a way in which logical statements are expressed in a branch of mathematics called *logic*. (It's really not as bad as it sounds.) In fact, as with straightforward conditional expressions, we also use boolean operators in our everyday speech. For instance, how about this one:

When I've learned HTML and I've learned JavaScript,
I'm going to take a vacation.

The two conditional expressions in the first line are linked together with an "and" to form one conditional expression. They both must be true for the whole expression to be true. Unless I've learned HTML *and* JavaScript, I'm not going to take a vacation. So boolean operators are used to combine conditional expressions together. You can use them to return true only if both conditions are true, or if either one or the other is true. These are the boolean operators you can use:

!	Not (tells you what value the variable *doesn't* contain).
&&	And. Condition x *and* condition y must be true.
||	Or (this is the "pipe" symbol, usually the Shift \ key). Condition x *or* condition y must be true.

Logical expressions evaluate to true or false as do conditional expressions. Let's see how these operators are used in conditional expressions.

Example 6.10

```
function function1() {
var dToday = new Date()
var nHours = dToday.getHours()
var nDay = dToday.getDay()
```

```
if ((nDay == 5) && (nHours >= 12)) {
   alert("Thank God it's Friday afternoon"  )
}
else {
   if ((nDay == 6) || (nDay == 0) ) {
      alert("Hey, it's the weekend" )
   }
   else {
      alert("Just another day")
   }
}
}
```

We've used a nested if statement here, just as in the previous example. But this time we're also using boolean conditional expressions. Here's the first one:

```
if ((nDay == 5) && (nHours >= 12))        {
```

This means, "If nDay is 5 *and* nHours is greater than or equal to 12, then it's Friday afternoon." If both conditions are true, the program executes the code immediately following the first {; you'll see the Alert message box with *Thank God it's Friday afternoon*. If they aren't both true, then the script moves on to the else statement, which contains the nested if statement, which contains the following line:

```
if ((nDay == 6) || (nDay == 0) )        {
```

This means, "if nDay is 6 *or* nDay is 0, then it's Saturday or Sunday." If it's Saturday or Sunday, the program executes the instruction starting after the {, displaying the Alert message box with the message *Hey, it's the weekend*. If neither expression is true, then the last Alert box is displayed, *Just another day*.

Note, by the way, that ((nDay == 6) && (nDay == 0))—which means "if nDay is 6 *and* nDay is 0"—is actually meaningless, because nDay cannot have two values (it can't be Saturday and Sunday at the same time). You wouldn't get an error message, but the statement would never return true—the script would always run the else statement.

Note also that the entire conditional expression must be enclosed in parentheses. The following expression,

```
if (nDay == 5) && (nHours >= 12)  {
```

would cause an error when the script loaded. So you must add the parentheses after if and before {, like this:

```
if ((nDay == 5) && (nHours >= 12))  {
```

As you can see, you can combine conditional expressions using boolean operators. You can also use these operators to combine boolean variables, as you learned in Chapter 5, "Expressions & Operators—Manipulating Values." These expressions can get to be quite complex and difficult to read, so it is best to use parentheses to group logical expressions into understandable units of code. Also note that if you combine many boolean variables using boolean operators, it is easy to get confused over what you actually mean!

BOOLEAN NOT—WHAT DOESN'T THE VALUE CONTAIN?

Earlier in this chapter, you saw what the != operator does. This is the *not equal to* operator, and you can use it to tell a script to do something if a variable is not equal to a particular value. You'll remember that we used it like this:

```
function function1() {
    if (sButton != "A")     {
        alert("The variable is not equal to \'A\' \n→
        It is \'" + sButton + "\'")
    }
}
```

If sButton does not equal A, the Alert is displayed. What if the variable is a boolean variable, though? You'll remember from Example 6.3 that simply placing the name of the boolean variable in the parentheses is the same as saying "if this variable contains true." Well, all you need to do is place an exclamation mark immediately before the variable name to say "if this variable does *not* contain true." For example, look at the following:

Example 6.11

```
var bStatus = true
function CheckStatus() {
    if (!bStatus) {
        alert("The value in bStatus is false")
    }
    else {
        alert("The value in bStatus is true")
    }
}
```

This script is the same as the one in Example 6.3 with three changes. We've placed ! immediately before the variable name. In the first alert line we changed true to false, and in the second alert line we changed false to true. Now, if bStatus is *not* true—that is, if it contains false—the first line will be displayed.

ANOTHER FORM OF IF STATEMENT

There's another, shorthand way to write an if statement, though it's important to note that this expression doesn't just compare values, it also assigns a value to a variable. It looks like this:

```
variable = (condition) ? value1 : value2
```

This expression uses the ? operator to assign values to a variable that is dependent on a conditional expression. If the condition in the parentheses (it could also be a boolean variable) evaluates to true, then the variable is made equal to value1. If it is false, then the variable is made equal to value2.

Here's an example:

Example 6.12

```
function function1() {
var dToday = new Date()
var nSeconds = dToday.getSeconds()
```

```
var sText = (nSeconds > 30) ? "MORE" : "LESS"
    alert("We are " + sText + " than halfway through→
this minute. Seconds=" + nSeconds )
    }
```

This example does exactly the same thing as Example 6.7. If nSeconds is greater than 30, then it makes the variable sText equal to MORE; if it isn't greater than 30, it makes sText equal to LESS. This variable is then used in the Alert box to display a message.

LOOPS

You've now seen how you can control which statements of your program are executed using the conditional expressions. You've learned, in effect, how to give your scripts decision-making abilities. Now let's look at how to repeat tasks—how to execute lines of your program over and over. As you'll learn, this provides a way for you to make a script carry out an operation over and over until a certain condition is reached, at which point you can make the script do something. These operations are known as *loops*, and we'll start by looking at the for loop.

THE 'FOR' LOOP

The for statement is one way you can write a loop into your program. Look at the next example:

Example 6.13

```
function function1() {
var i
    for (i = 1; i < 4; i++) {
        alert("The value in i is " + i )
    }
    alert("The loop has finished and i is " + i )
}
```

This is a `for` statement. Try it in the Online Companion. This loop counts up to three. Each time it adds one, it executes the line of code within the curly brackets. This code displays an Alert box showing the value of the variable `i`. The Alert box stops the program and waits for you to click the OK button. Then the loop continues.

TIP

> *There's nothing unusual about the action of this Alert box. Whenever a script opens an Alert box it always stops and waits for the user to click on the OK button.*

Let's look at the format of the `for` statement in more detail:

```
for(initial expression; conditional expression; update→
expression) {
    code to be run if conditional expression is true
}
```

The first part of the `for` statement, the *initial expression*, is executed the first time the loop is executed—before anything else is done. It is usual to initialize a "counter" here (a variable that will hold a number showing how many times the loop has been executed), and in this example it sets the counter `i` equal to 1.

The *conditional expression* is evaluated before the loop can be executed. If this expression is true, then the next cycle around the loop is started, and the code within the curly brackets is run (in the example, the Alert box is displayed). If the conditional expression is *not* true, then the code is not executed and the loop ends. The browser moves on to the next line of script immediately after the closing } of the `for` statement (which, in our example, displays an Alert box telling us that the loop has ended). In our example script the conditional expression is `i < 4`, which means "run the loop if the value of `i`—the counter—is less than 4."

The *update expression* is evaluated each time a cycle of the loop ends. In other words, the code in the curly brackets is executed before the update expression is executed. In our example, this expression increments the value in variable `i` by 1 using the increment operator, `++`. *Update expressions* are usually used to increment the counter, and the counter is used to determine how many times the loop will run.

You may want to play around with the values in the example. Copy the example to your hard disk and change the values to see how it works. Try changing the for loop to the following:

```
for (i = 0; i < 4; i++) {
```

The program will now execute the loop four times with i = 0, 1, 2, and 3, ending with 4.

Now try changing the conditional expression to

```
for (i = 0; i < 6; i++) {
```

The loop is now executed 6 times with i = 0, 1, 2, 3, 4, and 5, ending with 5.

Finally try changing the update expression to

```
for (i = 0; i < 6; i= i + 2) {
```

The counter is now incremented by 2 each time so that the loop is now executed 3 times with i = 0, 2, and 4. Try playing around with this code to get a good understanding of what is happening.

TIP

Be careful with the conditional and update expressions. If you get these wrong, you can get the script stuck in a perpetual loop. For instance, try i+2 as the update expression. Because this is faulty, and doesn't update the counter, the conditional expression is always true, so the loop goes on forever. You'll have to crash the browser to get out of it.

FOR = NESTED IF?

Many advanced statements in programming are really created as shortcuts. You don't need to use a for statement—you can do the same thing using nested if statements. The code in our example is more or less equivalent to this:

Example 6.14

```
function function1() {
var i = 1
   if (i < 4) {
       alert("The value in i is " + i )
       i++                         // i now equals 2
       if (i < 4) {
          alert("The value in i is " + i )
          i++                      //i now equals 3
          if (i < 4) {
             alert("The value in i is " + i )
             i++                   //i now equals 4
             if (i < 4) {          //i is not less than 4 so→
                                        this is false
                alert("The value in i is " + i )
                i++
             }
          }
       }
   }
}
```

This is a series of nested if statements that do the same thing. Clearly the for statement is much easier to create and understand. Also, it would be very difficult to replace a long and complicated for statement with nested if statements.

THE WHILE LOOP

Another way to create a loop is by using a while statement. You can perform exactly the same function as in Example 6.13 with the following statement:

Example 6.15

```
function function1() {
var i = 1
   while (i < 4) {
      alert("The value in i is " + i )
      i++
   }
   alert("The loop has finished and i is " + i )
}
```

The loop executes *while* the conditional expression in the parentheses is true. Once i = 4 and the condition evaluates to false, the
loop no longer executes and the program goes to the next line,
which is the last Alert box.

Here's the basic format of the while loop:

```
while (conditional expression) {
   code to run while conditional expression is true
}
```

As you can see, the while statement has a conditional expression.
If the expression is true (in the prior example, if i < 4, then the code
after the curly brackets is run. If it is not true, then the browser
moves on to the next line of the script. In this case, it displays an
Alert box telling us that the loop has finished. We still have a counter
in this example, but the counter is now placed in the code between
the curly brackets; while statements have no *update expression*.

Lets try another while loop, but this time without a counter:

Example 6.16

```
function function1() {
var sWord =""
   while (sWord != "Aardvark") {
      sWord = prompt("Input the word \'Aardvark\' in order→
to stop the loop","")
   }
   alert("The loop has finished")
}
```

This example uses a new element of JavaScript that we have not seen yet: the Prompt dialog box (see Figure 6-1). The `prompt` box "collects" something a user types into it. In this case it displays the message *Input the word 'Aardvark' in order to stop the loop*, and whatever the user types in will be put into the `sWord` variable when the user clicks on the OK button. This `while` loop will go around and around until `sWord` contains the word `Aardvark`. In the previous example, you used a counter as the condition on which the `while` statement depended. In this case you are using the contents of `sWord` as the condition. (We've actually told the `while` statement to continue as long as `sWord` *does not contain* `Aardvark`.) So until the user types in the correct text, the `while` loop will continue and will display another prompt box.

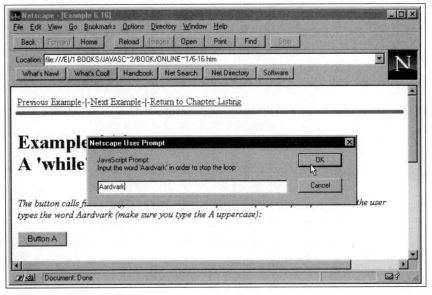

Figure 6-1: *The Prompt dialog box.*

DO WHILE LOOPS

Another common form of loop is the `do while` loop. This type of loop is important because it guarantees that the instructions will be carried out at least once, by placing the conditional expression *after* the instructions that must be carried out. (With other loops the conditional expression is checked first, so in some cases the instructions may never be carried out.) At the time of writing, there is no do while loop in JavaScript. However, do is a reserved word, and Java *does* use do while loops, so do while loops will probably be implemented sometime in the future. Here's an example of how do while loops should work. (It's not in the Online Companion, of course, as it won't function currently.)

```
function function1() {
var sWord =""
   do {
       sWord = prompt("Input the word \'Aardvark\' in order→
to stop the loop","")
   }
   while (sWord != "Aardvark")
   alert("The loop has finished")
}
```

Here's the basic do while format:

```
do {
   code to carry out
}
while (conditional expression)
```

In this example you can see that the do while statement begins by displaying the Prompt dialog box (even if sWord already contained Aardvark the Prompt dialog box would open). The data from the dialog box is placed into sWord. Next you see while followed by a conditional expression in parentheses. If this expression is true, the program loops back up to the do line. If it's false, the browser skips down to the next line; in this case it displays an Alert box.

You may be able to duplicate a do while loop in some cases, by repeating the code you want carried out. For instance, look at this example:

Example 6.17

```
function function1() {
var sWord ="Aardvark"
```

```
    sWord = prompt("Input the word \'Aardvark\' in order to→
stop the loop","")
    while (sWord != "Aardvark") {
        sWord = prompt("Input the word \'Aardvark\' in order→
to stop the loop","")
    }
    alert("The loop has finished")
}
```

Remember, the purpose of the do while is to make something run even if the while condition is false. So we started by initializing sWord with Aardvark. In this case the while loop wouldn't normally run at all, because the condition is false; sWord *does* contain Aardvark. So we simply put the same code that is inside the while loop just above the while loop. Now, even though sWord already contains Aardvark, the Prompt dialog box will open. Then, if the user doesn't type Aardvark, the while loop kicks in. (If the user clicks on OK without typing anything into the Prompt dialog box, sWord will be cleared.)

Another way to handle it (a more elegant way, perhaps) would be this:

```
while(true) {
    code to carry out
    if (!condition)
    break
}
```

By putting true in parentheses you are ensuring that the while loop at least begins. Then the if statement determines whether the loop should continue or not.

BREAKING OUT OF A LOOP—BREAK

In order to stop a loop from inside you can use the break statement. This statement makes the program skip to the line after the loop. There are times when using the conditional expression to stop a loop is not enough and you want your program to decide what to do from within the loop. You can use break from within for and while statements. Look at the following example to see what we mean. We've allowed the user to execute a break, by clicking on the Cancel button of a dialog box:

Example 6.18

```
function function1() {
var bResult
    for (i = 1; i < 4; i++) {
    bResult = confirm("i = " + i + "\nClick cancel to→
execute a \'break\' statement","")
        if (bResult == false) {
            break;
        }
    }
    alert("The loop has finished\ni = " + i)
}
```

The example is a `for` statement that will loop until i is equal to 4. The loop displays a Confirm dialog box as seen in Figure 6-2. You have seen how these work before, in Example 2.12. When the user clicks on a button, a boolean value is returned—true if he clicks on OK, false if he clicks on Cancel. That value is placed in the `bResult` variable.

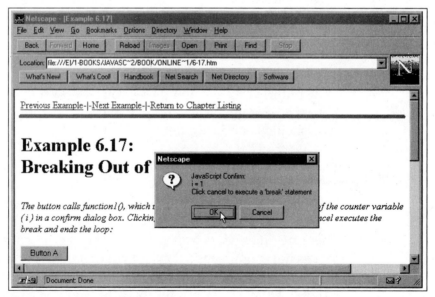

Figure 6-2: *The Confirm dialog box.*

The next instruction that is executed, immediately after the Confirm dialog box has closed, is an `if` statement. This statement checks the value in `bResult`; if the value is `false`, the conditional expression is true, so the instruction within the next curly brackets is run. That instruction is the `break`. And `break` simply means, "don't go back to the top of the `for` instruction; instead, go to the next line of the script, after the loop." The final line uses `alert` to display a dialog box to tell us that the loop has finished.

RETURNING TO THE TOP OF THE LOOP—CONTINUE

As with `break`, `continue` is a way of controlling `for` or `while` loops, except that the loop is not terminated. Instead the `continue` statement returns processing immediately back to the top of the loop and the next cycle starts. In other words, `continue` provides a way to stop the processing of the rest of the lines of code within the loop.

When the `continue` statement is executed, processing goes back to the conditional expression in a `while` loop, or the update expression in a `for` loop. Take a look at this `while` loop to see what we mean:

Example 6.19

```
var bResult
var i = 0
    while (i < 4) {
        bResult = confirm("i = " + i + "\nClick cancel to→
execute a \'continue\' statement","")
        if (bResult == false) {
            continue;
        }
        i++
    }
    alert("The loop has finished\ni = " + i)
}
```

The example is a `while` statement that will loop until i is equal to 4. The loop displays a Confirm box. Again, the result from the Confirm dialog box (`true` for OK, `false` for Cancel) is placed in the `bResult` variable.

The `if` statement takes a look at `bResult`. If `bResult` contains `false`—that is, if the user clicked on the Cancel button—the conditional expression is true, so the instruction immediately after { is run. That's the `continue` statement, which returns processing to the beginning of the `while` statement without running the `i++` operation. If `bResult` contains `true`—that is, if the user clicked on the OK button—the conditional expression is not true, so the instruction within the curly brackets is not run. Instead, the `i++` operation runs and *then* returns to the top of the `while` statement.

So if you continually click on the OK button the loop runs completely until the process has finished. If you click on the Cancel button, you will not get anywhere. You are simply stuck, because the value in `i` is never incremented. In fact the only way to get out of the loop is by completing it. At some point you must click on the OK button several times to finish.

MOVING ON

You've learned how to control the flow of a program. Conditional expressions and loops are very powerful. Without them programs would not accomplish much. With them programs can apply logical thought to problems.

Now it's time to find out more about functions. You already have seen a little basic information about functions—how to get functions to store little scripts that can be called and executed later. But there are a couple of things we haven't looked at yet; how to pass parameters to functions, and how to work with values that are returned by functions. And that's just what we'll look at in the following chapter.

CHAPTER 7

More on Functions

We have already had a quick look at functions in Chapter 3, "First Steps—Scripts, Functions & Comments," and have used them in many of our examples, but we need to discuss them a little more as there are a number of features of functions that we haven't looked at yet. We need to see where functions may be defined, how they can return values that can be used by other parts of the script, and how to pass information from other parts of the scripts to the functions.

Let's start again from the beginning, to make sure that we all get this straight. Let's take a look at how to define functions.

 ## DEFINING A FUNCTION

Defining a function is the process by which we state the function name and explain what it does. It is always in this format:

```
function functionname() {
    the instructions that the function carries out
}
```

A function definition always starts with the keyword `function` so that when the browser loads the page it knows which bits of script are functions. We have called a lot of the functions in our example `function1`, but it is a good idea to give your functions meaningful names like `DisplayMessage` or `GetText`. This will help you keep all those functions straight, and help you and others identify their purposes when reading through a script later. The lines of script between the outermost braces define what the function will do when it is called or used.

When your browser loads the page it will read in the function and hold it in the computer's memory ready for use, so that when the function is *called* by another piece of JavaScript—an actual script or an event handler—the browser can find it in memory and execute the instructions contained in it.

WHERE YOU PUT YOUR FUNCTION IS IMPORTANT

We have been putting our function definitions into the HEAD section of our HTML pages in the examples because it is the first part of the document to be loaded. (There's no danger of functions being called by a piece of JavaScript later in the document, before they have been loaded into memory.) You can define functions anywhere in a Web page, but you must take care to define them before you call them. This is not as straightforward as it sounds, so let's use some examples to see how JavaScript works with functions.

Example 7.1

```
<SCRIPT LANGUAGE="JavaScript">
<!--
function1()
function function1() {
  alert("This is function1 running.")
}
//-->
</SCRIPT>
```

You don't have to do anything on this page; there are no buttons to click. When the page is loaded into the browser, the function is executed and all it does is display an alert box with the text *This is function1 running*. Take a close look at this piece of code, though. The function call—the point at which the function is used—actually comes before the function definition, but the code works okay. This tells us that all of the code within the <SCRIPT> and <\SCRIPT> tags is read into memory before it is executed, so it doesn't matter in what order you put your functions within those tags.

Also note that the page is not displayed until you click the OK button on the Alert box (when you put an alert in a script like this you are, in effect, pausing the script while the Alert box is displayed), so the script in the HEAD section is not only loaded first, but it is also executed (if there is anything to execute) before the rest of the page is displayed. Now look at this example:

Example 7.2

```
<SCRIPT LANGUAGE="JavaScript">
<!--
function1()
//-->
</SCRIPT>
<SCRIPT LANGUAGE="JavaScript">
<!--
function function1() {
  alert("This is function1 running.")
}
//-->
</SCRIPT>
```

This is, in some respects, the same as the first example. The instructions are exactly the same, but we've split the instructions into two separate scripts. However, this example produces a load-time error and the error alert box is displayed with the message "function1 is not defined."

TIP

A load-time error occurs when the script is first loaded into memory. You'll learn more about this in Chapter 8, "Troubleshooting & Avoiding Trouble."

This is because the function is called from a block of script that is read before the block that contains the function definition. Although the call and the definition are in the same order, they are now in two completely different scripts. In the next example, we have swapped the two blocks of script and now it works fine.

Example 7.3

```
<SCRIPT LANGUAGE="JavaScript">
<!--
function function1() {
  alert("This is function1 running.")
}
//-->
</SCRIPT>
<SCRIPT LANGUAGE="JavaScript">
<!--
function1()
//-->
</SCRIPT>
```

These are the same scripts as before, but in a different order. So it looks like the browser will read in everything between a <SCRIPT> and <\SCRIPT> tag pair and then execute it. It then reads and executes the next block of script and so on. To make your life simpler, it is always best to define your functions in the HEAD section before anything else. That way you can be sure that your functions will have loaded before they are used.

FUNCTIONS CAN RETURN VALUES

We've used functions in a fairly simple way so far. Just to complicate the issue, though, we'd like to explain that functions can *return* values. This means that they can be used to assign values to variables by putting the function calls in the following format:

```
variable = functionname()
```

In the following example you can see how a function returns the text that has been typed into a prompt box. First, we define the following function in the HEAD, which uses the prompt method to open a Prompt dialog box.

Example 7.4

```
<SCRIPT LANGUAGE="JavaScript">
<!--
function function1() {
var sTypedText
    sTypedText = prompt("Type some text in, then click on→
OK", "")
    return sTypedText
}
//-->
</SCRIPT>
```

This script defines a function (function1()). The function declares a variable named sTypedText. sTypedText will contain a string. Where does the string come from? We've used the prompt built-in function to get the string from the user. We'll learn more about built-in functions in Chapters 10 and 11. All you need to understand right now is that when you use the prompt function in this manner, the text that appears within parentheses and quotation marks will appear as an instruction within a Prompt dialog box (see Figure 7-1). When the user clicks on the OK button in the Prompt dialog box, the text that has been typed is made available to the script. On the next line of the script we've used the return keyword to tell the script that we want the function to return something. What? The text currently held by sTypedText, of course.

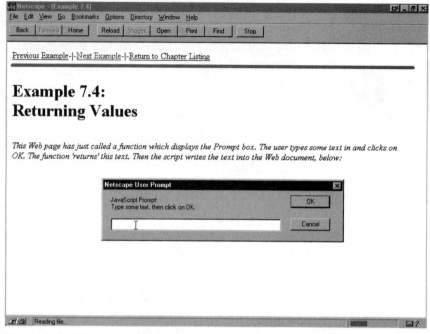

Figure 7-1: *The Prompt dialog box collects text from the user, and returns it to the script.*

Later in the document we've used this script:

```
<SCRIPT LANGUAGE="JavaScript">
<!--
var sText
sText = function1()
document.write("You just typed: <P><H3>" + sText + "</→
H3><P>")
//-->
</SCRIPT>
```

This script starts by declaring a variable named sText. Then we "initialize" the variable—that is, place data into it by assigning function1() to the variable. What data does function1() contain? It contains the text that we told the function to return. Finally, we used document.write to write some text into the Web page: *You just typed:*, followed by a new paragraph (<P>), and the text held by the sText variable. (We formatted that text, and ended the paragraph after the text, using the <H3>, </H3>, and <P> HTML tags.)

Where did we call function1() from? We called it by assigning it to sText. Because we used the return keyword when we defined the function, function1() returns a value to the line that called it— dropping it into the sText variable.

TIP

What happens if the user clicks on Cancel? The value null is returned (try it and see). What if the user clicks on the OK button without typing anything? An empty string is returned. Yes, there is a difference. In the first case, you'll see null *written into the Web page. In the second case, nothing is written into the Web page.*

You *must* use the return keyword to use this system. If you didn't use the return sTypedText line in the first script, what would happen? The Prompt dialog box would appear, but the text returned from prompt would not be stored anywhere, as you can see in the following example:

Example 7.5

```
<SCRIPT LANGUAGE="JavaScript">
<!--
function function1() {
var sTypedText
    sTypedText = prompt("Type some text in, then click on→
OK", "")
}
//-->
</SCRIPT>
```

We removed the return sTypedText line from this script (compare to Example 7.4). Try it in our Online Companion, and you'll see that the text is not written to the page.

It's interesting to consider that the text is actually being returned twice. First, we get the text from:

```
    sTypedText = prompt("Type some text in, then click on→
OK", "")
```

Remember, prompt is a built-in function, one that you don't have to define because it's already defined for you and built into JavaScript. The prompt function automatically returns the text from the Prompt dialog box (we don't have to tell it to do so). This return value is then assigned to the sTypedText variable. Then we used the following line:

```
return sTypedText
```

It tells function1() to return a value, and that the value it returns should be the value held by sTypedText. Finally, we get the text the second time from this line:

```
sText = function1()
```

This time function1() returns a value and assigns it to sText.

What would have happened if we hadn't assigned the returned value to anything? If, instead of this line:

```
sText = function1()
```

we had this line:

```
function1()
```

The function would still have worked. We would see the Prompt dialog box—but we wouldn't receive the returned value for any further use inside our program. The text typed by the user would be unused by our script.

Multiple Returns

You can have more than one return statement in your function so that you can return different things depending upon what has happened within the function. The following example illustrates this using another built-in function called confirm. This displays a dialog box with two buttons: OK and Cancel. If the user clicks on OK the confirm function returns true. If the user clicks on the Cancel button confirm returns false.

Example 7.6

```
<SCRIPT LANGUAGE="JavaScript">
<!--
function function1() {
var bResultReturned
    bResultReturned = confirm("Click OK or cancel.")
    if (bResultReturned)   {
        return "You pressed the OK button"
    }
    else    {
        return "You pressed the Cancel button"
    }
}
//-->
</SCRIPT>
```

This is very similar to the example we looked at earlier, in which the `return` keyword is used to tell the function to return something. This time, though, we haven't told the script to return text typed by the user. We can't do that, because the user doesn't type anything into a Confirm dialog box (see Figure 7-2). Instead, the `confirm` built-in function returns one of two values, a boolean `true` or a boolean `false`. So we've told the script to return a string literal, a line of text we've typed into the script. And we've used an `if` statement to determine *which* line of text should be used. You saw what `if (bResultReturned)` means in Chapter 6, "Conditionals & Loops—Making Decisions & Controlling Scripts." It means, "if the boolean variable `bResultReturned` contains the value `true`, carry out the instructions following. If not, go to the `else` statement and carry out the instruction following that." In each case the instruction is to return some text.

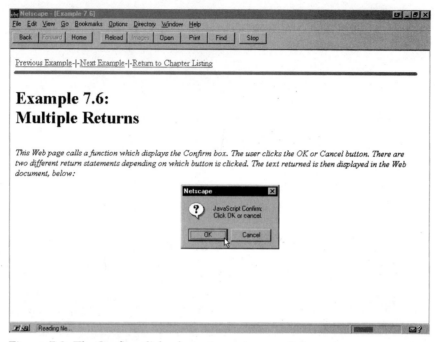

Figure 7-2: *The Confirm dialog box returns* true *or* false.

Later in the Web document, we used the script from Example 7.4 to write the return value into the Web document. So if the confirm function returns true—that is, if the user clicked on OK—the script writes You pressed the OK button into the document.

PASSING VALUES TO FUNCTIONS

You may have wondered why empty parentheses are always placed after function names. They are there to hold *arguments* or parameters. By putting values into the brackets, you can pass data into a function when you call it. In order to do this you must have already defined the function with variables in the brackets where it will receive the data, as in the following example:

Example 7.7

```
<SCRIPT LANGUAGE="JavaScript">
<!--
function function1(sText) {
    alert(sText)
}
//-->
</SCRIPT>
```

Notice that we've added (sText) after the function name. (We finally used those parentheses.) This means that the function will expect data to be passed to it, and this data will be made available to the function in the variable sText. We say that sText is an *argument* of the function function1. The function then displays the data from sText in an Alert box. Later in our example Web page, we call this function with this simple script:

```
function1("Text that is passed to the function")
```

We've used the parentheses again. This time we've placed a string literal into the parentheses. When the interpreter (the browser) runs this line it looks inside the parentheses, it will take this text and place the text into the sTextvariable inside the function. The function then uses alert to display the contents of the variable.

Why not just use a global variable? Well, using global variables can get confusing and programmers try to use them as little as possible to pass data to functions. If you have a global variable that is used and updated by many functions, it is difficult to know what has happened to it and where. This makes debugging more difficult. If you eliminate the need for global variables by passing your data to a function and receiving data back from it by "return," your program is much more structured, easier to read, and your functions are modular. You can easily use them from different places in your program without having to worry about the effect on other parts of the program through changes to the global variables.

PASSING MULTIPLE VALUES

You can pass many values into your function by separating the arguments with commas, as in the following example:

Example 7.8

```
<SCRIPT LANGUAGE="JavaScript">
<!--
function Percentage(nNum, nPerc) {
    return nNum * (nPerc/100)
}
//-->
</SCRIPT>
```

We've created a function that carries out a calculation. It has two arguments (or two parameters): nNum and nPerc. Each represents a numeric variable, the value for which will be passed to the function when we call it. The function takes those values and carries out a calculation; first it divides the value in nPerc by 100, then it multiplies the result by the value in nNum. Then the function returns the result of this calculation.

Later in the script the function is called like this:

```
<SCRIPT LANGUAGE="JavaScript">
<!--
var nValue1 = prompt("Type in a number","")
var nValue2 = prompt("Type in a the percentage you wish to→
calculate","")
var nPercent = Percentage(nValue1, nValue2)
document.write("<H3>" + nValue2 + " percent of " + nValue1 +→
" = " + nPercent + "</H3>" )
//-->
</SCRIPT>
```

We've started by declaring two variables, nValue1 and nValue2. In each case we've assigned a value to the variable using the prompt built-in function. In other words, a Prompt dialog box opens (the text within the quotation marks and parentheses is displayed in the box), then the user types something into the box and clicks on OK. When he does so, the number that was typed is returned from the prompt function, and placed into the variable.

The next line, `var nPercent = Percentage(nValue1, nValue2)`, declares another variable, `nPercent`. This time, though, we've assigned a value to the variable by calling the `Percentage` function that we defined earlier. You'll notice that we are passing two values to the function, `nValue1` and `nValue 2`—the values returned by the Prompt boxes. The browser takes those values and, as we've just seen, places them in `nNum` and `nPerc`, where the function uses them to perform the calculation, and returns the result which is assigned to the `nPercent` variable in the current script. Finally we've used `document.write` to write the result of the calculation to the Web page.

Note that the variable names we used when calling the function (`nValue1` and `nValue2`) are different from the names used within the function (`nNum` and `nPerc`). They don't *have* to be though, we could have used the same names in fact, as we'll see next.

TIP

This example will only work if numbers are put into the text boxes. If you put in non-numerics, or click on OK without typing anything, you will get an error. A program should really be able to process inputs in a sensible manner, but we've left out the error checking because this is just an example. We'll learn about error checking in Chapter 16, "Forms & JavaScript."

CALL BY VALUE

JavaScript uses a convention known as *call by value* when it calls functions. This means that the arguments a function receives are the same *value* as what was in the calling statement—but not *actually* the same *variable*. The received arguments are copies of the originals. In our last example, when the function is called the variables `nValue1` and `nValue2` are copied into temporary variables `nNum` and `nPerc`, which are separate from `nValue1` and `nValue2`. `nNum` and `nPerc` are said to be *local* to the function. The next example illustrates that if the function changes the values of the local variables `nNum` and `nPerc`, this has no effect on the values of `nValue1` and `nValue2`. In fact to make this quite clear, we've even changed the names of nNum and nPerc to nValue1 and nValue2, respectively. In other words, the names of the original variables are now the same as the names of the variables in the function to which the values are being passed.

Example 7.9

```
<SCRIPT LANGUAGE="JavaScript">
<!--
function Percentage(nValue1, nValue2) {
  var nResult = nValue1 * (nValue2/100)
  nValue1 = 0
  nValue2 = 0
  return nResult
}
//-->
</SCRIPT>
```

This example is the same as the previous example, except that after carrying out the calculation the script resets the values of nNum and nValue2 to 0. We added buttons to the page so you can view the values held by nValue1 and nValue2; you'll see that they remain the same as the values you typed.

WORKING WITH FUNCTIONS

Functions are useful for several reasons:

- When you have a piece of code that you may want to use from several places in your script, you can use a function so that you do not have to repeat the same code in several places.

- Functions are especially useful in JavaScript when used by *event handlers*. You can have lots of code in the event-handlers part of an object (a text box or button) on an HTML form, but it can easily become a mess. It's much clearer if you create a function instead, then call the function from the event handler. (We'll learn more about event handlers in Chapter 12, "JavaScript Events—When Are Actions Carried Out?").

■　Functions can be used to make your program more readable and tidier. You can split your program up into manageable chunks that are easier to understand than one mass of code.

Let's look at another version of the percentage calculator we just created:

Example 7.10

```
<SCRIPT LANGUAGE="JavaScript">
<!--
function GetNumbers(form) {
    var sNumber = form.txtNumber.value
    var sPercentage = form.txtPercent.value
    form.txtResult.value= Percentage(sNumber, sPercentage)
}
function Percentage(sNum, sPerc) {
    var nResult = sNum * (sPerc/100)
    return nResult
}
//-->
</SCRIPT>
```

We've created two functions in this script, so you can see how creating multiple functions lets you break your complicated scripts into smaller blocks. First we've created GetNumbers(form).

What is being passed to GetNumbers in parentheses? The form variable? No, this is the form *object*. Now, this is a little advanced and we'll be looking at some of these things later, in Chapter 10, "Objects, Properties & Methods." But what you need to understand here is that the form object contains information about the form held in the page (which we'll look at in a moment). The form object contains information about its components, txtNumber and txtPercent (we'll see these in a moment, too). This information is passed to the variables sNumber and sPercentage by naming the information like this: form.txtNumber.value and form.txtPercent.value. (In other words, the value held by the txtNumber box in the form, and held by the txtPercent box in the form.)

Now, look at this line:

```
form.txtResult.value= Percentage(sNumber, sPercentage)
```

This line means, place the value returned from the `Percentage`
function into `form.txtResult.value`. In other words, this function
is also writing to an object in the form. As you'll see in a moment,
`txtResult` is the Result text box. This value comes from the
`Percentage` function. As you can see, we're passing the variables
`sNumber` and `sPercentage` to the `Percentage` function, which you
can see lower in the script. This function is the same as the
functions we've seen earlier in this chapter—it calculates the
percentage, then returns the result (which goes to
`form.txtResult.value`).

Later in the Web page we've created this form, which you can
see in Figure 7-3:

```
<FORM>
Enter a number: <INPUT TYPE="text" NAME="txtNumber"
SIZE=6><BR>
Enter the percentage you want: <INPUT TYPE="text"
NAME="txtPercent" SIZE=6><P>
<INPUT TYPE="button" VALUE="Result"
onclick="GetNumbers(this.form)"> <INPUT TYPE="text"
NAME="txtResult" SIZE=10>
</FORM>
```

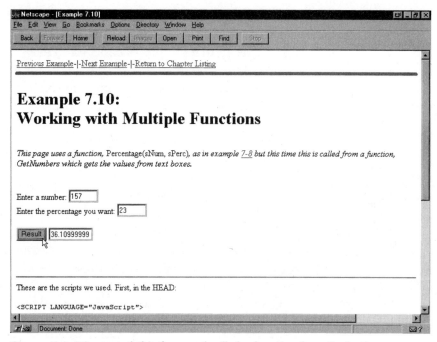

Figure 7-3: *We created this form and called a function from the button.*

The form has three text boxes: txtNumber, txtPercent, and txtResult. It also has a button, which calls the GetNumbers function using the onclick event handler. Notice that we've passed the values from the form to the function using (this.form). That means "pass a reference to the form through to the function." The function then uses the reference to get at the individual objects in the form with the dot notation (more on this in Chapter 16, "Forms & JavaScript").

So what happens when the user clicks on the button? The form reference is passed to the GetNumbers function, which then gets the values from the txtNumber and txtPercent boxes and passes them to the Percentage function, which returns the result of the calculation to GetNumbers, which passes the value back to the txtResult box.

Now, we could have done this all in the onclick event handler if we'd wished, but it would be a mess. Not only is it clearer this way, but it makes it easier to reuse bits of code, too. The Percentage function is like a tool that can be used in many places for many reasons. We just have to call it to use it, rather than rewriting it each time we need it. So we can actually use this function from several places within the script. You can create libraries of code like this, too—pieces that you can just plug into any of your scripts where required.

BUILT-IN FUNCTIONS

As well as being able to make your own functions there are several that come as part of JavaScript and are called *built-in* functions. In other words, you don't need to define these functions; they are automatically there, waiting for you to use them from any point in your script. These are the built-in functions available to you:

eval	Returns a number from an operation containing a string.
parseInt	Evaluates a string and returns an integer.
parseFloat	Evaluates a string and returns a floating-point number.
escape	Returns the ASCII-encoded value of a character.
unescape	Returns character represented by the ASCII encoding. The opposite of escape.
isNaN	Tells you whether a value is NaN (not a number). This currently only works in the UNIX versions of Netscape Navigator.

EVAL(STRING)

The eval function requires a string of some kind. This string is usually a mathematical expression, but it can be any JavaScript statement or expression, including variables and the properties of objects. (We'll look at objects in Chapter 10, "Objects, Properties &

Methods.") This function is especially useful when working with forms, because the data typed into a form is always a string, though a numerical value is often desired. For instance, look at this script:

Example 7.11

```
function GetNumbers(form) {
    form.txtResult.value= eval(form.txtCalc.value)
}
```

This is taking the value held by the txtCalc field in the form, carrying out the calculation in the form, and returning the result— a floating-point number—to the txtResult field. If you look at this example in the Online Companion (or see Figure 7-4), you can see that you can type an equation into the text box.

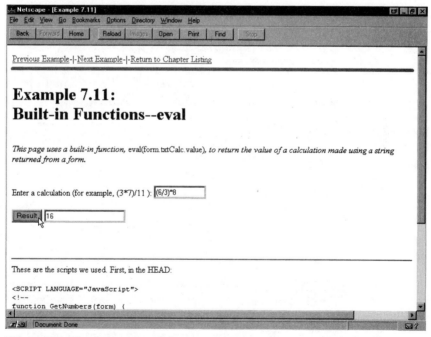

Figure 7-4: *The form we used for our* eval *example.*

The value from txtCalc is a string value. Form values are always strings. But this string contains more than numbers; in the example suggested in the Web page, you would have this: (3*7)/11. Without eval it would be very difficult to calculate this, as it's a mixture of numbers and special characters.

Why, then, did the previous examples work in which we took the results from form fields and carried out a calculation? Because those fields contained nothing but numbers and, as we saw in Chapter 5, "Expressions & Operators—Manipulating Values," JavaScript tries to "do the right thing" and carry out a calculation if it can. In the case of (3*7)/11, though, it needs a special function, eval, to help it with the calculation.

The eval function can be used for more than evaluating numerical expressions, however. Its argument string can also include object references and JavaScript statements—for re-setting initial values of data variables, for example.

PARSEINT(STRING, RADIX)

The word *parse* is used in programming to mean the process by which a computer examines a set of instructions and tries to make sense of it. JavaScript has a couple of "parse" functions: parseInt and parseFloat. Regardless of the name's origin, though, these are really functions that are used to get numbers out of strings before you use them in calculations. (Use a string in a calculation and you'll probably get a strange result.) All text entered into a form is regarded by JavaScript as a string—so if you have a form that collects numerical data, you need some way to ensure the string represents a number.

The parseInt function examines a string and tries to return an integer. The integer will be in the "radix" (the base) that you specify: in decimal, octal, or hexadecimal. We've created an example to show parseInt at work, but note that currently (in Netscape Navigator 3.0 beta 4), parseInt does not work correctly and returns the wrong numbers.

Example 7.12

```
function GetInteger(form) {
var nBase
    if (form.cmbRadix.selectedIndex == 0)nBase = 2;
    if (form.cmbRadix.selectedIndex == 1)nBase = 8;
    if (form.cmbRadix.selectedIndex == 2)nBase = 10;
    if (form.cmbRadix.selectedIndex == 3)nBase = 16;
        form.txtInteger.value= parseInt(form.txtNum.value,→
nBase)
    }
```

We start with a series of `if` statements. This series looks at the selection box named `cmbRadix`, and checks to see what is selected. (We'll learn more about this in Chapter 16, "Forms & JavaScript.") We are referring to the `selectedIndex` property of the selection box named `cmbRadix`. The `selectedIndex` is the position in the box of the selected item, starting at 0—that is, if the user clicks on the first item in the box, the `selectedIndex` value is 0; if he clicks on the second, the value is 1, and so on.

(`form.cmbRadix.selectedIndex` means "the `selectedIndex` position in the `cmbRadix` form element, in the `form`".) This tells us which base the user has selected (we'll see the selection box in a moment). So, this series of `if` statements figures out what value to place in the `nBase` variable. For instance, if the second item in the selection box has been selected, then `nBase` will be 8 (in other words, the user has chosen octal).

TIP

Okay, so we broke our rule. In Chapter 6, "Conditionals & Loops— Making Decisions & Controlling Scripts," we told you that it's not a good idea to write `if` statements like this, that it's better to use all the brackets correctly. Well, sometimes rules are made to be broken, and this is one case where creating `if` statements without brackets just seemed clearer.

Once that's been figured out, we use `parseInt` to look at the number in the txtNum field of the form (`form.txtNum.value` means "use the `value` in the `txtNum` field of the `form`"). It uses the `nBase` variable to determine what base should be used. The returned value—which should be an integer in the specified base—is then placed into the `txtInteger` field. (`form.txtInteger.value` means "the value in the `txtInteger` field in the form," and as we are using the assignment operator, this value is placed into the text box.)

Now, here's the form we've used:

```
<FORM>
Select a radix (base) you want to convert to--10 (decimal), 2
(binary), 8 (octal), 16 (hexadecimal):
<select name="cmbRadix" size="4">
<option>Binary (Base 2)
<option>Octal (Base 8)
<option selected value>Decimal (Base 10)
<option>Hex (Base 16)
</select><BR>
Type a number: <INPUT TYPE="text" NAME="txtNum" SIZE=12><BR>
<INPUT TYPE="button" VALUE="Result"
onclick="GetInteger(this.form)">
<INPUT TYPE="text" NAME="txtInteger" SIZE=20>
</FORM>
```

As you can see, we've created a selection box, two text boxes, and a button. The user selects the base in which he or she wants the result from the `cmbRadix` selection box (or simply leaves `Decimal` selected, as that's the default value). The user then types a number into the `txtNum` box and clicks on the `Result` button to use the `onclick` event handler to call the `GetInteger` function. The result from that function is passed to the `txtInteger` box, as you can see in Figure 7-5.

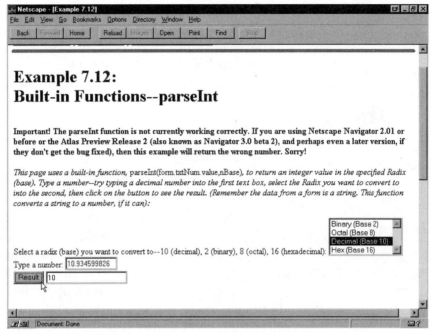

Figure 7-5: *The parseInt function at work.*

Try this in the Online Companion and see what happens. Here's what *should* happen (if parseInt worked correctly). The parseInt function takes the value in the text box—which is a string, remember—and tries to convert it to a number (in the selected base), the best it can. It will remove any portion of the number to the right of the decimal place (it doesn't round the number, it simply discards everything to the right of the decimal place). If the string includes any non-numeric characters, parseInt will use all the digits up to the first character that it can't recognize and then discard the rest. If it doesn't recognize the first character, it simply returns 0. For instance, assuming we are using base 10:

If you type this….	You'll get this…
23	23
23&	23
&23	0
23.9875634	23

PARSEFLOAT(STRING)

This function is almost the same as parseInt, except that it returns a floating point number—it won't discard the portion to the right of the decimal place, and you are not specifying a Radix to be used. Take a look at this example:

Example 7.13

```
function GetFloat(form) {
    form.txtFloat.value= parseFloat(form.txtNum.value)
}
```

We haven't worried about the if statements this time, as we don't have to select a base. All the user does is enter a number and click on a button. The text entered into the form is passed to parseFloat (form.txtNum.value, the value in the txtNum box). The parseFloat function then returns the floating-point number evaluated from the string, placing it into the txtFloat text box.

Here's the simple form we used:

```
<FORM>
Type a number: <INPUT TYPE="text" NAME="txtNum" SIZE=12><P>
<INPUT TYPE="button" VALUE="Result"
onclick="GetFloat(this.form)"> <INPUT TYPE="text"
NAME="txtFloat" SIZE=30>
</FORM>
```

The parseFloat is currently working okay, so you can use parseFloat instead of parseInt. The parseFloat function will not truncate the digits after the decimal point. It will also understand exponential values, and the – and + signs. For instance:

If you type this….	You'll get this…
23	23
23&	23
&23	0
23.9875634	23.9875634
-23	-23
+23	23
99e2	0.98999999999999999
99e-55	9.9000000000000004e-054

You can see an example in Figure 7-6.

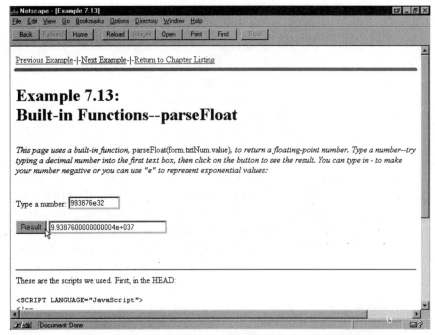

Figure 7-6: *The parseFloat function at work.*

ESCAPE(CHARACTER)

The escape function is used to return the ASCII encoding value of a character in the ISO Latin-1 character set. Use escape to evaluate ? (for instance (escape(?)) and %3F will be returned). Try escape(?>) and %3F%3E is returned. For instance, in the following example, we started with this function:

Example 7.14

```
function ConvertASCII(form) {
    form.txtASCII.value= escape(form.txtCharacter.value)
}
```

A simple function that takes the value in the `textCharacter` field of the form and evaluates it with the `escape` function. The result is then placed in the `txtASCII` field of the form. Here's the form:

```
<FORM>
Type any character: <INPUT TYPE="text" NAME="txtCharacter"
SIZE=12><P>
<INPUT TYPE="button" VALUE="ASCII Value"
onclick="ConvertASCII(this.form)"> <INPUT TYPE="text"
NAME="txtASCII" SIZE=20>
</FORM>
```

Type a character into the `txtCharacter` text box, click on the `ASCII Value` button, and the value from `txtCharacter` is sent to the `ConvertASCII` function where it is evaluated using `escape` and returned to the form. Try it in the example and see. Note, however, that you can only use nonalphanumeric characters—no letters or numbers. If you type D, for instance, `escape` will return D. And some nonalphanumeric characters won't work either: @, _, +, −, ., and /.

UNESCAPE

This function is the exact opposite of `escape`. It takes an ASCII encoding value, and returns the character that the value represents. In the following example we've used the same script as in the previous example, except that we've replaced `escape` with `unescape`.

Example 7.15

```
function ConvertASCII(form) {
    form.txtASCII.value= unescape(form.txtCharacter.value)
}
```

As you can see, this is the same as in the previous example, except that we used `unescape` instead of `escape`. Try typing **%3F** or **%27** and clicking on the button to see the character that the value represents.

TIP

You may see unEscape in some documentation. You must type unescapeall in lowercase, though, or it won't work

ISNaN(NUMBER)

This built-in function is only used on UNIX systems. It's used to evaluate an argument to see if it's NaN (not a number): the function returns true (it is not a number) or false (it is a number).

When you use the parseInt and parseFloat functions, if they evaluate a string that is not a number, they return NaN. (This happens on all but the Windows browsers.)

For instance, you might use isNaN in an if statement, like this:

```
if isNaN(FloatValue) {
  RunThis()
} else {
  OrThis()
}
```

In this if statement we use isNaN to look at the value held by the FloatValue variable, which holds the value returned by the parseFloat function earlier. If the value held by FloatValue *is* NaN (that is, it's not a number), then the RunThis function is called. If the value is not NaN, the OrThis function is called—this function presumably does something with the number in FloatValue.

TIP

There are other built-in functions. The ones we've just looked at, though, work independently; they are not linked to any object. The other built-in functions (and there are quite a few), are "methods" related to "objects." They are used in a different manner, so we're not going to look at them right now. We'll come back to them in Chapter 10, "Objects, Properties & Methods."

MOVING ON

We're going to take a break from programming for a while, and look at the problems you can run into while creating your script. In the next chapter we'll find out how good programming practices can help you avoid some problems in the first place and how—when you *do* run into trouble (and you will, regardless of how careful you may be)— you can track down the source of your problems.

We'll explain how you can save a great deal of trouble by simply taking care in the way you write your scripts by declaring variables correctly, by using sensible names, by using parentheses in calculations, and so on. You can also space your scripts in such a manner that they are easier to read; and we'll also look at how to use Alert boxes to help you "debug" your scripts.

CHAPTER 8

Troubleshooting & Avoiding Trouble

Don't expect to write bug-free programs. There's no such thing as a sophisticated bug-free program, because there's no such thing as a perfect programmer. While very simple programs or scripts—the sort of things that take up a line or two of code—can be made bug free, the more complicated your script the more likely it will contain bugs. So in this chapter you can take a break from learning about the different elements of JavaScript and instead learn how to figure out your mistakes, and how to avoid problems in the first place.

NOT JUST YOUR BUGS

There are two types of bugs you'll have to watch for: yours, and those in the JavaScript browsers. In other words, you may introduce bugs into the scripts you write, but you will also run into situations in which JavaScript just doesn't seem to work correctly whatever you do—because JavaScript is new and has bugs. Most of the JavaScript bugs will be removed with future versions of Netscape Navigator, but no product is completely bug free.

For example, the Netscape Navigator 3.0 beta has a bug in the Modulus calculation. (We looked at Modulus in Chapter 5, "Expressions & Operators—Manipulating Values.") When you use the

% symbol in place of the normal division symbol (/), JavaScript should divide the number on the left by the number on the right, and then discard any digits to the right of the decimal place in the result. As you saw in Example 5.5, JavaScript may not do that, depending on which browser you are using. For instance, 1500 % 40 should give a result of 37 (1500 / 40 = 37.5, remove everything from the right of the decimal place = 37). Yet you may get a result of 20.

To further complicate these bugs, they vary between platforms. A bug that appears in a JavaScript browser that runs on a Macintosh may not appear in the same browser running in UNIX or Windows.

There's not much you can do about these bugs, except try to keep informed. You'll find information about these bugs in the JavaScript newsgroups, mailing lists, and Web pages. In particular, at the time of writing the JavaScript FAQ Web page is a good source for information about bugs: http://www.freqgrafx.com/411/jsfaq.html. See Appendix H, "Finding More Information," for more sources of information about JavaScript.

AVOIDING TROUBLE

Better to avoid bugs in the first place than to track them down once they've found their way into your scripts. You can do this by following a few rules.

- Build your scripts a piece at a time, and test each piece before moving on to the next piece. It's easier to find a bug in 10 or 20 lines of script than in a few hundred.

- Use lots of comment lines to remind you what each piece is for, what data the variables contain, what functions do, and so on.

- Don't change variables types. As you saw in Chapter 4, "Variables & Literals—Storing Data," you can change variable types if you wish, but you'll probably get confused if you do and end up using a variable in the wrong way.

- Use good naming conventions. If you use logical variable names that help you to identify the data held by the variable, and the datatype (string, numeric, boolean), you'll find it easier to read your scripts and keep everything straight.

- Declare variables explicitly. As you saw in Chapter 4, if you don't declare variables correctly by using the `var` keyword, you can run into problems in which the wrong variable is used.

- Don't use a name for a variable that is inside a function if you've already declared the name globally to refer to something else. This is related to the previous suggestion; if you start mixing names, and not declaring variables explicitly, and you may find a variable being used at the wrong time. Mixing names like this is simply confusing.

- Be careful how you pass parameters. As you saw in Chapter 7, "More on Functions," you should try to change passed variables only, not global variables.

- Many, though not all, JavaScript names and keywords are case sensitive, so be very careful about how you type your scripts.

- Variable and function names are case sensitive. Naming your functions and variables in a consistent manner will help you avoid declaring a variable or defining a function, and then calling or referring to it later using the wrong case.

- As you saw in Chapter 6, "Conditionals & Loops—Making Decisions & Controlling Scripts," in some circumstances you can omit the { } braces in `if` statements. This may save a time now, but can lead to problems later—especially if you are creating nested `if` statements. Without the braces, `if` statements can be ambiguous and may not function in the intended manner. However, in some instances not using braces may actually make the script clearer—use your judgment.

- Put parentheses into logical expressions. Logical expressions can be very confusing. They may look like they do one thing, when in fact they actually do something quite different. By using parentheses you can be sure that your logical expressions do exactly what they are meant to do.

- Define functions and global variables in the HEAD. That way you can be sure that they will be created before the rest of the document loads. The user won't be able to do anything that uses the function or variable before it is available.

WATCH THE LAYOUT

As you've seen so far, scripts have been "spread" over several lines. For instance, take a look at this example that was used earlier in the book:

```
<SCRIPT LANGUAGE="JavaScript">
<!--
function function1() {
var dToday = new Date()
var nHours = dToday.getHours()
var nDay = dToday.getDay()
        if ((nDay == 5) && (nHours >= 12))        {
                alert("Thank God it's Friday afternoon"  )
        }
        else     {
                if ((nDay == 6) || (nDay == 0) )        {
                        alert("Hey, it's the weekend" )
        }
                else    {
                        alert("Just another day")
                }
        }
}
//-->
</SCRIPT>
```

The script above is exactly the same as the following script:

```
<SCRIPT LANGUAGE="JavaScript">
<!--
function function1() {
var dToday = new Date()
var nHours = dToday.getHours()
var nDay = dToday.getDay()
if ((nDay == 5) && (nHours >= 12))
{alert("Thank God it's Friday afternoon")}
else{if ((nDay == 6) || (nDay == 0) )
{alert("Hey, it's the weekend" )}
else{alert("Just another day")}}}
//-->
</SCRIPT>
```

In fact, you can remove most of the spaces in this script and string out this entire script into one block of text, like this:

Example 8.1

```
<SCRIPT LANGUAGE="JavaScript">
<!--
function function1(){var dToday=new Date()var nHours=
dToday.getHours()var nDay=dToday.getDay()if((nDay==5)&&
(nHours>=12)){alert("Thank God it's Friday afternoon")}
else{if((nDay==6)||(nDay==0)){alert("Hey, it's the
weekend")}else{alert("Just another day")}}}
//-->
</SCRIPT>
```

These last two examples are confusing, though. Better to write your scripts with lots of spaces and line breaks. As you can see in the first example, we've done several things to make the script clearer:

- We've placed each variable declaration on a new line. (We didn't have to, but it makes it much easier to find them!)

- When we placed an opening brace ({), we moved it to the right a bit—it's easier to see.

- After the opening {, we moved down a line and indented the instruction that is within the brackets. This makes it easier to see the instruction.

- When we placed a closing brace (}), we placed it on its own line. As we said before, you must make sure that for every opening { you have a closing }. This is one way to make it easy to count the braces.

- We indented the contents of if statements. The if and its corresponding else are at the same level. When we nested an if statement, we indented the if and else to the right of the if and else in which they are nested. Indenting means, in effect, "this bit of code is linked in some way to the bit of code under which it's indented."

- Although most (though not all) spaces are "unnecessary" we included spaces all over the place. We have spaces between variables, operators, and values, for instance (nHours >= 12), though we don't need them. They just make it easier to read the script.

- Another thing you may do—though we haven't—is place a semicolon at the end of each line. Some JavaScript programmers do this out of habit; you have to in C. In JavaScript it's optional, *except* when putting multiple statements within an event handler (we'll look at event handlers in Chapter 12, "JavaScript Events—When Are Actions Carried Out?").

We've done all these things for one reason—to make our scripts easier to work with and read. The clearer your scripts, the less likely you are to introduce mistakes. And the clearer your scripts, the easier it will be to track down problems.

TIP

Don't Type, Copy! You can be the world's most careful programmer, and still introduce bugs into your scripts by mistyping something. Typos are probably the most common source of program errors, so it's a good idea to type as little as possible. Whenever possible, copy a piece of script that you've already used somewhere else (and know to be good) and paste it into the script on which you are working. You can also use your text or HTML editor's tools to build "libraries" of scripts. Soon we'll see JavaScript-programming tools that help you create scripts by choosing commands from list boxes rather than typing.

A WORD ABOUT SPACES

How many spaces can you use? In general, as many as you want. You may want to simply press the Tab key to indent items—press several times if necessary. There's no limit to the number of spaces you can use. You also can enter extra blank lines whenever you want. As discussed in Chapter 2, don't use line breaks inside statements, though. The JavaScript interpreter simply ignores all these extra spaces and line breaks.

However, you will find a few situations in which you *must not* use spaces. In Chapter 14, "Controlling Windows & Documents With JavaScript," for instance, we'll examine how to open secondary windows, using *window features* to define what window components should be used, and the window size. For example, the following instruction opens a window and includes the Location bar and Toolbar, and allows the user to resize the window:

```
open("window.htm","Window1","location,resize,height=250,
width=450,toolbar")
```

You'll notice that there are no spaces between these window features. Each feature is separated with a comma, but if you use a comma followed by a space you will actually turn off all subsequent features. Because the window features is really one parameter—though it has several different parts—you cannot place spaces within it.

TIP

Adding a space somewhere it's not allowed is actually a good diagnostic tool. You can use it to "turn off" things while you check for a script problem in a particular case.

TRACKING DOWN PROBLEMS

However carefully you write your scripts, you are bound to introduce mistakes. Eventually you'll find you have a script that doesn't work quite correctly, and you will have to figure out why. Eventually? Well, okay, soon—probably your first and every subsequent script. In fact troubleshooting is an integral part of programming, in the same way that editing is an integral part of writing. You will almost *always* have to troubleshoot unless you've written a very tiny script. So let's see what you can do to track down problems.

There are basically two types of bugs:

- *Load-time bugs.* These bugs appear as soon as your Web page loads in the browser, and are caused by problems in the scripts that are read by the browser as soon as it opens the Web page.

These are often scripts that declare variables and define functions; they also may be problems with scripts designed to write information into the Web page, for instance. Generally, you'll see an error message when these errors occur. This type of bug occurs because there is something wrong with the script—it doesn't make sense to your browser.

■ *Run-time bugs.* These are bugs that appear later—when an event handler runs the script. For instance, the bugs may not appear until the user clicks on a button; or, if you are using the onunload event handler, until the user loads a different page. These bugs *may* or *may not* display an error message. (If there's a run-time bug in a script using the onload event handler, the bug will appear immediately after the page has loaded.)

Why do some bugs cause error messages to appear, while some don't? Quite simply, some bugs, such as syntax errors, can be recognized by the JavaScript interpreter (the browser), while others can't. When the browser reads the JavaScript it tries to make sense of it. If it can't, it displays an error message. For instance, if you have missed a closing }, or if you haven't used quotation marks when you should have, or if you used double-quotation marks when you should have used singles, or used the = assignment operator when you should have used the == conditional operator, or called a function that doesn't exist, the browser will get "confused." It can't understand your script, so it displays an error message telling you that you've got a problem.

On the other hand, the script may work perfectly as far as the interpreter is concerned. But that doesn't mean it does what you want it to do. For instance, in a calculation you may have used one numeric variable instead of another one, the one you really should have used. The browser can still make the calculation, as you've given it a numeric value. As far as you are concerned, the answer is wrong because the script uses the wrong value. But the browser has no way to know that, so it has to assume the script is good.

FINDING LOAD-TIME BUGS

Let's start by looking at load-time bugs. Say, for instance, that you've created a script and the script just loaded in your browser for the first time. Up pops an error message—the one in Figure 8-1, for instance. (This is the error message that appears when you use Example 6.2.)

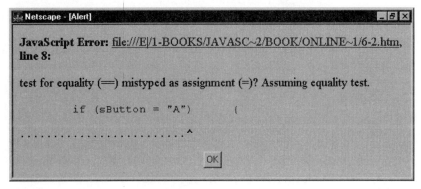

Figure 8-1: *The Error Message box.*

A load-time error can occur without an error message appearing. You may have made a mistake in the HEAD that the browser doesn't recognize as a mistake, so it doesn't display an error message. However, this mistake won't become apparent until an event runs the script. (We'll be looking at problems in the HEAD again in a few moments, when we look at run-time errors.)

What do you do? You read the error message, of course. In this case you can quickly see what you did wrong. The message says *test for equality (==) mistyped as assignment (=)? Assuming equality test*. The browser has found a situation in which it thinks that you probably want to check a variable to see if it matches a value, yet you used the = assignment operator instead of the == conditional operator. (It actually uses == instead of =, but warns you so that you can fix the error.) You'll also see that below the message is the line in which the problem occurred:

```
if (sButton = "A") {
```

And, indeed, you can see that = was used instead of ==. The browser will also try to provide more information. You'll notice that the message box tells you the line number on which the script error occurs. It also tells you the file in which the problem occurs. You might think that would be obvious, but if you are loading several documents into frames, this will help you not only identify in which document the problem lies, but even go directly to that document; the document name is a link, so click on it to load that document into the browser.

Notice that under the line of code is a series of periods and a caret (^) pointing up at the code. Also, notice that part of the code is colored red. These are indicators that are supposed to point directly at the part of the code that has a problem, though as you can see they're not always accurate. Still, they usually point in the general direction of the problem.

In this case the fix is quick and easy; simply replace the = with ==, save, and restore. In Figure 8-2 you'll see another example.

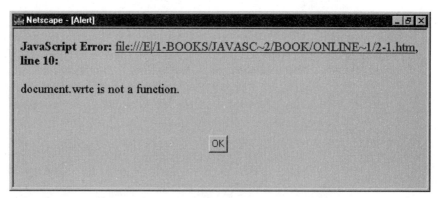

Figure 8-2: *A simple typo caused this problem.*

In this case you've got a typo; instead of typing `document.write`, you typed `document.wrte`. The browser thinks you are trying to use a function, but finds that you haven't defined that function anywhere. Again, the solution is simple—find `document.wrte` and correct the spelling.

Error messages are not always as easy to figure out. Sometimes the browser won't really understand what you've done wrong, but will tell you what *appears* to be wrong. For instance, we took Example 4.7, and removed one of the \ symbols preceding the quotation mark in the Mark Twain quote. We ended up with four error messages, one after another. Here are the messages we saw:

```
missing operator in expression
var twainA = ""I never write \'metropolis\' for seven cents
................^

twainB is not defined

twainC is not defined

twainD is not defined
```

Although you'll end up with four separate message boxes, with the last message box on top, you should look at the first box that appeared first. (The others may be caused by the problem addressed by the original message, so fix that first problem and you may not need to worry about the others.)

Now, in this case we're told that there's a missing operator in the expression. The browser hasn't realized that the second quotation mark is supposed to be part of the string literal, so it assumes it's part of the script itself. Still, if you look carefully at the message, you can quickly see what you did wrong. Replace the \ and save, close all of the message boxes, reload, and all the error messages will go away.

> **TIP**
>
> *Why did we get the* `twainB, twainC, and twainD is not defined` *messages? The actual error messages come from later in the script, where we're using* `document.write` *commands to write the contents of these variables into the Web page. But the source of the problem is in the first script—these variables weren't declared properly in that script. Because the browser got confused in the first line of the first script, it was unable to finish the script properly.*

FINDING RUN-TIME BUGS

Run-time bugs are problems that only appear when a script actually runs—when some kind of action occurs. As we said before, you won't always see error messages with these, because the browser may not consider the problem to be an error. While an error message helps you pinpoint the problem—by showing you the line number and even pointing at the error (or close to the error) in the line, you can still figure out bugs that don't cause messages to appear. You'll simply have to review your script carefully.

The first step is to figure out what ran the script. If, for instance, the problem lies in something being written into the Web page, you need to find where in your script you are writing to the page. If something strange happens as soon as the page has finished loading, take a look at the `onload` event handler in the Web page's `<BODY>` tag. If something goes wrong when you click on a button, find that button in the script. Then work your way back from there. If the event handler names a variable, check to see that it names the correct variable. Perhaps the most likely problem in a bug that doesn't display an error message is a variable with the wrong data. Find where the variable was declared, and look at all the places in the script where the variable has had data assigned to it. More important, look at the last point at which the variable had data placed into it. Carefully examine all the way back to the origins of that data: is it coming from the right place, is it being calculated correctly? What data will the variable have when you click on the button?

Your Own Debugger—Checking Values With Alerts

There's a problem with tracking down bugs in JavaScript—there's no *debugger*. A debugger is a special tool used by programmers to help them remove bugs. It runs through the program line by line, showing the programmer the status of the program as it proceeds. For instance, it will show the programmer what values are held by the variables as the program runs. In effect the debugger can look "inside" the program as it runs and confirm that each piece of the program works correctly.

In JavaScript you are on your own. There is currently no debugging tool, so you must do all the work for yourself. There is a good way to *duplicate* the actions of a debugger, though, using the Alert dialog box. When programmers debug code, they are basically looking at variable values inside their programs as they run. Using the Alert dialog box method allows you to do just that.

You can place lines of code (or code *stubs* as they're known to programmers) in your scripts to open Alert dialog boxes. These boxes display the contents of a variable at each point in the script. In fact we did this in earlier examples. Take a look at Example 6.13, for instance:

```
function function1() {
var i
        for (i = 1; i < 4; i++) {            .
                            alert("The value in i is " + i )
        }
        alert("The loop has finished and i is " + i )
}
```

We put an alert into a loop. The alert displays the value of the variable i each time the loop runs. When an Alert box opens, the browser stops at that line in the script. You can then read the value held by the variable to confirm that it's correct, then click on the OK button to continue the script. If you are debugging a loop that goes around many times, you can insert an if statement to limit the conditions under which you get the Alert box.

Remember to take out your code stubs when you have finished debugging the program.

COMMON ERRORS

Here are some common mistakes you should watch out for:

- You created a conditional expressions using the = assignment operator instead of the == conditional operator.

- You used a variable that you haven't yet declared.

- You used a variable that you've declared, but it hasn't been initialized—that is, it has no value.

- You forgot to include parentheses in the correct places, or didn't include the correct number (there must be an equal number; each opening (must have a closing)).

- You forgot to include braces, or didn't include the correct number (again, there must be an equal number; each opening { must have a closing }).

- You declared a variable inside a function, then tried to use it globally—that is, *outside* the function.

- You forgot to include () immediately after a function name.

- You didn't put quotation marks in the correct places, enclosing string literals, for instance.

- You used double quotation marks (" ") instead of single quotation marks (' '). Remember, if you are placing something that must be enclosed in quotation marks, and it's nested within something else enclosed between double quotation marks, then you must use single quotation marks.

■ You haven't explicitly declared a variable (using var) within a function, and when you tried to use it you ended up getting the value from a global variable of the same name. (See Example 4.5.) This demonstrates why you should not design programs to use local variables with the same name as global variables.

■ You mistyped a name or keyword, or typed it in the wrong case.

■ You accidentally changed a variable's type, and ended up using the variable in the wrong situation for its current type.

■ You created a Boolean expression that you didn't fully understand, and it works differently from the way you thought it would. Combinations of many Boolean variables and Boolean operators have different meanings depending on where you put the parentheses.

■ You created a calculation that doesn't work the way you think it should. Again, the calculation will vary according to operator precedence and where you put the parentheses.

■ You referred to something (a day of the week or an entry in an array) using its position number, but counted from 1, not 0. Remember that programmers often count from 0, not from 1. So in many cases when you have to specify a number—an item's position in a selection list, for instance—you must call the first item 0, the second 1, and so on.

■ You have multiple statements in an event handler (see Chapter 12, "JavaScript Events—When Are Actions Carried Out?"), and haven't placed a semicolon after each expression.

MOVING ON

Back to work. In our next chapter we're going to take a look at arrays. These provide a way for you to store many related values. You can think of an array as a multivalue variable; in fact, that's exactly what it is.

Arrays are very useful things. You can use two or more arrays in conjunction to link related data. One array might contain first names, the next second names, the next e-mail addresses, for instance. You can then search one array, and display the corresponding data from one of the other arrays. So turn to the next chapter and we'll show you how to do just that.

CHAPTER 9

Building Arrays

What is an *array*? A very useful thing, that's what. It's a collection of data, and it's an essential programming tool. Later you'll see just how useful an array can be when we create our area-code program in Chapter 18, "The Area Code Application." We'll be using examples from that application in this chapter as we examine how to create arrays.

As you already know, you can create variables that hold information. However, a variable can hold only one thing at a time. What if you want to store 10, or 100, or 500 items at once? And what if all these items are all similar (such as information related to a telephone area code)? Well, you could create 10, 100, or 500 variables, but this would be very clumsy. Better to create an array to hold all this information. In fact an array can be thought of as a multidata variable. Use one name for this array (rather than 10, 100, or 500 variable names), then place all the information into the array.

 ## CREATING AN ARRAY

Some programming languages have built-in array systems—JavaScript didn't until very recently. We'll look at the new `Array` object, introduced with Netscape Navigator 3.0 beta 3, at the end of this chapter, but because Netscape 2.0 can't use the `Array` object, we'll be looking at how to create an array *without* it.

If you want to use an array that will work with Netscape 2.0, you will need to create one. You can create an array in three steps:

1. First, create a new object class by writing a special function.

2. Call the function.

3. Then enter the data into the array.

STEP 1: CREATING THE ARRAY OBJECT

Let's start by showing you the "official" way to create an array. Then we'll discuss a much quicker "shortcut" method for creating an array.

The first step is to create a new *object class*. (You'll learn more about objects in Chapter 10, "Objects, Properties & Methods.") An object is simply a thing that describes something; the `document` object is a description of the document; a `form` object is a description of the form, and so on. JavaScript has objects that are already created for you, and you can also create your own objects. Creating an object is a little advanced; we'll discuss it in Chapter 13, "Advanced Topics," but even there we won't go into too much detail. It doesn't matter too much if you don't understand the full capabilities of object creation. As long as you can see how we use the object to create the array, that's enough.

In order to create an array, you must first create an object that describes the array. You can do that by defining a special type of function, like this example:

```
function makeArray(n) {
    this.length = n
    for (var i=1; i <= n; i++) {
        this[i] = null;
    }
    return this
}
```

We've created a function called `makeArray`. Notice that we are going to pass the value `n` to this function in the parentheses when we call it.

What does `this.length = n` mean? It simply means "place the value `n` into the `length` property of this object." Objects contain properties; a property contains information about the object. In this case, `length` is a keyword to represent the number of items that will be stored in the array. So the value stored by the length property is `n`, which will be passed to the function when it is called (as you'll see in a few moments). In other words, when we call this function to create our array, we're going to tell the function how many items will be stored in the array.

Next we have a `for` statement. This statement declares a variable, `i`. It initializes `i` with the value 1. Then it uses the conditional expression (go back to Chapter 6, "Conditionals & Loops—Making Decisions & Controlling Scripts," if you can't remember this stuff) to compare `i` with the value held in `n`; as long as `i` is equal to or less than `n`, the instructions within the { } are run: `this[i] = null`. This sets the value at the position `i` in the array to null.

TIP

We've initialized to null—that is, we've put the value null into the array positions. You can also initialize to other values: to 0, for example, which may be more appropriate in some scripts.

Then the *update expression* is run (`i++`); this increases the value held in `i` by one. The loop then continues. When the value in `i` is greater than the value of `n` (the number of items in the array), the `for` loop ends, and the last instruction is run. The instruction `return this` means "return the object that's been created."

So, we've created a function that describes the array object we want. But in order to use an object you need to create an *instance* of the object (the function is merely the "blueprint"). So to do that, we have to call the function.

Step 2: Call the Function

We create our array object instance by declaring a variable in a special way, as in this example:

```
var arrayname = new functionname(n)
```

For instance:

```
var area = new makeArray(187)
```

This creates an array called **area**. Notice that we are passing the number 187 to the **makeArray** function. That's because this array will contain 187 items. So, what do we have now? A special variable that can contain 187 items. Now we can put data into the array.

Tip

Okay, we've broken one of our rules, or a suggestion anyway. We suggested that you place a letter before a variable name to indicate the variable type (sArea, for instance, instead of area). However, in this case we didn't bother, for two reasons. First, we wanted to use a small name, because we're going to be using it many times. Second, because we're using it so often in the script, we're not likely to forget what type of data it holds.

Step 3: Placing Data into the Array

If we were assigning a value to a normal variable called area, we'd simply do this:

```
area = "Alabama             "
```

We've placed the string **Alabama** (plus a number of spaces afterward) into the variable **area**. But we want to put 187 items into this special variable, the **area** array. So we need to number each one, like this:

```
area[1] = "Alabama          "
area[2] = "Alabama          "
area[3] = "Alaska           "
area[4] = "Alberta          "
```

```
area[5] = "Antigua          "
area[6] = "Arizona          "
area[7] = "Arizona          "
area[8] = "Arkansas         "
area[9] = "Bahamas          "
area[10] = "Barbados          "
area[11] = "Bermuda           "
area[12] = "British Columbia  "
area[13] = "British Columbia  "
```

. . .

Each time that we placed an item into the variable, we gave it a number, so that the items are indexed. We can ask our script, "what's in position 9?," and we'll get the result Bahamas. (You'll learn more about this in a few moments.)

TIP

We've entered spaces to make the variables the same size. That's a simple way to make sure that when the program displays the results, they line up properly.

Now, why do we have multiple occurrences in some instances (two Arizonas and two Alabamas, for example)? Well, this comes from our Area Code example. This is an application that allows you to search for a state, province, or country in North America, and get a list of the associated telephone area codes. There are multiple area codes in some of these places, so we needed more than one entry. In fact we've created multiple arrays that are "parallel" to each other. For instance, there's another array called cde, which contains the actual area-code numbers. Here's how we created both area and cde together.

```
var cde = new makeArray(187)
var area = new makeArray(187)
area[1] = "Alabama          "; cde[1] = 205
area[2] = "Alabama          "; cde[2] = 334
```

```
area[3] = "Alaska          "; cde[3] = 907
area[4] = "Alberta         "; cde[4] = 403
area[5] = "Antigua         "; cde[5] = 268
area[6] = "Arizona         "; cde[6] = 520
area[7] = "Arizona         "; cde[7] = 602
area[8] = "Arkansas        "; cde[8] = 501
area[9] = "Bahamas         "; cde[9] = 242
area[10] = "Barbados         "; cde[10] = 246
area[11] = "Bermuda          "; cde[11] = 441
area[12] = "British Columbia "; cde[12] = 250
area[13] = "British Columbia "; cde[13] = 604
```

First we created both arrays: `var cde = new makeArray(187)` and
`var area = new makeArray(187)`. Then we entered all the data in
the same way. On each line we entered data into the same positions
in both arrays. The `;` symbol means that an entry into one array has
ended, and the entry into the other array has started. We don't have
to do it this way. We could simply create one array, fill the array,
then create and fill the next array below the first one. But doing
them together like this helps us read the script, and figure out what
is happening. We can quickly see, for instance, that the area code
for `Bermuda` is 441.

TIP

*The Netscape Navigator 3.0 beta and earlier releases have a bug that
limits line length to 255 characters or less in some cases. If you run into
this problem, you may not be able to put multiple array entries on one
line. Instead create each array separately, or simply move long variable
assignments down to the next line.*

GRABBING DATA FROM AN ARRAY

How can we get data out of our array? Well, think about how we could get data out of a normal variable. We could, for example, do this:

```
alert("normv")
```

That would simply open an Alert box and display the value held in the normv variable. You've probably already figured out how to get a value out of an array. You could do this:

```
alert("area[6]")
```

That would open the Alert box and display the value held in position 6 of the area array.

0 OR 1?

Elsewhere in this book you have learned that when you number a list of items in JavaScript you start from 0, and in most cases that's true. However, when you create an array in this manner, you must start numbering from 1. The 0 position contains the property length, a number that indicates the theoretical size of the array. (It's actually the number passed to the function in parentheses, which is not necessarily the same as the number of values that are stored in the array. In the earlier example, the value was 187.)

Note, however, that in most programming languages the entries in the array would begin at position 0. And indeed even in JavaScript the *real* array objects count up from 0. As you'll see in Chapter 10, "Objects, Properties & Methods," JavaScript has a series of array objects created for special purposes. The frames array lists all the frames in the document, the options array lists all the options in a selection box, and so on. These arrays work in the normal manner, counting from 0. But when you create your own arrays, you'll start counting from 1.

Take a look at the following example. We've created two small arrays:

Example 9.1

```
<SCRIPT LANGUAGE="JAVASCRIPT">
<!--
function makeArray(n) {
    this.length = n
    for (var i=1; i <= n; i++){
        this[i] = null;
    }
    return this
}

var acode = new makeArray(187)
var area = new makeArray(187)
area[1] = "Alabama          "; acode[1] = 205
area[2] = "Alabama          "; acode[2] = 334
area[3] = "Alaska           "; acode[3] = 907
area[4] = "Alberta          "; acode[4] = 403
area[5] = "Antigua          "; acode[5] = 268
area[6] = "Arizona          "; acode[6] = 520
area[7] = "Arizona          "; acode[7] = 602
area[8] = "Arkansas         "; acode[8] = 501
area[9] = "Bahamas          "; acode[9] = 242
area[10] = "Barbados         "; acode[10] = 246
area[11] = "Bermuda          "; acode[11] = 441
area[12] = "British Columbia  "; acode[12] = 250
area[13] = "British Columbia  "; acode[13] = 604
//-->
</SCRIPT>
</HEAD>
```

As you can see, we began by creating the array objects, then we put 13 entries into each array. (We still passed the number 187 to the array, meaning that the array will be 187 entries long. But that's okay. You'll see in a moment what happens if you try to get an entry from a position that has not been filled.) Then we created these buttons:

```
<FORM>
<INPUT TYPE="BUTTON" VALUE="What's in area Position 11?"
onclick="alert(area[12])"><P>
```

```
<INPUT TYPE="BUTTON" VALUE="What's in acode Position 11?"
onclick="alert(acode[12])"><P>
<INPUT TYPE="BUTTON" VALUE="What's in area Position 110?"
onclick="alert(area[110])"><P>
<INPUT TYPE="BUTTON" VALUE="What's in area Position 500?"
onclick="alert(area[500])"><P>
<INPUT TYPE="BUTTON" VALUE="What's in area Position 0
(area.length)?" onclick="alert(area.length)"><P>
</FORM>
```

Try the Online Companion example and you'll see that the first button displays *British Columbia* in the Alert box, the value stored in position 11 of area. The second shows *250*, the value stored in position 11 of cde. The third and fourth buttons, though, display *null*, because in both cases they are positions that haven't been filled (and we initialized it to null, remember).

TIP

In the second case not only is it empty, but we're also trying to find a value from an entry larger than the number (187), that we told the function would be held by the array. Actually, thanks to the rather informal way in which JavaScript works with arrays, this doesn't matter much. You'll learn more about that under "The Shortcuts," later in this chapter.

We've put the same arrays in another example in our Online Companion. This time we've added a function in the HEAD to figure out the position:

Example 9.2

```
function GetArray(form) {
var nBase
        if (form.array.selectedIndex == 0) sArray = area;
        if (form.array.selectedIndex == 1) sArray = cde;
      form.returninfo.value =
sArray[form.arraypos.selectedIndex]
      }
```

You saw a script similar to this in Chapter 7, "More on Functions." The reference to the form is passed to the function (you'll

see the form in a moment). The selection position from the array selection box (form.array.selectedIndex is checked; if the position is
0, the sArray variable is set to area. If it's 1, it's set to cde. (You'll
learn more about referring to a form element in this manner in
Chapters 16, "Forms & JavaScript.") Then we find the value in the
array. sArray[form.arraypos.selectedIndex] means "find the selected item in the selection box called arraypos; this is the position
in the array named in sArray." The information held in that position is then passed back to the form: form.returninfo.value,
which means "place this information in the returninfo text box."

Here's the form that was used:

```
<FORM>
Select array you want to check: <select name="array"
size="2">
<option selected value>area
<option>cde
</select><P>
Select an array position you want to check: <select
name="arraypos" size="2">
<option>
<option selected value>1
<option>2
<option>3
<option>4
<option>5
<option>6
<option>7
<option>8
<option>9
<option>10
<option>11
<option>12
<option>13
<option>14
</select><P>
<INPUT TYPE="button" VALUE="What's in this position?"
onclick="GetArray(this.form)"><P>
Here's the information in that position: <INPUT TYPE="TEXT"
NAME="returninfo">
</FORM>
```

We have two selection boxes; one in which you can select the array name, the other in which you select the position. When you click on the button, the function you just saw is called, and the information from the array position is placed into the text box, as you can see in Figure 9-1.

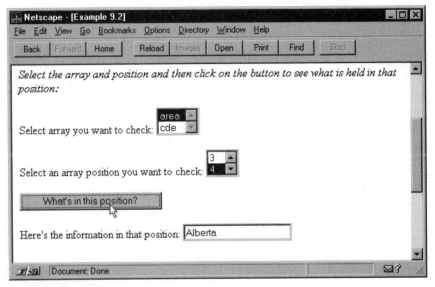

Figure 9-1: *Select the array name and the position, then click on the button to see the value held there.*

MATCHING ARRAYS

A powerful feature of arrays is the ability to match values; position *a* in array *x* represents position *a* in array *y*, for instance. In our example position 1 in the area array represents position 1 in the cde array, position 2 represents position 2, and so forth.

In this way you can refer to a position in one array, and see the information in that array and the associated array (or associated *arrays*, as you may have multiple arrays). For instance, in the following example you can select an area from a selection box, and see the corresponding area code. In other words, you are specifying a value in one array, and the script is displaying the corresponding value in the other array.

Example 9.3

```
<FORM>
Select the area for which you want to retrieve the area code:
<select name="area" size="14">
<option >
<option selected option>Alabama 1
<option> Alabama 2
<option> Alaska
<option> Alberta
<option> Antigua
<option> Arizona 1
<option> Arizona 2
<option> Arkansas
<option> Bahamas
<option> Barbados
<option> Bermuda
<option> British Columbia 1
<option> British Columbia 2
</select><BR>
<INPUT TYPE="button" VALUE="What's the area code?"
onclick="form.returninfo.value=cde[form.area.selectedIndex]">
<INPUT TYPE="TEXT" NAME="returninfo">
</FORM>
```

We built a form with a selection box in it. In the box we have a list of all the areas in our array. Notice, by the way, that there is a blank space at the top of the list. (There was a blank space in one of the selection boxes in the previous example, too.) The problem is that while arrays count from 1 up, selection boxes count from 0 up! If we put Alabama 1 in the first position, when we use the selectedIndex property (as you'll see in a moment), we would get the index value 0. Alabama is position 1 in the array, not 0. We could have converted the selection-box positions to array positions, as we did with the if statements in the array selection box in the last ex-

ample. However, we added a blank option at the top to shift the entries down into their correct positions as a quick fix.

Now, what happens when you click on the button? Here's the
`onclick` instruction again:

```
onclick="form.returninfo.value=cde[form.area.selectedIndex]"
```

As you can see, this time we are looking at the `cde` array; you selected an entry from the `area` array, but what we want is the matching
position in `cde`. We then take the position number and place it between the [ ] brackets; `form.area.selectedIndex` means "look in the
`area` selection box, and find the `selectedIndex` position (the position
of the selected item)." So if you selected the blank space at the top, we
would have, in effect, this:

```
cde[0]
```

If you selected the 5th position, you'd get this:

```
cde[4]
```

and so on.

So we find the information in the appropriate `cde` position, and
then place that information into the `returninfo` text box. You select
something in one array, but get an associated value from another
array, as you can see in Figure 9-2. Simple.

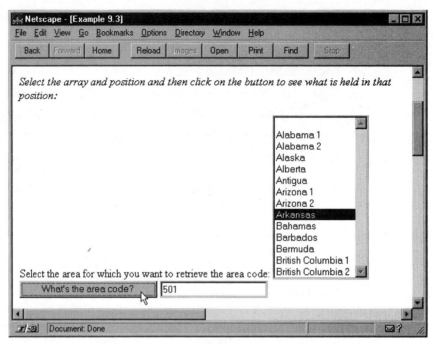

Figure 9-2: *You select from one array (area) and get a value from another array (cde).*

Actually there is a better way around the problem of the array index not being the same as the option index. You can use `selectedIndex +1` to index the array, like this:

```
onclick="form.returninfo.value=cde[form.area.selectedIndex + 1]"
```

THE SHORTCUTS

As you learned before, there's a quicker way to create an array. You see, JavaScript has what might be termed "loosely defined" arrays. In some programming languages, such as C, you have to define an array very carefully and specifically. The method for creating an array object shown above is a formal method for doing so:

```
function makeArray(n) {
    this.length = n
    for (var i=1; i <= n; i++){
        this[i] = null;
    }
    return this
}
```

We've named the array, set the array length, set all the array position values to null, and returned the array object. But JavaScript's rather loose array definition allows you to create this array object with just one line of script. You can see an example in the Online Companion. We've simply taken the first example from this chapter, and removed most of the lines from where the function was defined, leaving nothing but this:

Example 9.4

```
function makeArray(n) {
}
```

Try this page, and you'll find that almost all of it works exactly the same as in the first example (when we created the array more formally). Click on the buttons and you'll see the same information, with one exception, this button:

```
<INPUT TYPE="BUTTON" VALUE="What's in area Position 0
(area.length)?" onclick="alert(area.length)">
```

This button displays the area array's length property. But because we took out the this.length = n line, that property is no longer being set. So when you click on that button, you'll see *undefined* in the Alert box.

Let's see something else about this length property. In the next example, we've copied the first example again, and retained the formal method for creating the array. However, we have also done the following:

Example 9.5

```
var acode = new makeArray(3)
var area = new makeArray(3)
area[1] = "Alabama          "; acode[1] = 205
area[2] = "Alabama          "; acode[2] = 334
```

```
area[3] = "Alaska         "; acode[3] = 907
area[4] = "Alberta        "; acode[4] = 403
area[5] = "Antigua        "; acode[5] = 268
area[6] = "Arizona        "; acode[6] = 520
```

Notice that this time we've passed the number 3 to the function. In other words, we are saying, "this array will contain three items." But we've put more than that in there (in fact the Online Companion example has 13, not the 6 shown here—we didn't want to repeat that stuff).

Try the example. What happens? All the buttons work correctly. Even though we are asking for information in position 11—a position larger than the number we've told the function the array will contain—we still get the information. Note, however, the last button. When we ask for the `area.length` value we get 3, not 13. We get the value that we told the function the array would contain, not what it actually contains.

So, do we need to specify the `length`? The array works even if we don't set the `length` parameter; it doesn't seem to use it. In fact, we don't have to bother passing a number to the function and it still will work okay.

Well, it's a good idea to specify the length. Why? You may want to create a script that needs to know how long the array is. In Chapter 18, "The Area Code Application," you'll learn how you can search an array and you must be able to tell the search script when to stop.

In the release of JavaScript incorporated into Netscape 2.0, `length` is just an object property. You have to set it and make sure that it is correct if you wish to use it. As we will see in Chapter 13, "Advanced Topics," you can create an object's property simply by assigning it. This is similar to the way that you can create variables. In fact, assigning a value to an array element is actually the same as creating a new property for the object. In the latest release of JavaScript, though, there is a built-in `Array` object—this automatically sets the length for you. How about the rest of the formal array creation, though? These pieces:

```
for (var i=1; i <= n; i++){
        this[i] = null;
    }
    return this
```

You can generally do without these. The for loop is used to set all the positions in the array to null or 0. But if you are about to place data into all those positions anyway (and you probably are), you need not do this. And the last piece, return this, is also unnecessary, as the array will be returned without it.

TRUE ARRAY OBJECTS

The latest beta (Netscape 3.0 beta 4) has a built-in array object, though you probably shouldn't use it quite yet. If you create an array using this new object, earlier browsers won't be able to use your scripts.

What do we mean by a built-in array object? It's one that's already there, waiting for you to use; it saves you the first step of array creation—you no longer have to create an object class. Now you just go straight to the second step, and create an *instance* of the object. (Remember, the *class* is the blueprint, the *instance* is the actual usable object. We'll learn more about this in the following chapter.)

In our example, for instance, we could create an array called area like this:

```
var area = new Array()
```

Then we could begin placing data into the array in the way we did before:

```
area[0] = "Alabama          "
area[2] = "Alabama          "
area[3] = "Alaska           "
area[4] = "Alberta          "
```

Note one big difference with the Array object, though; we started at 0, not at 1. Also, this object will keep track of how many elements it has, and automatically set the length property for you.

Moving On

Arrays are really quite simple. The next subject we want to look at is a little more complicated, though. We're going to explain how to work with objects. Objects are "things" that can be described and manipulated using properties and methods. For instance, there's a `document` object, which describes the currently open document. This has a range of properties (such as `lastModified`, which we've used before and which is the date that the document was saved) and methods (such as `clear`, which clears the window, and `write`, which we've used a number of times as well).

We're going to learn about the different objects available to you, the way they are linked together in a hierarchical system, about object classes and object instances, and more in the following chapter.

CHAPTER 10

Objects, Properties & Methods

So far we have tried to avoid talking about objects as much as possible. You may have heard of *Object Orientation* (OO) and wondered what all the fuss was about. Object Orientation is a way of building programs that "reflects" or models the real world more closely than in earlier programming languages. Programs are built using objects that have properties or data associated with them and also have behavior or methods that belong to them as well.

For instance, let's consider an object in the real world—a house. It has properties, such as the number of rooms, number of windows, and so on. It also has behaviors associated with it—things that you can do to it and with it:

- People can *live* in the house

- The house can be *painted*

- The house can be *sold*

- The house can be *rented*

If you owned many houses you might want a program that could help you manage them. The program would have "house" objects in it, one such object for each house you wanted to manage. For each house there would be values for each of its properties: the number of rooms, the rental value, the house's dimensions, and so on. You would probably want to create forms for the input of each house's properties. You could also have functions or *methods* associated with each house object, which would represent behavior associated with that particular house. You might have a method that lists materials needed to paint the house or a method that calculates the rent to be collected.

There is much more to full object-oriented programming (OOP) than this, but JavaScript is not full OOP. JavaScript provides various objects for you to use and even allows you to create your own objects, but it does not implement more complicated OO concepts. (This is just as well, because OOP can get very complicated, especially for people with little or no programming experience. In fact many programmers don't understand OOP, either.)

So, in summary, an object has a collection of *properties* and *methods* associated with it.

The Object	The House
The Object's Properties	Rooms, doors, windows, fire places, etc.
Methods (which are types of functions), behaviors associated with the object itself and with the object's properties	You can sell the house You can rent the house You can paint the house (and the rooms, doors, etc.) You can clean the house (and the windows, floors, etc.)

JavaScript provides a number of objects for you to use. We have already used the document object a few times earlier in this book. The document object is the Web page that your HTML and JavaScript produces. There are other objects such as the window object and the form object.

PROPERTIES—VARIABLES BELONGING TO OBJECTS

The properties of an object are variables belonging to the object. They are specified using the dot notation (.) in the following way:

```
objectname.propertyname
```

where `objectname` is simply the name of the object and `propertyname` is, yes, you've guessed it, the name of the property. For instance, in our house example, if we wanted to refer to the house's basement we could call it this:

```
house.basement
```

Simple, eh? We're going to look at the `navigator` object now. This object is used to describe the browser viewing the Web document that contains the script. It is a simple object in that it currently has only four properties. The following example displays each of the properties:

Example 10.1

```
<SCRIPT LANGUAGE="JavaScript">
<!--
function DisplayProperties() {
    document.write("<P><B>navigator.appCodeName =</B> " +→
navigator.appCodeName)
    document.write("<P><B>navigator.appName =</B> " +→
navigator.appName)
    document.write("<P><B>navigator.appVersion =</B> " +→
navigator.appVersion)
    document.write("<P><B>navigator.userAgent =</B> " +→
navigator.userAgent)
}
//-->
</SCRIPT>
```

This is a fairly simple script. We created a function, called `DisplayProperties`, which is called later in the source document (the script above is in the HEAD). The `DisplayProperties` function writes several lines to the Web page, using the `document.write` method. (A method is simply a function associated with a particular object.) In this case the `write` method is associated with the `document` object, and is used to write text to the Web page. The example does this for all the properties, one after another. First it uses HTML tags to start a new line and begin bold text, then it writes the name of the property followed by = (notice that all the HTML tags, the name, and the = are enclosed in quotation marks), and then it writes the property name.

Later in the source document the function is called from this simple script:

```
<SCRIPT LANGUAGE="JavaScript">
<!--
DisplayProperties()
//-->
</SCRIPT>
```

You can see the result in Figure 10-1 (your output may look different—this is from the Windows 95 Netscape 3.0 beta 4).

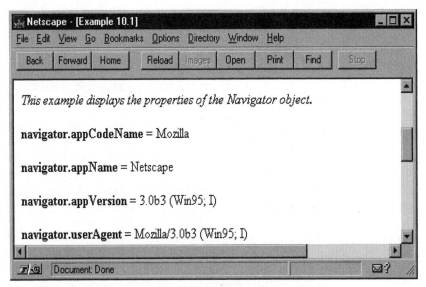

Figure 10-1: *We've written the contents of the navigator properties to the Web page.*

What are all these properties? Let's see:

Property	Description
navigator.appCodeName	The browser's code name. Mozilla is the code name given to the Netscape Navigator family of browsers.
navigator.appName	The browser's application name. The Netscape Navigator family of browsers identifies itself by providing the word Netscape as the appName.
navigator.appVersion	This is information that identifies the browser version number, in this format: releaseNumber(platform;country). For example, you might see something like 3.0B4 (Win95; I)—that's beta 4 of Version 3 of the Netscape Navigator browser; it's the Windows 95 version; and it's an International release (if there'd been a U rather than an I, it would have been a US release). Unfortunately there's currently some inconsistency over this information—you might see 2.01(Win95; I; 32bit), for instance, which means Version 2.01, Windows 95 version, International release, 32-bit program.
navigator.appUserAgent	This is the information sent from the browser to the server in the user-agent header when the browser requests a Web page from the server. In some cases it's a combination of the appCodeName and the appVersion (though it doesn't have to be). For instance, you might see this: Mozilla/ 3.0B3 (Win95; I).

TIP

Later versions of JavaScript may have a property called `javaEnabled`, or it may be a boolean method (that is, a function associated with the object that returns a boolean value). This will indicate whether the browser is capable of working with Java applets and, if so, whether the capability is enabled or disabled. Which raises an important issue: JavaScript is continually developing. You should always work with the latest copy of the "JavaScript Authoring Guide" from Netscape Communications (see Appendix H, "Finding More Information," for details).

NAVIGATOR OR BROWSER?

Currently the only JavaScript browsers are the Netscape Navigator family of browsers. So the Netscape developers have a lead on other browser companies and will define, to a great degree, the future of JavaScript. Netscape Communications calls its browsers "navigators," which is why this is the `navigator` object rather than of the `browser` object. But remember that this is really referring to the browser—any JavaScript-compatible browser. Another company could use the `navigator` object to provide information about its browser, even if it doesn't refer to its browser as a "navigator" (which must amuse the Netscape developers, if only a little). Microsoft, for instance, will be forced to use the `navigator` object—using the name chosen for a browser by its major browser rival—in order to identify the Internet Explorer browser to JavaScripts.

You've seen how you can write the value held by an object's property directly by naming the property. But you can also get an object's properties by assigning them to variables, like this:

```
variable = objectname.propertyname
```

We could have assigned the property values to a variable in the previous example, and then placed the variable name into the `document.write` instruction, for instance. In some cases, you can also set a property's value, like this:

```
objectname.propertyname = value
```

The next example uses the `document` object to illustrate this. Every Web page has a `document` object—in the same way that our "house" object contained all the information about our house, the `document` object contains all the information about the page.

The `document` object can be used to change how that page is displayed. The following example sets the background color (`bgColor`) property of the document to `indigo`, but then the user can select red, green, blue, or white using the buttons.

Example 10.2

```
<SCRIPT LANGUAGE="JavaScript">
<!--
document.bgColor = "indigo"
//-->
</SCRIPT>
```

This first script is in the HEAD and immediately sets the color of the page to `indigo`. Notice that we have the property name (`document.bgColor`), the assignment operator (=), and the value we want to assign to the property (`indigo`). There's a huge list of colors you can choose from; you can find this list in Appendix G, "Color Values"; you can also read more about document colors in Chapter 14, "Controlling Windows & Documents With JavaScript."

In the BODY, we've created these buttons:

```
<FORM>
<INPUT TYPE="button" VALUE="Red" onclick="→
document.bgColor = 'red'">
<INPUT TYPE="button" VALUE="Blue" onclick="→
document.bgColor = 'blue'">
<INPUT TYPE="button" VALUE="Green" onclick="→
document.bgColor = 'green'">
<INPUT TYPE="button" VALUE="White" onclick="→
document.bgColor = 'white'">
</FORM>
```

As you can see, the buttons use the `onClick` event handler to set the `document.bgColor` property to the specified color. Click on the buttons and see; the color of the document changes each time you click (see Figure 10-2).

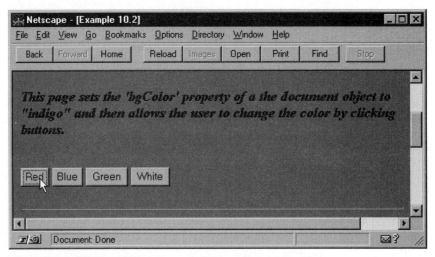

Figure 10-2: *Click on a button to change a color.*

TIP

Note that some properties of objects are read-only. You can't change the `navigator` *object's properties, for example.*

METHODS—FUNCTIONS BELONGING TO OBJECTS

Methods are functions that are associated with objects. Remember our house example? The house is the *object*. Cleaning the house would be the *method*. Methods are simply another class of function. In Chapter 7, "More on Functions," we looked at two classes of functions: those you create yourself, and the built-in functions. Well, methods are the third class of functions. They are also built-in—you don't have to define them, they are just there waiting for you to use—but they are dependent on objects, while the built-in functions we saw in Chapter 7 are independent of objects.

We used a method in the last example when writing to the Web page:

```
document.write("<P><B>navigator.appCodeName =</B> " +→
navigator.appCodeName)
```

This line uses the `write` method of the `document` object to write to the page. The parameters for the `write` method go in the brackets and, in this case, the method needs one string as its argument—the text that is being written. The general format for using a method is:

```
objectname.methodname(parameters for method)
```

TIP

As with the other functions we've looked at (see Chapter 7), methods can return values.

STRING VARIABLES ARE OBJECTS

We've worked a lot with string variables already and because string variables are actually objects, string objects have properties (well, one property to be precise, the length of the string variable is its only property) and methods. We can, therefore, use one of the string methods to convert between upper- and lowercase as we did in the following example:

Example 10.3

```
<SCRIPT LANGUAGE="JavaScript">
<!--
var sText
var sUpper
sText = prompt("Input a string in lower case","")
sUpper = sText.toUpperCase()
document.write("The string in Upper case is: <P><H3>" +→
sUpper + "</H3>")
//-->
</SCRIPT>
```

We declared two variables, sText and sUpper. Then we initialized sText using the prompt method (prompt is actually a method of the window object, though in this case we don't need to say window.prompt, just prompt will do). We've used this method before—the user types something in the Prompt dialog box, and when he clicks on OK that text is returned and assigned to sText.

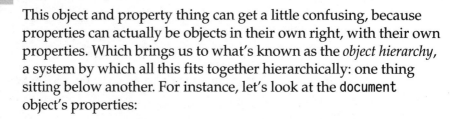

> *Here's another method we used a lot earlier in this book: the alert method. Again, this is really window.alert, but you don't need to include the window. piece—it's assumed (unless you are putting the script in an event handler, in which case you must include it—see Chapter 12, "JavaScript Events—When Are Actions Carried Out?"). Another method we've used is window.confirm.*

Next we used the sText.toUpperCase() method. (Note that we are using the parentheses at the end of the method name because a method is a type of function, and functions always end with parentheses; and, as we saw in Chapter 7, we can pass information to functions using these parentheses.) sText is our string variable—but as we've said, string variables are objects, and string objects can use the toUpperCase method. So this method simply takes the text from the sText variable and converts it to uppercase, then returns the result to the sUpper variable. The final line uses the document.write method to write the contents of sUpper to the Web page.

OBJECT HIERARCHY—THE DOCUMENT OBJECT

This object and property thing can get a little confusing, because properties can actually be objects in their own right, with their own properties. Which brings us to what's known as the *object hierarchy*, a system by which all this fits together hierarchically: one thing sitting below another. For instance, let's look at the document object's properties:

Property	Description
alinkColor	The color of the text used in a document to display an active link—a link that the user has clicked on, but the user has not yet released the mouse button (the HTML ALINK attribute).
anchor	Each anchor in the document (the <NAME= tags) is a property of the document, though each anchor has its own properties, so they are also objects.
anchors	This is an array (we learned about arrays in Chapter 9, "Building Arrays") which lists all of the anchor objects in the document.
bgColor	The color of the document background (the BGCOLOR attribute).
cookie	A piece of text related to this page stored in the cookie.txt file. You'll learn about cookies in Chapter 13, "Advanced Topics."
fgColor	The color of the document's text (the TEXT attribute).
form	Each form (the <FORM> tags) in the object is a property of the object. Again, as each form contains its own properties, each form is also an object.
forms	This is an array which lists all of the form objects in the document.
image	Each <IMG> tag is an object within the document object. This is a new object, added to JavaScript in Netscape 3.0 beta 3.
images	This is an array which lists all the image objects in the document.
lastModified	The date that the document was last modified (based on the host computer's date setting).
linkColor	The color of the text used in this document to display a link to a document that the user has not yet viewed (the LINK attribute).
link	Each link (the <A HREF= tags) in the form is a property and, as with each form and anchor, an object.
links	This is an array which lists all of the link objects in the document.

Property	Description
location	The complete (absolute) URL of the document.
referrer	The URL of the document containing a link that the user clicked on to get to this document. If the user didn't get to this document via a link, this is empty.
title	The text between the document's <TITLE> and </TITLE> tags.
vlinkColor	The color of the text used in this document to display a link to a document that the user has already viewed (the VLINK attribute).

ARE THESE REALLY PROPERTIES?

Are the anchor, image, link, and form objects really properties of the document object? Strictly speaking, some might claim, no they're not! We could tell you that while these objects are *descendants* of the form object, they are not *properties* of the object. We'd then have to discuss two different hierarchical systems. We've chosen to simplify the situation, and regard these objects as properties.

Why? Because they are indeed descended from the document object, and you will refer to them using the same sort of notation. For instance, to refer to the title property you would refer to document.title. To refer to a form named formB you would refer to document.formB. We have done the same elsewhere. When we talk about the radio object, for instance, we treat it as a property of a form object. It's descended from the form after all, and is referred to in the same way. We believe that it's simpler to regard these things as properties, and to list them as properties in various tables—as a beginning programmer you don't need to worry about the distinction between a property and an object that is a descendant but not a property.

Each of these properties contains information about the Web document currently displayed in the browsers. We've seen the `lastModified` property before—it's the date that the document was last saved. The `fgColor` property is the color of the text in the document (the `TEXT` attribute in the `<BODY>` tag). The `title` property is the document's title (`<TITLE>`).

But how about the `forms` property? This is a special property, because it's also a list (or an array) of objects. The array lists each `form` object in the document, so it contains its own properties. But each individual `form` is also an object, because each `form` object contains its own properties. In fact each individual `form` object has a property called the `elements` array. This array contains a list of the elements contained by the form: buttons, text boxes, and so on.

Objects having properties that are objects is what the object hierarchy is all about. The object that is a property of another object is said to be a *descendant* of the first object. A `form` is a *descendant* of the `document` object. The `document` is said to be a `form` object's *parent* or *ancestor*. The `form` object can be said to be the *child* or *descendant* of the `document`. When you read the Objects reference in Netscape's "JavaScript Authoring Guide" (see Appendix H, "Finding More Information"), you'll notice that for each object there's a `Property` section—a listing all the properties of that object—but there's also a `Property of` section that states the name of the parent of the object, which is the name of the object of which the current object is a property.

This part of the object hierarchy can be shown like this:

```
Object          Properties       Properties            Properties
                of               of the                of a
                window           document object       form object
     |              |               |                     |
     v              v               V                     V
window------ default
            document---------- alinkColor
            frame              anchor
            frames array       anchors array
            history            bgColor
            length             cookie
            parent             fgColor
            self               form ----------------- action
            status             forms array            elements array
            statusname         image                  button
            top                images array           checkbox
            window             lastModified           hidden
                               linkColor              password
                               link                   radio
                               links array            reset
                               location               select
                               referrer               submit
                               title                  text
                               vlinkColor             textarea
                                                      encoding
                                                      length
                                                      method
                                                      target
```

As you can see from this hierarchy, document is a property of window. But because it has its own properties, it's also an object. A form is a property of a document, but it also has a number of properties of its own. The form property, then, is an object. Notice also the arrays. The arrays are lists. The forms array lists each form in the document. The elements array is a list of all the elements in the form. The frames array lists the frames in a window, and so on. (We'll come back to arrays in a little while.)

The elements in a form may be text boxes, select boxes, buttons, and so on—depending on what you've created. For example, if you have a radio button in a form, then you have a `radio` object, which is a property of the `form` object, which is a property of the `document` object, which is a property of the `window` object. (Remember our sidebar earlier; we are using the term *property* loosly, to mean any property of an object, or any object descended from an object.)

If you wish to refer to a `property` or a method belonging to an object you must specify the complete path through the object hierarchy (with the exception of the `window` object, which is assumed and can be left out). In the following example there is a form called `Customer` (its `name` property is `Customer`) and it has an text box object called `Lastname`. In order to refer to a property of the `Lastname` object, we must specify the entire path through the hierarchy, like this:

```
document.Customer.Lastname.propertyname
```

In the following example the value property of the `Lastname` text box is set to Smith when the button is clicked:

Example 10.4

```
<SCRIPT LANGUAGE="JAVASCRIPT">
<!--
function ChangeText() {
   document.Customer.Lastname.value = "Smith"
}
//-->
</script>
```

This function simply places the text `Smith` into the `value` property of the `Lastname` form element (in the `Customer` form). Later in the page we have the form:

```
<FORM NAME="Customer">
<INPUT TYPE="button" NAME="But1" value="Change the text box's→
value property" onclick="ChangeText()">
<INPUT TYPE="text" NAME="Lastname" value="">
</FORM>
```

When you click on the button the `ChangeText( )` function is called. The text box `value`—that is, the contents of the text box—is then changed.

You can see from the example above that we specify the name of the object using the object hierarchy by first putting `document`, then the form name (`Customer`), and then the element object's name (`Lastname`).

Note that you do not need to specify the `window` in the object reference even though it is at the top of the hierarchy. Generally you don't need to use the window object's name unless you are referring to another window.

USING ARRAYS

You can also refer to an object by its array position—if it's one of the objects that is listed in an array. An array is a property of an object that contains a list of descendent objects. For example, you can refer to a form using the `forms` array. This array contains a list of all of the `form` objects contained by the document. Similarly, the `elements` property of a `form` can be used to refer to an element object in the `form`. The following example has two functions that loop around incrementing a variable `i`, which is used as the index to the `elements` array.

Example 10.5

```
<SCRIPT LANGUAGE="JAVASCRIPT">
<!--
function DisplayElementNames( ) {
    for (i=0; i<4; i++)    {
        alert("The element[" + i + "] name is " +→
document.Customer.elements[i].name)
    }
}
function DisplayElementContents( ) {
    for (i=0; i<4; i++)    {
      alert("The element[" + i + "] value is \'" +→
document.Customer.elements[i].value + "\'")
    }
}
```

```
//-->
</script>
```

We've started with the `DisplayElementNames` function. This uses a `for` statement to loop around, displaying an Alert box for each element. Notice that we have a variable called `i`, which is initialized to the value 0. The first element in the form has the number 0 (remember, we count from 0 up, not 1 up). As long as the value in `i` is less than 4, the loop continues, and each time the loop goes around it increments the value in `i` (that's what `i++` means, remember?; see Chapter 6, "Conditionals & Loops—Making Decisions & Controlling Scripts" for information about `for` loops). Now, what happens during each pass through the loop? The `alert` method is used to display the Alert dialog box. In that box we have some text, but we also included the array number of the element (`i`) and, more important, we included the contents of the `name` property. The `name` property is, not surprisingly, the `name` of the form element; whatever appears after `NAME=` in the HTML tag.

Now, how have we referred to this `name` property? See the following:

```
document.Customer.elements[i].name
```

Which means the `name` property of element `i` in the `elements` array, in the form named `Customer`, in the `document`. As you can see, we used the object hierarchy and the `elements` array to specify exactly the element we are talking about. (Of course we've used the `i` variable to specify the element number, because as we pass through the loop over and over again, the value in `i` goes from 0 to 1 to 2 to 3 and then stops, because we've told the `for` statement to stop as soon as `i` is no longer less than 4.)

The second function (`DisplayElementContents()`) works in exactly the same way, using a `for` loop to display the contents of the elements one by one. What do we mean by contents? The value held by the element. Here's how we referred to the value:

```
document.Customer.elements[i].value
```

Again, this means the `value` property of element `i` in the `elements` array, in the form named `Customer`, in the `document`. This time `value` means either the text that appears after VALUE= in the HTML tag, or the actual value typed by the user into the text box.

Later in the page we have this form:

```
<FORM NAME="Customer">
<INPUT TYPE="button" NAME="But1" value="Display the elements→
names" onClick="DisplayElementNames()">
<INPUT TYPE="button" NAME="But2" value="Display the elements→
contents(Value)" onClick="DisplayElementContents()"><p>
Lastname: <INPUT TYPE="text" NAME="Lastname"><p>
FirstName: <INPUT TYPE="text" NAME="Firstname">
</FORM>
```

This form has four elements. You can type text into the two text boxes. When you click on the first button, the DisplayElementNames() function runs. As you've seen, that function displays the name of each element in the form, one after the other. If you click on the second button, the DisplayElementContents() function runs, so you'll see the value property of the elements, one after the other (in the case of the text boxes, whatever you typed in; in the case of the buttons, you'll see what appears after value=).

ARRAYS & OBJECTS

Don't get confused between the arrays and objects, between the elements array and an element object, for instance. Both are properties. The elements array is a property of a form object and is an array—a list—of the element objects that the form contains. An element object is also a property of a form object, but it is an individual element: a button, selection box, or whatever. There is a similar distinction between the forms array and a form object. When a property has a plural name, then it contains an array of objects. When it has a singular name, then it's a single item. If we talk of forms, we are talking about an array; if we talk of form, we are talking about a single object. You might think of the hierarchy like this:

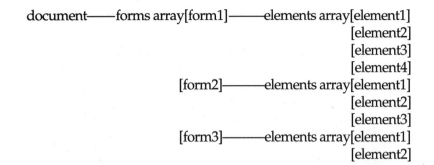

```
document——forms array[form1]———elements array[element1]
                                              [element2]
                                              [element3]
                                              [element4]
                      [form2]———elements array[element1]
                                              [element2]
                                              [element3]
                      [form3]———elements array[element1]
                                              [element2]
```

The `formn` and `elementn` listings are the individual objects, as listed in the `forms` and `elements` array.

Here's another example: the `anchors` property in a `document`. This is an array of anchor objects. The hierarchy looks like this:

```
document————anchors array[anchor1]
                         [anchor2]
                         [anchor3]
                         [anchor4]
```

This structure is used for any case in which a parent may have more than one child of a particular type. A `document` may have many `forms`; a form may have many `elements`. Note, then, that there are two ways to name an object that is listed in an array. You can name a form in the following two ways. Let's say you have a form called `secondForm`, and it's the second form in the HTML document (counting down from the top). You want to refer to the `length` property (the number of elements in the form). You can refer to the form like this...

Example 10.6

```
document.forms[1].length
```

...or like this:

```
document.secondForm.length
```

The first method uses the array; `forms[1]` means the second form in the array. (We start counting at 0.) The second method uses the `forms` name. The example in the Online Companion shows that whichever method you use, you get the same result.

Similarly, we can refer to elements within a form by name or by element array position. Here's how we might grab the value from a text box called Lname, in a form called `secondForm`:

Example 10.7

```
document.secondForm.Lname.value
```

We refer to the element's `value`—that is, the property that contains the actual text displayed in the text box.

> **TIP**
>
> *The full hierarchy would be `window.document.secondForm.Lname.value`. However, you can omit the `window` bit (although if you are referring to another window, you would need to use the window name).*

We could also refer to the element like this:

```
document.secondForm.elements[3].value
```

assuming that the text box is the fourth element in the form.

We could even refer to it in this way:

```
document.forms[1].elements[3].value
```

> **TIP**
>
> *The `elements` array is a different from the `anchors`, `forms`, `frames`, `links`, and `options` arrays. While all these other arrays have objects of the same name (minus the s: `anchor`, `form`, `frame`, `link`, `option`), there is no element object. Rather, there are several different objects—the `button`, `checkbox`, `hidden`, `password`, `radio`, `reset`, `select`, `submit`, `text`, and `textarea` objects—which are listed in the `elements` array.*

OBJECT CLASSES & INSTANCES

You need to understand the difference between object *classes* and object *instances*. An object *class* is the definition of an object. The `document` object is a class; the string `object` is a class; the `Date` object is a class, and so on. A class is like a blueprint for something. But you can't use a blueprint—you have to use the blueprint to create something before you can use it. So before you can use an object, an *instance* must be created.

Let's go back to the house analogy we used earlier in this chapter. Remember that we were using a house object. The blueprint for a four-bedroom house may be thought of as an object class. We may talk about our four-bedroom house object class—a type of house that we'd like to live in. But you can't live in an object class, it's just a blueprint, remember. So before you can live in your four-bedroom house you (or someone else) has to create an actual house—an *instance* of the house—from the object *class*. The class is the blueprint, the instance is the one you actually own and live in.

So although JavaScript has all sorts of objects available to you, these objects cannot be used until an instance is created. There are two ways to create an instance. In most cases, the instance is created for you. For example, when you open a Web document, the browser automatically creates a `document` object instance. If there are links in the document (`<A HREF=>`), it also creates a `link` object instance for each link, and a `links` array, too. However, in some cases the instance is not created automatically. For example, if you want to use the `Date` object, you must create the instance yourself (as we'll see, that's done using the `new` keyword).

TIP

It's important to understand the distinction between an object class and an object instance. But also understand that when people talk about "using an object" in their scripts, they are, of course, talking about using the object instance.

Let's take a quick look at all the objects, their purpose, and whether the object instances are automatically created or must be created by you.

Object name	The object contains information about...	How is the instance created?
anchor	An anchor in the document (<A HREF=> and <A NAME=>).	Automatically, if the document loaded contains anchors.
Array	A new object (Netscape 3.0 beta 3 and later versions) used to create arrays; see Chapter 9, "Building Arrays," for more information.	Using the new keyword.
button	A button in a form (<INPUT TYPE="BUTTON")	Automatically if the document contains a button.
checkbox	A checkbox in a form (<INPUT TYPE="CHECKBOX")	Automatically.
Date	The date	Using the new keyword.
document	The currently displayed document.	Automatically when the document is loaded.
form	A form in a document	Automatically if the document contains a form.
frame	A window frame	Automatically when the window opens.
hidden	A hidden text object in a form (<INPUT TYPE="HIDDEN")	Automatically if the document contains a hidden form element.
history	The browser's history list	Automatically when the window opens.
link	A link (<A HREF=>)	Automatically if the document contains a link.

location	The URL of the current document	Automatically when the document opens.
Math	Mathematical constants and functions	Automatically, built-in.
navigator	The browser viewing the Web page.	Automatically when the page loads into the browser.
password	A password text field in a form (<INPUT TYPE="PASSWORD")	Automatically if the document contains a password field.
radio	A set of radio buttons in a form (<INPUT TYPE="RADIO")	Automatically if the document contains a radio button.
reset	A reset button in a form (<INPUT TYPE="RESET")	Automatically if the document contains a reset button.
select	A selection list in a form (<SELECT>)	Automatically if the document contains a selection list.
string	A string	Automatically when you create a string.
submit	A submit button in a form (<INPUT TYPE="SUBMIT")	Automatically if the document contains a submit button.
text	A text box in a form (<INPUT TYPE="TEXT")	Automatically if the document contains a text box.
textarea	A textarea in a form (<TEXTAREA>)	Automatically if the document contains a textarea box.
window	The current window, or a window you have created. The window object is the top-level object in the hierarchy for document, location, and history objects.	Automatically when the window opens.

WHAT'S A BUILT-IN OBJECT?

You may run across the term *built-in object* now and again. So what's a built-in object? The term "built-in" is used ambiguously to mean different things. The JavaScript documentation sometimes uses it to mean objects that are not created by you (as you'll see in Chapter 13, "Advanced Topics," you can create your own objects). It's also used to refer to the Date, Math, and string objects, which are built-in to JavaScript in the sense that they are not dependent on a particular document or window.

As you can see from this table, the object hierarchy is dependent on the circumstances. Many of these objects only appear if certain conditions are present in the document. If the document has no forms, for instance, there will be no instances of the button, checkbox, form, hidden, password, radio, reset, select, submit, text, or textarea objects.

A CONFUSING CASE—LOCATION

There are a few confusing names in this hierarchy, because they appear more than once in the hierarchy. First, there's location. This is both a property of the document object (document.location), and a property of the window object (window.location). To make things really confusing, both contain similar information. The document.location property contains the URL of the current document (the location of the document). The window.location property also contains a URL. But while document.location cannot be changed—in the same way that the document title is fixed, so is the document location—you *can* change the properties of the window.location object.

The window.location object is used to modify the contents of the window, loading a different Web page. This is also an object, as it has several properties, such as href, protocol, and host. The document.location property is used to tell you what is currently loaded. Here's an example that demonstrates the difference:

Example 10.8

```
function WinOpen() {
    NewWindow  = open("2-1.htm","Window1","toolbar=yes,→
height=250,width=450,");
}
```

We started with this simple script in the HEAD. The function
WinOpen creates a new window (using the open method). (We've
looked at how to open windows before, and we'll return to the
subject in Chapter 14, "Controlling Windows & Documents With
JavaScript.") NewWindow is the name we gave the new window (so is
Window1, but Window1 is intended to be used when referring to the
window as a target in HTML tags; when we refer to the window in
our scripts we use the name preceding the = assignment operator,
as you'll see in a moment). The file 2-1.htm is loaded into this
window. Then we have a form with these four buttons:

```
<FORM>
<FORM>
<I>Click on this button to create a new window:</I><BR>
<input type="button" name="WindowButton" value="Create→
Secondary Window and place Example 2.1 in the window"
onclick="WinOpen()">
<P>
<I>Click on this button to view the value held by the→
</I>document.location<I> property:</I><BR>
<input type="button" name="Button3" value="Show secondary→
document.location property" onclick="alert('document.→
location = ' + NewWindow.document.location)")"><P>
Click on this button to view the value held by the→
</I>window.location<I> property:</I><BR>
<input type="button" name="Button3" value="Show secondary→
window.location.href property"
onclick="alert('window.location.href = ' +→
NewWindow.location.href)")"><P>
<I>Change the </I>window.location<I> object's </I>href<I>
property:</I><BR>
<input type="button" name="Button2" value="Change the→
secondary window.location object to example 2-2"
```

```
onclick="NewWindow.location.href = '2-2.htm'")><P>
<I>Try changing the </I>document.location<I> property (it→
won't work):</I><BR>
<input type="button" name="Button2" value="Change the→
secondary window's document.location object to example 2-3"
onclick="NewWindow.document.location = '2-3.htm'")
</form>
```

Click on the first button to run the `WinOpen` function. The new window opens, and loads file `2-1.htm`. The second button opens an Alert box that shows you the `NewWindow.document.location` property. The third button opens an Alert box showing you the `NewWindow.location.href` property. Click on these and you'll see that the URL shown is the same in both cases; in fact they are always the same.

> **TIP**
>
> *Remember that earlier in this chapter we told you that there's no need to use the* **window.** *part of a hierarchical name. Here's a case when you* must *use the window name* **NewWindow.location.href**, *for instance. We're referring to another window, not the window holding the buttons, so we have to name it.*

The fourth button lets you change the contents of the window. It modifies the `href` property of the `window.location` object (`NewWindow.location.href`). You can go to the secondary window to see that the contents have changed. Use the two previous buttons to see that the `document.location` and `window.location.href` properties have changed.

Finally, the last button tries to change the `NewWindow.document.location` property. Try it, and you'll find that it doesn't do anything—you can't change that property.

> **TIP**
>
> *There's another confusing property: the* **window.window** *property. We'll cover this in the next chapter.*

THE HIERARCHY

Example 10.9

The object and property hierarchy can be a little confusing when you first get started. We created a hypertext document that you can use to go through the hierarchy; start at the top level, then work your way down the hierarchy seeing what properties are associated with what objects, and which of the properties are themselves objects. You can find this in the Online Companion. Also, see Appendices B and C for reference information about objects and properties. Finally, you should understand that there is an enormous amount of information related to all these objects and properties, more than we could possibly squeeze into this book. So make sure you are working with the latest Netscape "JavaScript Authoring Guide." At the time of writing the latest version was at http://home.netscape.com/eng/mozilla/3.0/handbook/javascript/.

SUMMARY

Before we move on, let's just go over this stuff to make sure that we have it straight.

An *object* is a thing: a house, or a `document`, or a `form`. An object has *properties*, other things associated with the object. The house has rooms; the `document` has forms; the `form` has buttons and text boxes.

Properties may be objects, too. A form is a property of a document. But a form is also an object, because it has its own properties.

Objects have *methods* associated with them. A method is simply another type of function. The `document.write` and `window.alert` functions we've used so often are methods.

In most cases you can forget the `window.` part of an object name, as `window.` is assumed to mean the window in which you are working. You only need to name the window when referring to a different window, or when writing a script in an event handler.

An *array* is a list of objects. The forms array lists all the forms in the document. You can refer to an object by its actual name, or by its position in the array.

An *object class* is a description of an object—a sort of blueprint. An *object instance* is an actual object that has been created and can be used in your scripts.

MOVING ON

Objects provide a very powerful programming tool, as you'll find out in the next chapter. In this chapter we explained the basic structure and purpose of objects and arrays. Now we need to look at a number of particular objects in more detail. We're going to start by looking at the date, math, and string objects in the next chapter. Then, later in the book, we'll cover other objects in more detail.

CHAPTER 11

More About Built-in Objects

Now that you've learned the basics about working with objects—properties, the object hierarchy, arrays, and so on—let's take a look at a different breed of objects, the ones that are often described as *built-in* objects: `date`, `math`, and `string`.

THE DATE OBJECT

The `Date` object enables you to work with dates and times. In order to work with the `Date` object, you must begin by creating an object instance (as we discussed in Chapter 10, "Objects, Properties & Methods"). You use the `new` keyword to do this. For example, you could create a `Date` object instance called `TodaysDate` like this:

```
TodaysDate = new Date()
```

Notice that the `Date` object ends with parentheses. This is so we can pass information to the object. That means that when we create the `Date` object we can do one of two things: grab the current date and time (that's what we've just done), or create an object instance that holds a particular date and time. We can do that in three different ways:

```
name = new Date("may  day, year hours:minutes:seconds")
name = new Date(year, month, day)
name = new Date(year, month, day, hours, minutes, seconds)
```

Notice that the first method is creating a string (we've put the information between quotation marks). The other methods use numeric values, as shown in the following example:

Example 11.1

```
LaunchDate1 = new Date("1, 15, 1997 12:02:00")
LaunchDate2 = new Date(1997, 1, 15)
LaunchDate3 = new Date(1997, 1, 15, 14, 02, 02)
```

TIP

There are currently problems with the **Date** *object. You'll find that some dates are not created correctly. The* **new Date( )** *works correctly (you'll get the current time and date, according to what's set on the computer on which the script is running). But our* **LaunchDate1** *variable may contain the wrong date. And you'll find that in the last two methods the month counts forward from 0. January is month 0, February is month 1, and so on.*

You can see these dates in the example in the Online Companion. We've created buttons that display the values held by the Date objects.

DATE METHODS

Now let's see what methods (functions) are available for the Date object.

Object	Function
getDate()	Looks in the Date object and returns the day of the month.
getDay()	Returns the day of the week.
getHours()	Returns the hours.
getMinutes()	Returns the minutes.
getMonth()	Returns the month.

getSeconds()	Returns the seconds.
getTime()	Returns the complete time.
getTimeZoneoffset()	Returns the time-zone offset (the number of hours difference between Greenwich Mean Time and the time zone set in the computer running the script).
getYear()	Returns the year.
parse()	Returns the number of millisconds in the Date string since January 1, 1970 00:00:00 (the Date object stores times and dates in the form of milliseconds since this date). Note, however, that this method is not currently working correctly.
setDate()	Changes the Date object's day of month.
setHours()	Changes the hours.
setMinutes()	Changes the minutes.
setMonth()	Changes the month.
setSeconds()	Changes the seconds.
setTime()	Changes the complete time.
setYear()	Changes the year.
toGMTString()	Converts the Date object's date (a numeric value) to a string in GMT time, returning something like the following: Weds, 15 June 1997 14:02:02 GMT (the exact format varies depending on the operating system running on the computer).
toLocaleString()	Converts the Date object's date (a numeric value) to a string, using the particular date format the computer is configured to use.
UTC()	Use Date UTC(year, month, day, hrs, min, sec) to return that date in the form of the number of milliseconds since January 1, 1970 00:00:00 (the hrs, min, and sec are optional).

As you can see, you can both retrieve and set different portions of the Date object that you've created. You also have several special methods for manipulating dates. Remember that you refer to a method in this form:

```
objectname.methodname( )
```

For example, look at this example:

```
TodaysDate.getMonth( )
```

Here's an example. First we created a Date object called TodaysDate:

Example 11.2

```
TodaysDate = new Date( )
```

Then we created these buttons:

```
<FORM>
<INPUT TYPE=BUTTON VALUE="Get the hour held by TodaysDate"
onclick="alert(TodaysDate.getHours())"><P>
<INPUT TYPE=BUTTON VALUE="Get the year held by TodaysDate"
onclick="alert(TodaysDate.getYear())"><P>
<INPUT TYPE=BUTTON VALUE="Set the year held by TodaysDate to→
99" onclick="TodaysDate.setYear(99)"><P>
<INPUT TYPE=BUTTON VALUE="Get Greenwich Mean Time"
onclick="alert(TodaysDate.toGMTString())">
</FORM>
```

As you can see, we've used the methods to see the hour held by the object (TodaysDate.getHours( )); to get the year held by the object (TodaysDate.getYear( )); to set the year to a different value (TodaysDate.setYear(99)); and to convert the date held by the object to Greenwich Mean Time (TodaysDate.toGMTString( )). (So, if you are not in the Greenwich Mean Time time zone, you'll see a different time in the Alert box.)

THE MATH OBJECT

The Math object provides properties and methods that are used to carry out mathematical calculations. The object's properties are mathematical constants (pi, Euler's constant, the base 10 logarithm of e, and so on). Its methods are mathematical procedures: functions use round numbers to check for the largest number, to calculate cosines, and so on. Of course we've already seen how to carry out mathematical operations using the math operators: +, -, /, and so on. But the Math object is more advanced, providing many mathematical "shortcuts."

Here are the math properties. They contain constants that are useful for people who like to mess with this sort of thing (if that includes you, then you already know what they are and what they are for).

Properties	Value
E	The base of natural logarithms, Euler's constant (approximately 2.718).
LN2	The natural logarithm of two (approximately 0.693).
LN10	The natural logarithm of ten (approximately 2.302).
LOG2E	The base 2 logarithm of e (approximately 1.442).
LOG10E	The base 10 logarithm of e (approximately 0.434).
PI	The ratio of the circumference of a circle to its diameter (approximately 3.14159).
SQRT1_2	The square root of one-half (approximately 0.707).
SQRT2	The square root of two (approximately 1.414).

Here are the methods you can work with:

Methods	Result
abs()	Returns a number's absolute value (its "distance from zero"; for example, both 2 and –2 have absolute values of 2).
acos()	Returns the arc cosine of a number (in radians).
asin()	Returns the arc sine of a number (in radians).
atan()	Returns the arc tangent of a number (in radians).
ceil()	Returns an integer equal to or immediately above a number (ceil(-22.22) would return 22; ceil(22.22) would return 23; and ceil(22) would return 22).
cos()	Returns the cosine of a number (in radians).
exp()	Returns e^{number}.
floor()	The opposite of ceil. (ceil(-22.22) would return 22; ceil(22.22) would return 22; and ceil(22) would return 22).
log()	Returns the natural logarithm (base e) of a number.
max()	Returns the greater of two numbers.
min()	Returns the lesser of two numbers.
pow()	Returns $base^{exponent}$.
random()	Returns a pseudo-random number between zero and one. (Only works on Unix versions of Netscape Navigator).
round()	Returns a number rounded to the nearest integer.
sin()	Returns the sine of a number (in radians).
sqrt()	Returns the square root of a number.
tan()	Returns the tangent of a number.

Here are a couple of simple examples:

Example 11.3

```
<FORM>
Type two numbers:
<INPUT TYPE="text" NAME="num1">
<INPUT TYPE="text" NAME="num2"><P>
<INPUT TYPE="button" VALUE="Find the largest number"
onclick="form.result.value = Math.max(form.num1.value,form. →
num2.value)"> <INPUT TYPE="text" NAME="result">
</FORM>
```

You type numbers into num1 and num2. Then, when you click on the button the Math.max(form.num1.value,form.num2.value) methods are used to compare the values in the num1 and num2 fields. The maximum value is then placed into the text box, result.

TIP

We could also have written Math.max(this.form.num1.value, this.form.num2.value). *We've referred to the text boxes,* num1 *and* num2; this.form *means "the information in* this *form, the same form the button is in." However,* form.num1.value *is a sort of shorthand; we can drop the* this. *bit if we want.*

Example 11.4

```
<FORM>
Enter the radius of a circle: <INPUT TYPE="text"
NAME="num1"><P>
<INPUT TYPE="button" VALUE="Find the circumference"
onclick="form.result.value = 2*Math.PI*form.num1.value">
<INPUT
TYPE="text" NAME="result"><P>
<INPUT TYPE="button" VALUE="Find the square root of the
first number" onclick="form.result2.value = →
Math.sqrt(form.num1.value)"> <INPUT TYPE="text"
NAME="result2">
</FORM>
```

We're doing two things here. First we are calculating the circumference of a circle, which is based on the radius that the user types into the first text box: `2*Math.PI*form.num1.value`, which is the same as multiply 2 by pi, by the value in the text box `num1`.

The second calculation simply finds the square root of the value in the first text box: `Math.sqrt(form.num1.value)`, which means return the square root of the value in the text box `num1`. You can see an example in Figure 11-1.

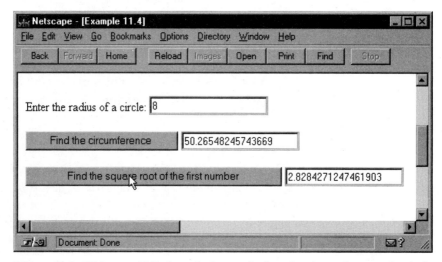

Figure 11-1: *We've used Math methods to calculate the circumference of a circle and a square root.*

THE STRING OBJECT

Each string in a script is an object as we saw in Chapter 10, "Objects, Properties & Methods." The methods related to these objects provide lots of ways to manipulate your strings. A `string` object has only one property, though, `length`, which is the number of characters within the `string`.

TIP

The length properties are always related to an object's size, even though the size is not always what you'd think of as a length in plain English; anchors.length is the number of anchors in a document; links.length is the number of links in a document; and select.length is the number of options in a selection box, and so on.

There are quite a few string object methods, though:

Method	Result
anchor(*Name*)	Used to turn the string into an HTML anchor tag (<A NAME=), using *Name* as the anchor name.
big()	Changes the text in the string to a big font (<BIG>).
blink()	Changes the text in the string to a blinking font (<BLINK>).
bold()	Changes the text in the string to a bold font (<B>).
charAt(*index*)	Finds the character in the string at the *index* position (0 is the first character, 1 is the next character, and so on).
fixed()	Changes the text in the string to a fixed-pitch font (<TT>).
fontcolor(*color*)	Changes the text in the string to a color (<FONT COLOR=*color*>).
fontsize(*size*)	Changes the text in the string to a specified size (<FONTSIZE=*size*>).
indexOf (character,*from*)	Used to search the string for a particular character, and then returns the index position of that character (the first character is index position 1). You can specify the index position *from* which you should begin the search.

italics()	Changes the text in the string to italics (<I>).
lastIndexOf (character, *from*)	Like indexOf, but searches backward to find the last occurrence of the character. The *from* position is the number of characters from the end.
link(*href*)	Used to turn the string into an HTML link tag (<A HREF=), using *href* as the anchor name.
small()	Changes the text in the string to a small font (<SMALL>).
strike()	Changes the text in the string to a strikethrough font (<STRIKE>).
sub()	Changes the text in the string to a subscript font (<SUB>).
substring (*indexA, indexB*)	Returns a portion of the string—a subset—starting with the character at *indexA* and finishing with the character at *indexB*.
sup()	Changes the text in the string to a superscript font (<SUP>).
toLowerCase()	Changes the text in the string to lowercase.
toUpperCase()	Changes the text in the string to uppercase.

USING STRING METHODS

How, then, do we refer to a string object? By the name of the variable holding the string. Take a look at this example. We started by creating these functions:

Example 11.5

```
function GetLength(form) {
var stextLength = form.string1.value
        form.result.value= stextLength.length
}
function Position(form) {
var sPos = form.string1.value
        form.result2.value= sPos.charAt(5)
}
```

The GetLength function takes the value from a text box called string1 and places it in a variable called stextLength. Then it finds how many characters are in the string using the length property: stextLength.length. Then it returns that value to the result text box in the form.

The Position function takes the same value, placing it in the sPos variable. Then it uses the charAt method to find out which character is at position 5 (the sixth character in the string). Then it returns that value to the result2 text box in the form.

As you can see in the Online Companion, we have two buttons in the form. The first takes the text that you typed and counts the number of characters in the string. The second finds out what character is at position 5, as you can see in Figure 11-2.

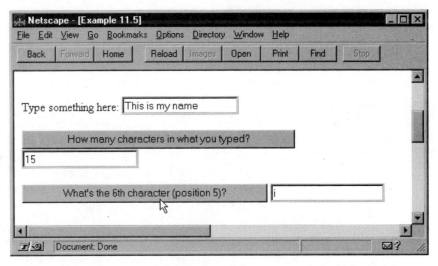

Figure 11-2: *We've counted the number of characters and checked a position, using the length property and the* charAt *method.*

Of course these string methods are mostly used for modifying how text is written to a page. So let's have a quick look at what can be accomplished:

Example 11.6

```
function function1() {
var sTypedText
    sTypedText  = prompt("Type some text, then click on→
OK.", "")
    return sTypedText
}
```

This is a function we've used before. When function1() is called a Prompt dialog box opens. When the user types in some text and clicks on OK, the text is assigned to the sTypedText variable. The value in sTypedText is returned by the function.

```
<SCRIPT LANGUAGE="JavaScript">
<!--
var sText
    sText  = function1()
    document.write("You just typed: <P>" + sText)
    document.write("<BR> This is big: " + sText.big())
    document.write("<BR> This is a link: " + sText.link→
("11-6.htm"))
    document.write("<BR> This is blinking text: " + →
sText.blink())
    document.write("<BR> This is bold: " + sText.bold())
    document.write("<BR> This is colored: " + →
sText.fontcolor("green"))
    document.write("<BR> This is italics: " + →
sText.italics())
    document.write("<BR> This is small: " + sText.small())
    document.write("<BR> This is strikethrough: " + →
sText.strike())
    document.write("<BR> This is subscript: " + sText.sub())
    document.write("<BR> This is superscript: " + →
sText.sup())
    document.write("<BR> This is lowercase: " + →
sText.toLowerCase())
    document.write("<BR> This is uppercase: " + →
sText.toUpperCase())
//-->
</SCRIPT>
```

When this script runs a variable, sText is declared. Then we use the document.write instruction to write the text in sText to the Web page. But notice that after each occurrence of sText you will find a method name: big( ), blink( ), sub( ), and so on. You can see the effect of all this in Figure 11-3.

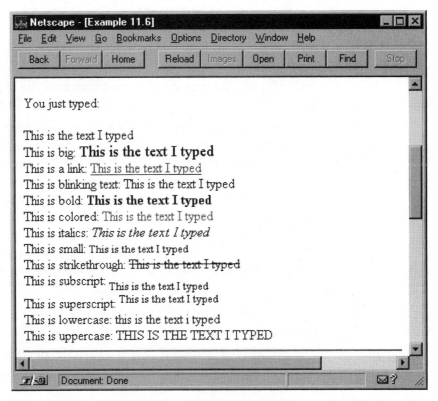

Figure 11-3: *We've used the string methods to write the text from the Prompt dialog box in a variety of ways.*

USING STRING METHODS WITH OBJECT PROPERTIES

It's worth noting that many object properties are actually strings. That means that you can use these string methods with those properties. Here's an example. There are a few features in JavaScript that vary between the different operating systems. If you want to place several lines of text into a textarea box, the code you must use to break the lines depends on the type of computer on which the browser is running. If it's a Windows browser, you must use \r\n. If it's a Unix browser you should use \n, and for the Macintosh you must use \r.

Well, there's a special property that we've seen before, `navigator.appVersion`, which tells us the application version of the browser. Neither `navigator` nor `appVersion` have any methods of their own—but it just so happens that `appVersion` is a string, so we can apply any of the string methods we want to this property.

What we need to do, then, is find out which browser is being used, and then pick the newline character accordingly. We can apply the `lastIndexOf` method to the `appVersion` to do this. The `lastIndexOf` method searches a string for some specified text. For instance:

```
navigator.appVersion.lastIndexOf('Win')
```

This simply means, "start at the end of the `appVersion` string, and look for `Win`." If it finds it, it will return the position of the text within the string. But if it can't find it in the string, it returns –1. So we can create a little routine like this:

```
var nl=null
    if (navigator.appVersion.lastIndexOf('Win') != -1) {
        nl = "\r\n"
    }
    else      {
        if (navigator.appVersion.lastIndexOf('Mac') != -1)→
        {
                nl = "\r"
        }
                else {
                        nl = "\n"
                }
    }
```

We've declared a variable called nl. Then we have an if statement. The statement uses lastIndexOf to see if Win is in the string. If
it is, it returns some number. If it isn't, it returns −1. Then, we compare this result to −1. The != −1 piece means, "not equal to −1." If the
letters Win appear in the appVersion string, we get a number—but
not −1, so the next line is executed and we place \r\n into the nl variable. If the letters Win *don't* appear in the string, we get −1, so the else
line is executed. The else contains a nested if. This time we're
checking to see if we can find the letters Mac in the string; if we can,
we place \r into nl. If we can't, the browser must be a UNIX
browser, so we go onto the next else, and place \n into nl.

We've created an example of how this works:

Example 11.7

```
<SCRIPT LANGUAGE="JAVASCRIPT">
<!--
var nl=null
    if (navigator.appVersion.lastIndexOf('Win') != -1) {
        nl = "\r\n"
    }
    else    {
        if (navigator.appVersion.lastIndexOf('Mac') != -1)→
    {
            nl = "\r"
        }

        else {
                nl = "\n"
            }
    }

function placeText()        {
var text1=prompt("Type over this line if you wish", "This is→
the default first line of text")
var text2=prompt("Type over this line if you wish", "This is→
the default second line of text")
var text3=prompt("Type over this line if you wish", "This is→
the default third line of text")
var text4=prompt("Type over this line if you wish", "This is→
the default fourth line of text")
var text5=prompt("Type over this line if you wish", "This is→
the default fifth line of text")
document.text.codes.value= text1 + nl + text2 + nl + text3 + →
nl + text4 + nl + text5
    }
//-->
</SCRIPT>
</HEAD>
<BODY onload=placeText()>
```

We started with the `nl` variable we've just seen, placing the appropriate code into the variable depending on what's in the `appVersion` string. Then we created a function that runs when the document loads (notice the `onload` event handler calling the function from the last line; we'll learn more about the event handlers in the following chapter).

This function displays five prompt boxes and takes the text you typed (or the default text, if you haven't typed anything), and places it into five variables, `text1` through `text5`. Finally, it writes the text to the `codes` textarea (`document.text.codes.value` means "the `value` held by the `codes` element in the `form` in this `document`"). Notice that it intersperses the `textn` variables with the `nl` variable, to place the line-break code that will make the lines "stack" rather than chain together into one long line.

So remember, many properties are strings, and can have the string methods applied to them.

MOVING ON

Way back in Chapter 3, "First Steps—Scripts, Functions & Comments," you learned about how you get a script to run. Since then we've been looking at *what* happens when a script runs, but now it's time to return to the *when* question. In the next chapter we're going to examine the event handlers again. We've used a few of them throughout the book—most notably the `onclick` handler. We want to look at the others, though, and learn a little more about the ones we've used before.

JavaScript Events— When Are Actions Carried Out?

How do you make something happen in a JavaScript? We've made a lot happen already, so you know that you can drop a script straight into HTML document to be run as soon as the browser reads it. You also know how to use *event handlers* to run scripts at a particular time. Up to this point, we've mostly used the `onclick` event handler, which runs a script when the user clicks on a button. In this chapter we're going to look more closely at all the event handlers.

By an *event* we mean something that happens when the user does something: opens or closes the Web document, moves the mouse pointer over something, clicks on something, presses the Tab key, and so on. In some cases, events are automatic such as when a page loads or unloads—that is, when a page is replaced by another Web page.

You'll place event handlers into HTML tags—the tags used to create links and form elements, for instance. You'll use the following basic syntax:

```
<TAG tagattributes eventHandler="JavaScript Code">
```

`Tag` represents the HTML tag name, while `tagattributes` represents the normal attributes used to create the item. The `eventhandler` is, of course, the name of the JavaScript event handler you want to use. `JavaScript Code` is the JavaScript instruction that you want to carry out when this event occurs.

Each event handler is designed for a specific HTML tag. For instance, the `onload` and `onunload` event handlers are placed into the `<BODY>` tag (you can also place it in the `<IMG>` tag if you are writing scripts for Netscape 3.0 beta 3 or later). There's no point putting them elsewhere. The `onclick` event handler will only work with the `button`, `checkbox`, `radio`, `reset`, and `submit` form elements, and with links (`<A HREF=`). There's no point trying to use the event handler with a `text` or `textarea` form element, for instance.

TIP

We've written all event handlers in lowercase: `onclick`, `onblur`, `onmouseover`, and so on. You'll often see these in mixed case: `onClick`, `onBlur`, `onMouseOver`. You can use whatever case you want when putting an event handler into an HTML tag, as HTML is not case sensitive. However, a new JavaScript feature (added to Netscape 3.0 beta 3), allows you to modify event handlers from scripts. As JavaScript is case sensitive, you have to use the correct case when naming event handlers in scripts—and the correct case is all lowercase.

THE EVENT HANDLERS

There are nine event handlers available to you. Here are their names and the event that sets off each one:

- onblur   When focus moves away from a form element.
- onchange   When focus moves away from a form element, after the contents of the element have changed.
- onfocus   When focus moves to a form element.
- onclick   When the user clicks on a form element or link.

- **onload**   When the Web page loads (or when an image loads, if using Netscape 3.0 beta 3 or later).
- **onmouseover**   When the user points at a link with the mouse pointer.
- **onselect**   When the user selects something in a form element.
- **onsubmit**   When the user submits a form.
- **onunload**   When the current Web page is replaced with another.

There are two new event handlers, added to JavaScript with Netscape 3.0 beta 3:

- **onerror**   When an image is unable to load.
- **onabort**   When the user aborts an image load.

Now, let's take a detailed look at the different event handlers available to you.

ONBLUR

This event handler is used to carry out an event on a *blur*. A blur is the event in which the *focus* moves away from the form element using the event handler. In other words, when the user does something to move away from the form element onto another by clicking on another form element—or even simply clicking outside the form somewhere—or by pressing Tab.

The onblur event handler works with the selection list (<SELECT>), multi-line text input (<TEXTAREA>), and text input (<INPUT TYPE="TEXT">) components. You might use onblur to confirm that the user has placed the correct information into a form. For instance, look at the following example, which is in two parts, a function definition in the HEAD and a function call in the BODY. First the function:

Example 12.1

```
function testAge(form) {
var nAge = form.ageBox.value;
    if (nAge >= 18) {
```

```
        if (nAge >=100)       {
                alert("You entered an age of " + nAge +".→
Are you sure this is correct?")
        }
    }
    else {
            alert("You entered an age of " + nAge + ". You→
must be 18 or over to use this service!")
    }
}
```

As you can see, the function is called testAge. We are passing information to it from a form. We take form.ageBox—the value typed into the text box in the form—and place it into the nAge variable. Then we use an if statement to check the value held by the variable (the age originally typed into the form, as you'll see in a moment). If the number is 18 or over, we check to see if it's 100 or over. If it is, we display an Alert box that asks the user if the age is correct. If it isn't 100 or over, we do nothing; the age must be okay. If the number is less than 18, though, we run the second else instruction, displaying an Alert box warning the user that he must be 18 or over (see Figure 12-1).

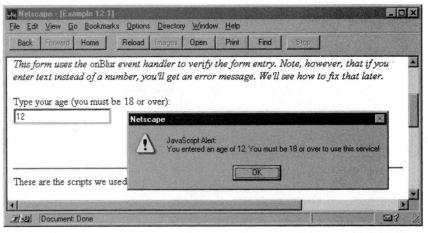

Figure 12-1: *The onblur event is displayed this Alert box.*

TIP

There's a problem with onblur. If the user swaps to another application, then swaps back, the focus changes so the user may see a message at an inappropriate time.

In the body of the document we created this form:

```
<FORM>
Type your age (you must be 18 or over): <BR>
<INPUT TYPE="text" NAME="ageBox" onblur="testAge(this.form)">
</FORM>
```

As you can see, this form only has one element, a text box. The user types something into the box. Notice the onblur event handler. When the user moves the focus away from this element, the onblur instruction runs which passes the contents of the form to the testAge function. Anything the user does to move focus sets off the onblur event handler: pressing the Tab or Enter keys, clicking elsewhere in the Web document, using the Back or Forward commands, using the history list or bookmarks, or clicking on a toolbar button or in the Location box.

TIP

Pressing the Tab key only sets off an event handler if there is more than one form element. If there's no element to Tab into, the event handler won't work. Other ways of setting off the event handler will work, though.

Try this example at the Online Companion. You'll see that if you enter an age below 18 or above 99 and then click somewhere out of the text box, you'll see an Alert message. Type anything from 18 to 99, though, and nothing happens when you click outside the box.

> ### TIP
>
> *There's a problem with this script. If the user enters text instead of a number, he'll get an error message. We can fix the problem using the* parseFloat *function (or* parseInt *in a later version of JavaScript— it's not functioning correctly in Netscape 3.0 beta 4 or earlier now). You can see an example of how we used* parseFloat *later in this chapter (Example 12.3), and when we discuss form validation in Chapter 16, "Forms & JavaScript."*

ONCHANGE

The onchange event handler is very similar to onblur, except that something must have changed in the form element before the user moves focus from the element—the user must have selected something different from the selection list, or must have entered or modified text in the text box or textarea elements. If you use onchange and the user moves from the element without changing anything, nothing happens.

Again, this event handler will work with the selection list (<SELECT>), multi-line text input (<TEXTAREA>), and text input (<IN-PUT TYPE="TEXT">) components.

Here's a simple illustration. We've modified the previous function call by placing a default value representing an age of 25 in the ageBox. And we added a line in the function itself to display an Alert message, even if you change the age from 25 to another valid one of 18 to 99.

Example 12.2

```
<FORM>
Type your age (you must be 18 or over): <BR>
<INPUT TYPE="text" NAME="ageBox" VALUE="25"→
onchange="testAge(this.form)">
</FORM>
```

As you can see, we've placed a value in the text box (25), and we've used the onchange event handler instead of the onblur to call testAge.

You'll find, when you use this example, that if you click inside the text box and then outside the text box nothing happens. But if you click inside, change the number to something under 18 or over 100, then click outside, you'll see an Alert box.

> **TIP**
>
> *In some browsers **onchange** may work a little prematurely. It may be set off as soon as you select something in a selection box, rather than after you move focus from the selection box. You can't rely on this as a feature, though, because in some browsers the user must still move focus away from the selection box.*

ONCLICK

The onclick event handler can be used to execute JavaScript when the user clicks on something: a button (<INPUT TYPE="BUTTON">), checkbox (<INPUT TYPE="CHECKBOX">), option (radio) button (<IN-PUT TYPE="RADIO">), a link (<A HREF=>), a Reset button (<INPUT TYPE="RESET">), or a Submit button (<INPUT TYPE="SUBMIT">). We've used dozens of onclick examples throughout this book, so we'll skip to the next event handler.

ONFOCUS

The onfocus event handler is the exact opposite of onblur. It carries out an action when the focus is moving *to* the element, not away. It works with the same form elements: the selection list (<SELECT>), multi-line text input (<TEXTAREA>), and text input (<INPUT TYPE="TEXT">) components. How do you move focus to an element? There are only two ways: by pressing the Tab key, or by clicking inside the element.

There's a problem with using onfocus, though. You can get stuck in a loop. Here's how. You click on the element and the script associated with the onfocus event handler runs. If that script does something that moves the focus from the form element, when the script has finished and focus moves back to the element, the onfocus event handler runs again. So the script runs again, finishes, and returns focus, so the script runs again. And so on.

In fact you have to be very careful about using onfocus. Only use it if you are absolutely sure that you have a script that cannot go wrong. Test it over and over. Test everything that could possibly go wrong: the user enters something too long or too short, text is entered instead of a number, the user switches programs and then returns to the previous program, and so on. If you create a program that has an error-message-producing bug at an onfocus event handler, you'll have some very unhappy users. The error message will appear. The user will click on OK. The focus will move back to the form element. So the error message will reappear...

So you can only use onfocus to do something that doesn't change focus away from the element, and only use it with a script that can't go wrong. You'll often find it's easier to use onblur to carry out an event when the focus is moving away from the previous element onto this one—although that only works if the user is working through the form in the correct order, of course, which cannot usually be assumed.

Here's one example of an onfocus script:

Example 12.3

```
function runTotal(form) {
    var nNum1 = parseFloat(form.num1.value)
    var nNum2 = parseFloat(form.num2.value)
    form.total.value = nNum1 + nNum2
}
//-->
```

We've used this script to place the sum of two values into a text box. The runTotal function is passed information from the form. We've created two variables, nNum1 and nNum2. We used the parseFloat built-in function (which we looked at in Chapter 6, "Conditionals & Loops—Making Decisions & Controlling Scripts"), to convert the values from the forms to numbers. Remember, anything entered into a form is regarded as a string. The parseFloat function will take that string and, if possible, convert it to a numerical format—so nNum1 and nNum2 are numerical, even though the values in num1 and num2 are strings.

Then we add nNum1 to nNum2, and place the result into the form's total field.

Here's the form we used:

```
<FORM>
Type number 1: <INPUT TYPE="text" NAME="num1" VALUE="0"><BR>
Type number 2: <INPUT TYPE="text" NAME="num2" VALUE="0"><BR>
Click in this box to see the total: <INPUT TYPE="text"→
NAME="total"
onfocus="runTotal(this.form)">
</FORM>
```

The user enters numbers into the first two text boxes. Then he tabs to the last box (the total text box), or clicks inside it. The onfocus event handler calls the runTotal function, passing the information from the form to the function. The function then replaces the contents of the total box with the result of the addition, as you can see in Figure 12-2.

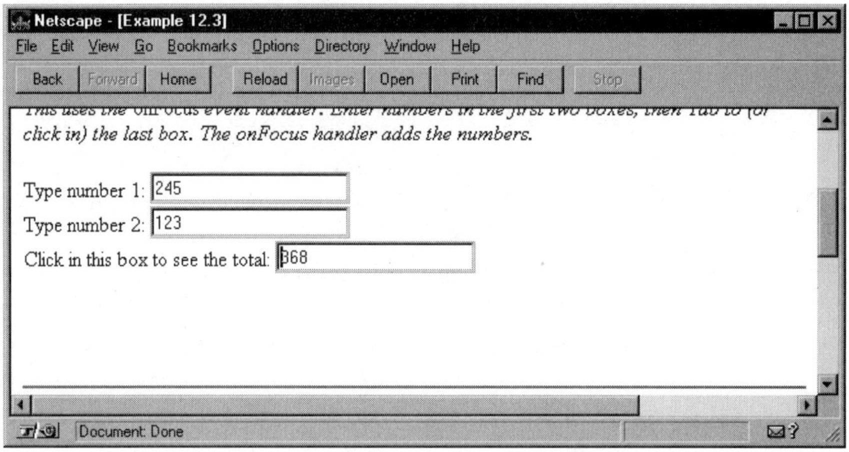

Figure 12-2: *Simply tabbing into the last text box causes the* onfocus *event handler to add the numbers.*

ONLOAD

Using the onload event handler causes the browser to execute the script when the page is loaded into the browser (specifically, once the browser has finished loading the page and any frames). This event handler can only be placed into the <BODY> or <FRAMESET> tags in this format:

```
<BODY onload="the script you want to run">
```

A common use for this event handler is to display an opening message, such as this:

Example 12.4

```
<SCRIPT LANGUAGE="JavaScript">
<!--
function confirmEntry() {
    if (confirm("As you have a JavaScript browser, you can go→
to our JavaScript enabled site. Click on OK to do so, or→
click on Cancel to remain at this (non-JavaScript) page.")){
```

```
            location='12-4a.htm'
            }
    }
//-->
</SCRIPT>
</HEAD>
<BODY onload="confirmEntry()">
```

We've created a function called `confirmEntry()`. This function uses an `if` statement to display the Confirm dialog box. If the user clicks on the OK button the first statement after the { is run (`location='12-4a.htm'`). In other words, if the user clicks on OK, the browser is redirected to another Web page. If the user clicks on Cancel, though, no action is taken.

Then notice how we call the function—using the `onload` event handler in the `<BODY>` tag (you can put it anywhere in the tag, before or after other attributes). Notice also that the instructions after = must be in quotation marks.

More recent versions of JavaScript—Netscape 3.0 beta 3 and later—allow you to place the `onload` event handler in the `<IMG>` tag, too, so you can do something when an image loads.

TIP

There's another way to get a script to run when the page loads, of course—simply place the script in the HEAD. Unlike the `onload` *event, though—which loads the entire page and frames and* then *runs the script—any script in the HEAD will run* before *the Web document is loaded, which may be useful in some cases.*

ONMOUSEOVER

Simply pointing at a link that contains the `onmouseover` event handler runs the script. This is commonly used to display messages in the status bar. However, as with `onfocus`, there are significant problems with `onmouseover`.

First, many people find those cute little status-bar messages rather irritating. Unfortunately they block the view of the URL, and many Web users *want* to see the URL when they point at a link. It often gives them information that helps them decide whether or not to click on the link. If you block their view, they may not be too happy.

TIP

There may be times when you want *to hide a link from users. I've just seen a site that has a series of multiple-choice questions. Each possible answer has a link to another page—the wrong answers link to a document called* wrong.html...*which means that the user can quickly see which answers are wrong! JavaScript could be used to hide this fact.*

The other problem is that although you can run any script you want from an onmouseover event, it may not be a good idea to do so. The user may not realize that the mouse pointer was over the link, and when something happens unexpectedly, may wonder what on earth is happening. For instance, let's say that you've used onmouseover on a link to open a Prompt dialog box. The user isn't at your Web page right now, but was a few minutes ago. The user employs the keyboard shortcut for the Back command to move back through the history list, eventually arriving at your site— where the mouse pointer just happens to be sitting over the link with an onmouseover event built in. The Prompt dialog box opens automatically, and the user thinks, "What did I do?"

Still, here's an example of using the onmouseover event. We've already gone through an example that uses status bar messages (see Example 2.9), so we'll do just what we said you should beware of doing: use the onmouseover event handler to open an Alert box.

Example 12.5

```
SCRIPT LANGUAGE="JavaScript">
<!--
function confirmMove() {
```

```
    if (confirm("Are you sure you want to use this link? I→
really don't think you should.
Well, if you insist, click on OK and I'll take you to the→
referenced page. Otherwise click on Cancel and leave the→
link alone!"))        {
        location='12-5a.htm'
        }
}
//-->
</SCRIPT>
```

First, we created a function called confirmMove( ). This is very similar to the previous example. It uses an if statement which uses the built-in function confirm to decide whether to display another page (12-5a.htm) or do nothing, returning the user to the current page. Next we created this link.

```
<A HREF="12-5A.HTM" onmouseover="confirmMove()">Click right→
here. <I>Not!</I></A>
```

The onmouseover event handler runs the confirmMove( ) function. So, when the user points at the link, the Alert box opens (as you can see in Figure 12-3). If the user clicks on OK, the browser loads 12-5a.htm. If the user clicks on Cancel, the box closes and the user returns to the current document.

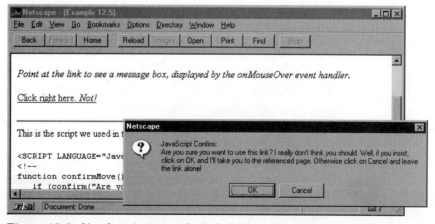

Figure 12-3: *Simply pointing at the link displays this Alert box. Clicking on OK takes the user to another page.*

You should note, however, another problem with `onmouseover`; you can get into the same sort of loop that you can get into with the `onfocus` event handler. You might try this for yourself. Copy the page containing this example to your hard disk. *Don't* copy the file to which the `confirm` function forwards you. Then try pointing at the link. You'll find that the Alert box opens, but when you click on the OK button it opens again…and keeps opening over and over. Your only way out is by clicking on Cancel several times. So you'd better make sure that the document you are linking to is always available!

ONSELECT

The `onselect` event handler makes the browser execute the JavaScript when the user selects text in a text (`<INPUT TYPE="TEXT">`) or textarea (`<TEXTAREA>`) form element. This is probably a fairly limited use. The problem is that right now there's no way for a script to grab the text that the user selected.

Here's a very quick and simple example that shows the handler at work, though:

Example 12.6

```
<FORM>
<INPUT TYPE="TEXT" VALUE="Select part of this text. Select
part of this text. Select part of this text." SIZE="50"
onselect="alert('That\'s it, you highlighted something.')">
</FORM>
```

In theory when the user selects any of the text, an Alert box will open. Right now, though, `onselect` is still in development and probably won't work on your browser.

ONSUBMIT

The `onsubmit` event handler executes the script when the user clicks on a Submit button to submit a form. This is typically used for form validation. The event handler isn't placed in the Submit tag, though, it's placed in the `<FORM>` tag, like this:

```
<FORM NAME="formname" onsubmit="instructions">
```

When the user clicks on the Submit button, the `onsubmit` instructions run. For instance, here's how you could display an Alert box when submitting a form:

Example 12.7

```
<FORM NAME="submittest" onsubmit="alert('Thanks for your→
information; remember to check back with us next week.')">
Type your age (you must be 18 or over): <BR>
<INPUT TYPE="text" NAME="ageBox"><P><BR>
<INPUT TYPE="SUBMIT">
</FORM>
```

That's simple; the `onsubmit` event handler simply calls the `alert` function when the Submit button is clicked (`<INPUT TYPE="SUBMIT">`).

But the `onsubmit` event handler can be used for more than this; it's also a handy way to verify a form's input. You can use it to send the information from the form to a function which can then verify that the information has been entered correctly. Then, if the data is not correct, the form will *not* submit the information.

For instance, remember the `onblur` event handler we used earlier in this chapter when we validated the input of a text box? Let's do the same, using the `onsubmit` event handler:

Example 12.8

```
function testAge() {
var nAge = document.age.ageBox.value;

    if (nAge >= 18) {
        if (nAge >=100)     {
                alert("You entered an age of " + nAge +". →
Enter an age from 18 to 99.")
                return false
        }
        else {
                return true
        }
    }
    else {
        alert("You entered an age of " + nAge + ". You→
must be 18 or over to use this service!")
```

```
            return false
            }
     }
```

This is very similar to the onblur example we used, except that we are using return false and return true—if the user enters an incorrect date, we return false; if the date's okay, we return true.

Then we have this form:

```
<FORM NAME="age" onsubmit="return testAge()">
Type your age (you must be 18 or over): <BR>
<INPUT TYPE="text" NAME="ageBox"><P>
<INPUT TYPE="Submit" NAME="Submit">
</FORM>
```

You can see that the onsubmit instructions are "return testAge()". This means, "call the testAge function, and return a value." Either true or false is returned. If false is returned the form is not submitted.

Although this isn't connected to an actual CGI script in our Online Companion, you can still see it at work (see Figure 12-4). Notice that if you enter an incorrect number, you see an Alert box. When you click on the OK button, the number in the text box remains. But if you enter a correct number, the page "flashes" and the number is removed—it's been submitted.

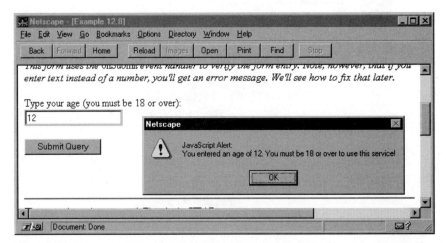

Figure 12-4: *We used the* onsubmit *event handler to call a function that verifies the form input; if the input's incorrect, the form is not submitted.*

ONUNLOAD

The onunload event handler runs when the user does something to
load another page into the browser—that is, when he unloads the
current page. The user may click on a link to load a new page, enter
a URL into the Location text bar and press Enter, use the Back and
Forward commands, or select a page from the history list or bookmarks, for instance. Anything that replaces the current page with
another page will cause the onload event handler to run.

The onload handler is placed in the <BODY> or <FRAMESET> tags,
just as with the onload event handler. The only difference is that the
script form onunload is placed in memory and does not run until
the page is unloaded. However, there are currently limits to what
can be accomplished with onunload. You can open another window, for instance, but you can't put anything into it. In fact, if you
try to do so, you may crash your browser.

The onunload event handler currently has a lot of problems, and
is really only useful for displaying the sort of goodbye message we
saw in Example 2.8. This event simply can't do much—you can't
use objects and, in fact, trying to do so can make the browser crash
in some cases.

TIP

*Remember also that when the user reloads a document, the current
document is unloaded, so the onunload event handler runs.*

Here's an example of this onunload weirdness:

Example 12.9

```
<SCRIPT LANGUAGE="JavaScript">
<!--
function Bye() {
var sAname = document.AccountForm.account.value
    alert("Please make a note of your account name→
(" + sAname + "), and remember to bookmark this Web page");
}
//-->
```

```
</SCRIPT>
</HEAD>
<BODY onunload="Bye()">
```

This is a simple little function. The value held in the account text box of the AccountForm is placed into the sAname variable. Then an Alert box opens and displays a message, including the value in sAname. Notice also that the onunload event handler should run the Bye() function when you load a different page.

Now, here's the text box and a button:

```
<FORM NAME="AccountForm">
Type your account name: <INPUT TYPE="TEXT " NAME="account">
<INPUT TYPE="BUTTON" NAME="TEST" VALUE="TEST" onclick="Bye()">
</FORM>
```

You can see the text box named account (the value of which we refer to as document.AccountForm.account.value in the Bye() function). The button also calls the Bye() function. Why? Well, try this in the Online Companion. Open the page, then type something into the text box. Don't click on the button, though. Open another page—click on the Back button, for instance. The Alert box may not appear (if you are using Netscape 3.0 beta 4 or later it probably will; in earlier versions it won't). In fact, your browser may actually crash.

Now return to the page and click on the button. This time the Alert box *will* appear. Now leave the document. Again, the Alert box appears, with the text from the text box included in the message.

What has happened? Clicking on the button sets the value in the sAname variable, so when you unloaded the Bye() function it already had the value. On the other hand, when you *didn't* click on the button, the objects had been destroyed, so Bye() was unable to get past the first line of the script. As you can see, the onunload event handler has problems which can really limit what you can do with it. Clearly certain onunload bugs have been fixed in more recent versions of Netscape.

THE NEW EVENT HANDLERS

A number of new event handlers were added to JavaScript with Netscape 3.0 beta 3:

- `onunload` This now works with the `<IMG>` tag. You can run scripts when an image loads.

- `onerror` The JavaScript is executed if an image could not be loaded. This event handler works with the `<IMG>` tag.

- `onabort` The JavaScript is executed if the user stops an image from loading (by clicking on the Stop button or loading another document, for instance). This works with the `<IMG>` tag.

Should you use these? Not immediately. Remember, you are writing scripts that will be used by visitors to your site. Until most people are using a version of browser that has these event handlers, they won't do you much good. So you should probably avoid them until Netscape 3.0 is in wide use.

Also Netscape 3.0 beta 3 introduced the ability to reset event handlers from scripts. You could, for instance, have several functions that you want to use from an `onclick` event handler. You could use a script to assign a particular function to that event handler in a particular situation: `document.Form1.Button1.onclick = function3` means "assign `function3` to the `onclick` event handler in `Button1`, in `Form1`. Notice by the way that we have `function3`, not `function3()`. If we used `function3()` at this point in the script the browser would try to actually call `function3()`; all we want to do is assign `function3()` to the event handler, so we drop the parentheses.

MOVING ON

You've learned about the basics of the JavaScript language. But there's a lot more than the basics. There are all sorts of complicated things that you can do with JavaScript. This book is an introduction to JavaScript, not an attempt to turn you into a master programmer. Still, we are going to cover a few advanced subjects in the following chapter.

You'll learn how to create your own objects, properties, and methods, work with *cookies*, and test and optimize your scripts. And once that chapter's over, we'll move on to the next part of the book and look at some more practical examples of how to put JavaScript to work.

CHAPTER 13

Advanced Topics

You have now seen all the basic features of the JavaScript programming language—but there's more. What we've squeezed into this chapter are the fairly advanced techniques—things you may want to try once you are more comfortable with the basics of the language.

We're going to look at how to create your own objects—that's right, not only does JavaScript provide you with a slew of ready-to-use objects, but you can create more as needed. We'll also talk a little about a new JavaScript feature, the capability to link JavaScripts to Java applications, and we'll examine the use of *cookies*, bits of data that are stored on the user's hard disk in a file called `cookies.txt`. We also will discuss how to make your scripts smaller (by breaking programming rules), and talk a little about testing your programs.

 ## CREATING YOUR OWN OBJECTS

Let's begin by learning how to create objects. You actually have done this before, back in Chapter 9, "Building Arrays." You'll remember that we had to create an array object before we could use an array. (The latest beta version of JavaScript has a new built-in `array` object, but the Netscape 2.0 browsers do not.)

Objects are created in two steps:

1. First define your object class by writing a *constructor* function. This function will have the same name as the object you are creating.

2. Create an instance of the object using the new keyword.

The constructor function defines the object class. (You can review classes and instances in Chapter 10, "Objects, Properties & Methods.") A class is not an actual object—it's the "blueprint" for that object. We use the class to create the actual object instance.

You use the constructor function to create properties for your new object. You use the this keyword, which refers to the current object, in order to give it properties. For example, take a look at this constructor function:

Example 13.1

```
function product(nam, p)   {
    this.name = nam
    this.price = p
}
```

This code by itself has not created any objects. In effect the function is the object class. In this case, we created an object class called product. This object has two properties: name and price. Where will the information for these properties come from? You can see that the information will be passed to the object in the parentheses when we call this object-creating function; nam will be the first value passed in the parentheses, and the function will put this into the name property; and p will be the second value passed in the parentheses, which will be put into the price property. In other words, this.name = nam means "give this object instance a property called name, and give name the value passed to the function as nam."

Remember that a function does not do anything until it is *called*. So you haven't created an object instance until you call the constructor function. But we call the function in a slightly different way. In earlier chapters you saw how to call a function by simply naming it (making sure that you include the parentheses after the name). When we call a function that we are using to create an object instance, though, we use the new keyword. But we are also creating an object variable of sorts. We actually create a variable, then assign the object function to the variable. So in this case we create object instances of the product object like this:

```
var product1 = new product("TimeSaver", "$23")
var product2 = new product("MoneySaver", "$11")
var product3 = new product("Time n'MoneySaver", "$99")
```

We now have three new object instances, product1, product2, and product3. Yes, they are variables, but special ones that contain more than one piece of information. You can see the name and price properties we are passing to the products, too. The name property of product1 is TimeSaver, while its price is $23, for example.

VIEWING OBJECT PROPERTIES

You can now get at the object's properties by specifying it's property names using the dot notation we've already seen. The following example writes the values of these properties to the page:

Example 13.1

```
document.write(product1.name + " " + product1.price + "<BR>")
document.write(product2.name + " " + product2.price + "<BR>")
document.write(product3.name + " " + product3.price + "<BR>")
```

CREATING AN OBJECT HIERARCHY—PROPERTIES CAN BE OBJECTS

As with some of the JavaScript objects we've looked at before, you can create objects whose properties can themselves be objects. We begin our next example with two object classes, product and order. The order class has a property called ProductType which is used to hold an object of the class product.

Example 13.2

```
function product(nam, p)   {
    this.name = nam
    this.price = p
}
function order(custname, prod, numbof)   {
    this.customer = custname
    this.ProductType = prod
    this.quantity = numbof
    this.OrderDate = new Date()
}
```

We've just created the two object classes, product and order. The product class is exactly the same as before, but our new order class has four different properties. However, note that we are only passing three values to the function: custname, prod, and numbof. The fourth property, OrderDate, is being created from one of the built-in JavaScript objects, the Date object; new Date() means "create a new Date object instance." In effect, when we call this function it creates a property from another object.

Now let's create the object instances:

```
var product1 = new product("TimeSaver", "$23")
var product2 = new product("MoneySaver", "$11")
var product3 = new product("Time n'MoneySaver", "$99")

var order1 = new order("Mr Brainless", product2, 5)
var order2 = new order("Mr Bonkers", product3, 22)
var order3 = new order("Mr Bozo", product1, 1)
```

First we created the product1, product2, and product3 instances—exactly as before. Then we created the order1, order2, and order3 object instances. Notice that when we created order1, product2 was passed as the second value, the prod value. In other words, another of order1's properties is also an object; not only is the OrderDate an object in its own right, but ProductType is also an object—this time one that we created. As you can see, in this manner we can create our own object hierarchy.

We can reference properties lower down in this hierarchy in the same manner we've already used. For example, if we want to see the price of the product in order1, we would refer to order1. ProductType.price. No, not order1.ProductType.product2.price, as you might imagine. In effect product2 *is* ProductType; when we passed the values from product2 to ProductType it loses its original name.

We could write out information from our objects like this:

Example 13.2 (continued)

```
document.write("NAME: " + order1.customer + "<BR>QUANTITY: "→
+ order1.quantity + " ")
document.write("<BR>DATE: " + order1.OrderDate)
document.write("<BR>PRODUCT TYPE: " + order1.ProductType.name→
+ "<BR>PRICE: " + order1.ProductType.price + "<P>")
document.write("NAME: " + order2.customer + "<BR>QUANTITY: "→
+ order2.quantity + " ")
document.write("<BR>DATE: " + order2.OrderDate)
document.write("<BR>PRODUCT TYPE: " + order2.ProductType.name→
+ "<BR>PRICE: " + order2.ProductType.price + "<P>")
document.write("NAME: " + order3.customer + "<BR>QUANTITY: "→
+ order3.quantity + " ")
document.write("<BR>DATE: " + order3.OrderDate)
document.write("<BR>PRODUCT TYPE: " + order3.ProductType.name→
+ "<BR>PRICE: " + order3.ProductType.price + "<P>")
```

You can see what this looks like in Figure 13-1.

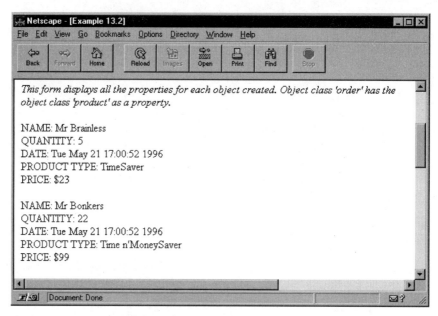

Figure 13-1: *We've written all the values from our objects and their associated properties.*

CREATING METHODS FOR YOUR OBJECTS

As you've already learned, objects have methods in addition to properties. You can create methods for your objects by creating yet another function and referring to it in the constructor function, in a manner similar to the way in which we created object properties:

```
objectname.methodname = functionname
```

Of course a method *is* a function, as you'll remember from our earlier chapters; it's simply a function associated with a particular object. You can then use the method in this manner:

```
objectname.methodname(function parameters)
```

For example, let's create a method called OrderAmount. First, we have to define a function called OrderAmount:

Example 13.3

```
function OrderAmount()      {
    return (this.quantity * this.ProductType.price)
}
```

Notice that this function will return a value. When we call the function we want it to send something back to us. And again, we've used the this keyword to refer to the current object; this.quantity means "the quantity property of this object—the object that has called the method." So what's the method doing? It's taking the quantity and price properties, multiplying them, and returning the result.

Next, we associate this method with the order object in the last line of the order object's constructor function:

```
function order(custname, prod, numbof)    {
    this.customer = custname
    this.ProductType = prod
    this.quantity = numbof
    this.OrderDate = new Date()
    this.OrderAmount = OrderAmount
}
```

Notice that we haven't passed another value to the function. We've simply added the this.OrderAmount = OrderAmount line which means "create a method based on the OrderAmount function."

This method is then used like any other method, by calling it:

```
order1.OrderAmount()
```

We added the following line to our example to display the total cost for each product:

```
document.write("TOTALCOST = " + order1.OrderAmount() +→
"<BR>")
```

In other words, order1.OrderAmount() means the value obtained when you use the OrderAmount() method of order1."

Okay, so we cheated a little. We used integers rather than floating-point numbers. We could have used prices like 22.99, 10.99, and so on. However, some versions of Netscape Navigator, including the 3.0 betas and earlier, have problems working with numbers such as these—instead of seeing 22.99 you'd see 23.989999999999998, or something similar. This little problem will be fixed in a later version of Netscape.

USING COOKIES

JavaScript is limited in the way that it can save information to the user's client computer hard disk. This is for security reasons. If JavaScripts were allowed to write to the hard disk it would make the work of those busy virus writers too easy. Scripts could be set up to destroy important files as soon as someone opened a Web page. This is a serious limitation, however, reducing JavaScript's capabilities. So there is *one* way you can write to the hard disk; you can write to a file called `cookie.txt`, which is stored in the main Netscape directory. This is actually something that was in use before JavaScript. (CGI scripts can write to `cookie.txt`, too.)

When you write to this file you are creating a *cookie*. You may have already seen scripts that do this. For example, if you go to the Netscape Create Your Personal Workspace page (http://home.netscape.com/custom/show_page.html), you'll see the dialog box in Figure 13-2 when you start creating a customized home page. This is to warn you that a cookie is being sent, and the message asks you if that's okay. If it is, the information setting up your customized page will be stored as a cookie.

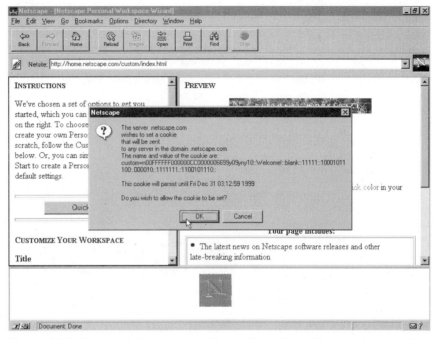

Figure 13-2: *You are being sent a cookie, and have the option to not receive it.*

Because `cookie.txt` is a text file (and because it's size is limited) it can't do any harm. Text files are not executable files, so they can't run programs. On the other hand a script that sends a cookie might overwrite information that was already in `cookie.txt`.

Actually cookies are not always stored in `cookie.txt`. When Netscape Navigator initially stores a cookie it stores it temporarily in memory, not in `cookie.txt`. Then, when you close the browser, it stores it in the text file *if* an expiration date has been set for the cookie. If not, it just throws it away. So cookies can be used to store data for a single session, or over long periods so that the next time a user comes to your site that information will still be available on the user's machine. It's very easy to do this, as the `document` object has a `cookie` property which is a string that holds cookie data for that document.

There are some restrictions on cookies. The browser is not allowed to create more than 300 cookies, each 4KB, so the **cookies.txt** *file is restricted to 1,200KB. Also, no one Web site may have more than 20 cookies.*

Let's set and display a cookie:

Example 13.4

```
function SetCookie(name, form) {
    document.cookie = name + form.txtCookie.value + ";"
    form.txtCookie.value = ""
}

//
=========================================================

function ShowCookie(form) {
    form.txtCookie.value = document.cookie
}
```

The first function, SetCookie( ), takes the name and information from the form that is passed to it when it is called. It then sets the document.cookie property, placing the name value inside it plus the text that the user types into the form.txtCookie.value text box, followed by a semicolon (;). Then it clears the form.txtCookie.value text box.

The second function, ShowCookie( ), simply takes the text from the document.cookie property and places it into the text box.

Here's the form we are using:

```
<FORM>
<INPUT TYPE="Text" NAME="txtCookie" size=50 ROWS=10→
COLS=73></TEXT><P>
<I>Now click on this button to copy the text into the→
cookie.txt file:</I><BR>
<INPUT TYPE="button" VALUE="Create Cookie" NAME="butSet"→
```

```
onclick="SetCookie('Cookie1', this.form);"><P>
<I>Now click on this button to copy that cookie from the→
cookie.txt file back into the text box.</I><BR>
<INPUT TYPE="button" VALUE="Display Cookie" NAME="butDisplay"→
onclick="ShowCookie(this.form);">
</FORM>
```

Type some text into the txtCookie text box, then click on the first button to call the SetCookie( ) function. Notice that we pass Cookie1 (the name of the cookie), and this.form (information from the form) to the function. When you click on this button you'll see the dialog box in Figure 13-3. This dialog box is asking if it's okay to save something to the cookie. Click on OK and that information is saved. Then click on the last button, to call ShowCookie( ). The information is grabbed from the document.cookie property—which in turn has to look in cookie.txt to find it. It is then displayed, along with the cookie name in the text box.

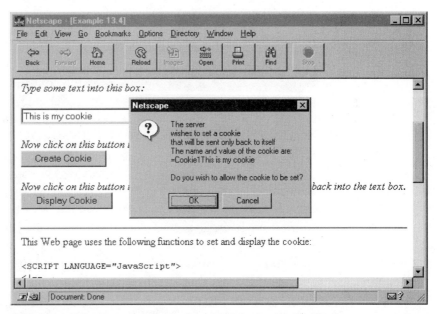

Figure 13-3: *Setting a cookie is as easy as placing a value in the* document.cookie *property.*

If you'd like to know more about working with cookies, see the "Netscape Authoring Guide" and go to http://www.netscape.com/newsref/std/cookie_spec.html. Also, check the JavaScript pages listed in Appendix H, "Finding More Information," for public domain cookie functions that you can use.

PERFORMANCE

JavaScript is unlike other programming languages in that it is not compiled. When a program is compiled all of the comments are stripped out and are not included in the executable file (the .EXE files), and the variable names are replaced with numbers that point to their location. Comments and long variable names are of use only to programmers and are found only in the source code. This means that it doesn't matter how long your variable names are or how much commented text you put into your program, the .EXE file is unaffected by these things.

JavaScript, however is different. JavaScript must be transmitted over the Internet and then transferred to the user's computer, comments and all. This means that comments and large variable names in JavaScript have a cost, in that they increase the amount of text to be transmitted. For the most part, users of your Web page will not want to read comments in your code, but those comments will increase the time it takes to transmit the page. For small bits of code this won't be significant, but for applications like our Area Code program (see Chapter 18), it can affect the time it takes to load the page.

If you build a large application you may like to keep your variable names and comments to a minimum. We have not because our programs have been designed as part of a tutorial. There are other ways to reduce the size of your script. For example, you can use the ?: conditional operator and some of the assignment operators such as += or *=, operators that are shorthand techniques.

Also, if you need to reduce the size of your scripts, you may want to consider breaking all or many of the rules that we have given you for making your code easier to read. It's probably not a good idea to do when you are first learning JavaScript. However, if it becomes essential to cut the size of a script, you can do so by leaving out unnecessary spaces, removing blank lines, not indenting lines, and so on. All things that make the code harder to read, but quicker to transmit.

TESTING YOUR SCRIPTS

Although programmers don't like testing, good ones know that it is an integral part of the development of programs. It is the inherent nature of programming that when you write code—because you are human and not a computer yourself—you will inadvertently put bugs into your program. Programs more than a few lines are just too complex to comprehend in their entirety. So when you change something in one part of the program, you may be causing, under certain circumstances, unexpected things to happen in another part of the program. You must, therefore, test your programs. Test them while developing them. Test them once they are complete, and test them as fully as you can if you make changes. And when JavaScript editors appear on the scene, as they surely will, find one you like and use it. JavaScript tools will probably be included in HTML editors, soon. Using them will help you to avoid syntax errors.

Unfortunately the different JavaScript interpreters don't all work in exactly the same way, so programs should be tested with as many different browsers as possible. Although Java and JavaScript are said to be portable, there are differences between how the different platforms (Windows 3.1, Windows 95, Macintosh, and various flavors of UNIX) work. Situations may arise where the code you have written will need to take into account the platform on which it is running as the code's behavior may be different for each. If you need complete confidence in your code, you should test it on different platforms.

Web pages containing JavaScript may well be read by users who have non-JavaScript Browsers as well. It would be a good idea to test your scripts with these types of browsers. Another approach is to set up your Web site so that you can steer non-JavaScript users away from your JavaScript pages. (If you are doing anything fancy with JavaScript, there's just no way to make the page useful for non-JavaScript browsers at the same time.)

Finally, as we've said elsewhere in this book, stay a few steps behind, not ahead. It may be fun playing with the very latest JavaScript features, but most of your audience will be using older browsers.

USING JAVA APPLETS WITH JAVASCRIPT

Shortly before this book went to press, Netscape released a beta version of Netscape Navigator that had an important new feature built in, one which allows JavaScript to be integrated with Java applets. This means that complicated applets can be built by Java experts and then made available for those using JavaScript. The JavaScript programmer will write the code that sends information to the Java applet and the code then returns information from the applet.

This is a path now taken by many areas of software development, where objects are written using a language which requires a high level of programming knowledge and then the objects are made available to users in a language which is easier to use. JavaScript will be the "glue" for sticking Java objects together. This is similar to the Visual BASIC/C++ system where VBXs and OCXs are built in C++ by one set of programmers and used in Visual BASIC by another set.

JavaScript will be able to access variables and methods of applets in an HTML document like this:

```
document.appletName
```

Where `appletName` is the name of the Java applet. The Java applet is embedded into a HTML page using the <APPLET> tag, like this:

```
<APPLET CODE=animate.class NAME=appAnimate WIDTH=10→
HEIGHT=10>
</APPLET>
```

In this example, the `appAnimate` Java applet, your JavaScript will be able to access it using this:

```
document.appAnimate
```

This is all part of what Netscape refers to as *LiveConnect*, a system in which JavaScript, Java, and Netscape plug-ins are all related and can work with each other. JavaScript will be able to access Java variables, methods, packages, classes, and objects. Java will be able to access JavaScript methods and properties, too.

To work with these systems you'll need to wait a while—it's not fully functioning at the time of writing. You'll also need to know more about Java programming, and you'll need a lot more information. Refer to the "Netscape Authoring Guide" for more details.

PROPERTIES ARE ARRAY ELEMENTS OF OBJECTS

We learned about arrays in Chapter 9, "Building Arrays." You may not have realized then that the properties of an object in JavaScript can be considered to be items in an array. You can, therefore, access an individual property using an index as in `object[i]`, provided you know the right index to use. For instance, if we displayed the value of `Math[0]`, we'd see `2.7182818284590451`, the value of `E`, the first `Math` property.

We created a little program so you can see this at work. We used the `for...in` statement which can be used to access all the properties of an object. In this example, you can select one of several different objects to look at, and the `for..in` statement loops around to display each property in the object:

Example 13.5

```
function show_properties(form, obj, obj_name) {
var sDisplay = ""
var i = 0
  for(i in obj){
      sDisplay = sDisplay + obj_name + "." + i + " = " +→
obj[i] + nl
  }
    form.txtObjectList.value = sDisplay
}
```

Notice that we are referring to the object property that we want to see using obj[i], where i is the index value. You can see this program in use in Figure 13-4. Try it for yourself; select the object you want to look at, then click on the button to see that object's properties in the textarea. (However, note that some browsers will crash when using this program, thanks to a bug in JavaScript in those versions. Netscape 3.0 beta 3, for instance, will crash if you use the Window option button. Netscape 3.0 beta 4 seems to work fine.)

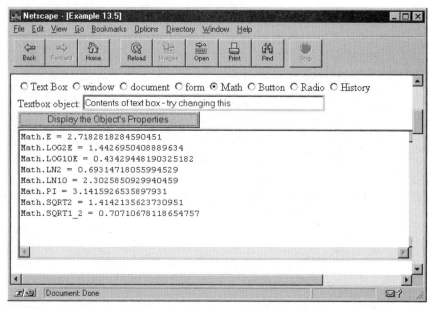

Figure 13-4: *This little program lets you view object properties using the array method of addressing the property.*

MOVING ON

We've finished with the theory, and we're going to move on now to specific ways in which you can use all the techniques you've learned. We'll start, in the next chapter, by looking at ways to control windows and the documents within those windows. We'll learn about opening secondary windows, and writing to them. Then, in subsequent chapters, we'll move on and look at how to work with frames and forms, and how to communicate with the user.

Controlling Windows & Documents With JavaScript

In this chapter you're going to learn all about working with windows—how to open them, how to write to them, how to close them, and so on. In order to work with windows, though, we need to understand the window and document objects, so we'll begin there, with a bit more theory.

THE WINDOW OBJECT

Your JavaScripts always have a window object. The window object sits at the top of the object hierarchy and contains properties and methods designed to provide information and help you manipulate both the window itself and the document within the window. For example, there are properties that contain information about the status-bar message and the number of frames in the document.

WINDOW OBJECT PROPERTIES

Let's take a look at the window properties:

Property	Description
defaultStatus	The default text in the window's status bar. A read-only property.
history	The window's history list.
length	The number of frames in the window.
name	The window's name.
opener	Refers to the window in which a script used window.open to open the current window. A property of the window object. This is a new property, introduced with Netscape Navigator 3.0 beta 3).
parent	A synonym for the parent window in a frameset. (We'll discuss this, along with self, top, and window, in a moment.)
self	A synonym for the current window.
status	The text currently displayed in the window's status bar. For example, you can set the following:: status="calculation complete".
top	A synonym for the top window. If you have frames within a window, top refers to the main window— the parent of all of the windows.
window	The current window.

It also has the following properties that are objects in their own right:

Property	Description
frame	A frame object contains information about a frame contained by the window.
frames array	This array contains a list of all the frame objects in the window. You can refer to a frame object using the frames array, like this: window.frames[indexnumber]; or by using the object's name, like this: window.framename.
location	An object that contains information about the URL of the document displayed in the window.
history	An object that contains information about the history list of the current window or frame.
document	An object that contains information about the document displayed in the window.

TIP

These property and method tables are not intended to replace the Netscape JavaScript documentation (see Appendix H, "Finding More Information," for information on where to get this). There's way too much detailed information in that documentation to be squeezed into this book. Use these tables to get an idea of what can be accomplished, then refer to the full documentation for the complete details.

REFERRING TO WINDOWS

There are several properties that are used to refer to particular windows. From "inside" a window—that is, when referring to the window containing the document in which the JavaScript is placed—you can use the window property; or, you can use nothing at all. If you don't name the window, JavaScript assumes you are talking about the window holding the document in which the JavaScript is placed. If you want to refer to a secondary window, though, you will have to name it.

> **TIP**
>
> ***Important:*** *When you refer to the current window from an event handler, you* must *include the* `window.` *part.*

As we'll see later in this chapter, when you create a window you will name it. In fact, the window will get *two* names. One name is used by HTML tags in the TARGET attribute to define where a document should be placed. The other name is the one that you will use in your JavaScripts to refer to the other window.

So, here's how to refer to a window. For example, let's say you want to set a value in a text box (`text1` in the form named `form1`). If the form that contains this text box is in the current document, you can use any of these methods to refer to the text box:

```
form1.text1.value="Wednesday"
window.document.form1.text1.value="Wednesday"
self.document.form1.text1.value="Wednesday"
```

You don't have to specify which window at all (unless you are running this script from an event handler, in which case you must use one of the last two formats). But you may want to, just to make the script more readable and to keep all these window references clear in your mind. You can refer to the window as `window` or `self`—it's the same thing.

Now, how do we refer to frames within a window? Each frame in a window is considered to be a *child* of that window. And it's a `window` object in its own right, having the same properties and methods as the parent window. If the form you want to modify is in the another frameset, you can refer to it by referring back to the parent window, like this:

```
parent.frame1.document.form1.text1.value="Wednesday"
```

We're going to be looking at forms in more detail in Chapter 15, "Using JavaScript With Frames."

REFERRING TO OTHER WINDOWS

You can refer to one window from another. For example, let's say you have a script in the parent window; how would you refer to a child window (a window that was created from that parent window)? You do this in the same way that you would refer to a child frame:

```
Win1.document.form1.text1.value="Wednesday"
```

This places a value into the `text1` text box in `form1` in a child window named `Win1`. What about a child of a child (a "grandchild"). That is, a child of a window created from the current window? Well, you'll have to name both windows, like this:

```
Win1.Win2.document.form1.text1.value="Wednesday"
```

`Win2` (the child of the child window) is, in effect, a property of `Win1`, so you must use the complete hierarchy and name. You cannot simply name `Win2`. The parent window knows nothing about `Win2`, because it was created by a different window.

When you refer to windows from a script, think about whether the current window will know anything about the other window. If you are referring to a child, it will. If you are referring to a window created from somewhere else, though, it won't. It won't know about a grandchild or a sibling—the grandchild was created by a child, the sibling by a parent. In fact, you can only refer to windows "down" the family tree, not "up" the family tree. You can refer to a child, or a grandchild, or a greatgrandchild. You can't refer to a parent window (except in the case in which you are referring from a *frame* to the frame's parent; you can't refer from a window back to the window that created it). You can't refer to a grandparent. You can't even refer to a "sibling," which is another window created by the same window that created the current window.

We have an example that shows how this window address system works. We created a document with a button that opens two secondary windows. One of the secondary windows has a button that opens another child window. Within the first document we have several buttons that modify the `defaultStatus` property in the three windows. (Right now don't worry about how windows are opened; we'll come back to that in a few moments.)

Example 14.1

```
<INPUT TYPE="BUTTON" VALUE="This window's status bar:→
self.defaultStatus" onclick="self.defaultStatus='This is the
current window\'s status bar'">
```

This button modifies the first window's status bar; notice that we've used `onclick="self.defaultStatus=`. We had to state `self.defaultStatus` because in an event handler you must state which window you are referring to, even if you are referring to the current window. (We could have used `window.defaultStatus` too, which means the same thing.)

```
<INPUT TYPE="BUTTON" VALUE="The child window's status bar:→
Win1.defaultStatus" onclick="Win1.defaultStatus='The child
window\'s status bar'">
```

The second button modifies the child window's status bar; we've used `Win1.defaultStatus` this time, `Win1` being the child window's name.

```
<INPUT TYPE="BUTTON" VALUE="The grandchild window's status→
bar: Win1.Win2.defaultStatus"
onclick="Win1.Win2.defaultStatus='The grandchild window\'s→
status bar'">
```

The third button modifies the grandchild's status bar, a child window of one of the current window's child. This time we named both windows (`Win1.Win2.defaultStatus`). If you want to try an experiment you can close the child window, then try this button. It won't work, because once the `Win1` window has closed there's no way to address `Win2`. The script has to address *through* `Win1`.

There are also two buttons used to close the child and grandchild:

```
<INPUT TYPE="BUTTON" VALUE="Close the grandchild window:→
Win1.Win2.close()" onclick="Win1.Win2.close()">
<INPUT TYPE="BUTTON" VALUE="Close the child window:→
Win1.close()" onclick="Win1.close()">
```

You'll find that if you use the second button and *then* the first button, the first button won't work. Why? Again, because once you've closed the child, there's no way to refer to the grandchild.

(The current window doesn't know the grandchild's name, but has to refer to it "through" the child.)

The grandchild also has several buttons, but they won't all work correctly:

```
<FORM>
<INPUT TYPE="BUTTON" VALUE="The current window:→
self.defaultStatus" onclick="self.defaultStatus='This is the→
current window\'s status bar'"><P>
<INPUT TYPE="BUTTON" VALUE="The parent window:→
Win1.defaultStatus" onclick="Win1.defaultStatus='The previous→
(parent) window\'s status bar'"><P>
<INPUT TYPE="BUTTON" VALUE="The parent window:→
parent.defaultStatus" onclick="parent.defaultStatus='The→
previous (parent) window\'s status bar'"><P>
<INPUT TYPE="BUTTON" VALUE="The top window: top.defaultStatus"→
onclick="top.defaultStatus='The top (most-ancient ancestor)→
window\'s status bar'"><P>
</FORM>
```

These all try to write to various status bars. The first one works, because it's writing to `self.defaultStatus`, the status bar in the grandchild window. The second creates an error message. We've named the previous window (`Win1.defaultStatus`), but the grandchild doesn't know that name, so it won't work. The third actually works; it does set the parent window's status bar, but this window is, in effect, it's own parent! Because when we use `parent`, we are actually talking about the parent window containing a frameset (you might think of it as the *main* window), not the window that created this window. So the current window's status bar is modified. (No, our window doesn't actually have any framesets in it; still, parent doesn't refer back any farther than the main window.)

And finally, we tried `top`. Again, though, when we use `top` we are referring to a situation in which a window contains nested framesets—not to a window that created another window. So again, this changes the current window's status bar.

WINDOW OBJECT METHODS

Now let's look at the window methods—the functions associated with the window object.

Method	Description
alert()	Opens an Alert message box.
clearTimeout()	Used to stop the setTimeout method from working.
close()	Closes the window.
confirm()	Opens a Confirm message box; the user has two choices: OK and Cancel. The method returns true if the user clicks on OK, false if the user clicks on Cancel.
blur()	Moves the focus away from the specified window. (This is a new method, introduced in Netscape Navigator 3.0 beta 3.)
focus()	Brings the specified window to the foreground. (Another new method.)
open()	Opens a new window.
prompt()	Opens a Prompt message box; the user can type into this box, and the typed text is returned to the script.
setTimeout()	Waits a specified number of milliseconds, then runs the instructions.

TIP

We've used the prompt, alert, and confirm methods a number of times, so we won't repeat them here. Just remember that if you use one of these methods from an event handler (as opposed to putting it in a function and then calling the function from an event handler), you must write window.prompt, window.alert, window.confirm.

Now that we've got the basic information, let's take a look at what we can do with all this.

OPENING SECONDARY WINDOWS

We'll begin with the basics. How can you open another window using JavaScript? Simple. Let's take a look again at Example 2.4, which we saw back in Chapter 2, "A Few Quick JavaScript Tricks." First, we had this in the HEAD:

Example 2.4

```
<HEAD>
<SCRIPT LANGUAGE="JAVASCRIPT">
<!--
function WinOpen() {
    open("window.htm","Window1","toolbar=yes");
}
//-->
</script>
</HEAD>
```

Then we placed the following piece in the body:

```
<form>
<input type="button" name="WindowButton" value="Secondary→
Window--Click on me" onclick="WinOpen()">
</form>
```

As you can see, we began by defining a function in the HEAD; we called this function WinOpen( ). The function uses the open method to open a window (called Window1), to load the file window.htm into the window, and to add the toolbar to the window.

Why would you want to create secondary windows like this? Well, secondary windows have been used in hypertext for a long time. The earliest forms of hypertext were too simple. If you clicked on a link you saw another document. Click on another link to see yet another document, and so on. The people developing hypertext soon learned two things: that there would be many times when the reader would want to see a bit of information for a moment, then continue in the current document; and that it's very easy to get lost in hypertext! Readers reported getting totally confused about "where" they were in the network of interlinked documents.

Secondary windows were one of the things developed to make hypertext easier to use. They were intended for situations in which the developer could be fairly sure that the user would want to keep the original document open. For instance, in a glossary you might have one document with a large list of entries; the user would click on an entry and a secondary window would open containing the definition of the entry on which you clicked. The original list would remain in view, of course, so the user could click on another one, modifying the contents of the secondary window to show the next definition.

Here's another use of secondary windows. Perhaps the developer feels that the user may want to branch off in a particular direction, but keep the original window open for some reason. In other words, the user may click on a link in the first window, opening the second. The user can then navigate through the document in the second window, going from page to page, while the original document remains open in the first window.

There are many reasons for using secondary windows and, as you've seen, secondary windows are very easy to create.

TIP

When you create secondary windows, make sure that you check them in a low-resolution mode, such as VGA. If you create windows in a high-resolution mode, such as 800 x 600 or 1024 x 768, they may fit nicely on your screen, but change to VGA and you may find that they are partly off screen. Also, a window that doesn't need a scroll bar in high resolution, may need one in a low resolution.

CONFIGURING THE WINDOW

JavaScript provides a number of ways for you to configure your
windows. You can do so by modifying the parameters of the open
method. So let's look at open. This is the basic format used by the
open method:

```
[windowVar = ][window].open("URL", "windowName",→
["windowFeatures"])
```

windowVar This is a window name. In effect, the open method
"returns" the window to this name. We didn't use this in our earlier
example, and you don't have to always do so. However, if you plan
to refer to this window from another window in your scripts, then
you must use this.

window   The open method is a method of the window object, so
you can include window. here if you wish, but it's not necessary.
(Unless, of course, this script is in an event handler, in which case
you must include window..)

The URL is the URL of the document you want to place into the
window. (Leave this empty—""—if you want an empty window, or
if you want to write to the secondary window. We'll see how to do
that later in this chapter.)

The WindowName is a name you give to the window. In this instance, however, this is the name used by the HTML <FRAME> and
<A> tags, not by your JavaScripts.

Finally, there are the WindowFeatures; you can define exactly
what the window should look like—whether it should have a
toolbar, location bar, directories bar, and so on, and what size it
should be.

The following features are set *on* using yes, 1, or by simply
naming the feature. They are set *off* using no, 0, or by omitting the
feature in its entirety.

TIP

If you omit all feature names, JavaScript assumes you want them all. So if you want none of these features, simply name one like this: toolbar=no.

- toolbar—Use this to include the browser's toolbar in the window. For example, toolbar, toolbar=1, or toolbar=yes means "place a toolbar in the secondary window."
- location—Use this to include the browser's location or URL bar.
- directories—Use this to include the browser's Directory Buttons bar. (The Netscape family of browsers have a Directory Button bar. Many browsers don't have such a bar, so later JavaScript browsers from other companies may simply ignore this window feature.)
- status—Use this to include the browser's status bar.
- menubar—Use this to include the browser's menu bar.
- scrollbars—Use this to place scroll bars in the window. (The scroll bars will only appear in the window if necessary; if the contents of the window are all visible within the window, the scroll bars won't be there.)
- resizable—Use this to allow the user to resize the window. If this is set *off*, the window size will be fixed.

The following features control the size of the window, and are set by entering a pixel value:

- width—This sets the width of the window, in pixels. For example, you might enter width=400.
- height—This sets the height of the window, in pixels.

TIP

It's a good idea to put scroll bars into your window if you are unsure as to whether all the data will fit. If you don't put scroll bars in, you won't get them even if they are needed to view all the contents.

There used to be another feature, `copyhistory`, but it's currently not working, as it was disabled for security reasons. This feature would grab the history list from the first window and give it to the new window, so the user could move back and forth through the history from that window. The Back and Forward buttons and the Go menu would then work using the original window's history list. For the present, this feature has been removed from JavaScript, perhaps for good—though it's a handy feature to have.

You can use all or any of these options, separating each with a comma (but *no* space between them), all enclosed within the same quotation marks. The quickest way to create a complete window is to leave all this stuff out, like this:

Example 14.2

```
<SCRIPT LANGUAGE="JAVASCRIPT">
<!--
function WinOpen() {
    open("window.htm","Window1");
}
//-->
</SCRIPT>
```

Try this example in the Online Companion and you'll find that you get a complete window (see Figure 14-1): all the toolbars and the status bar, it's sizeable, and it's full size. Remember, if you don't name any window features, you get them all.

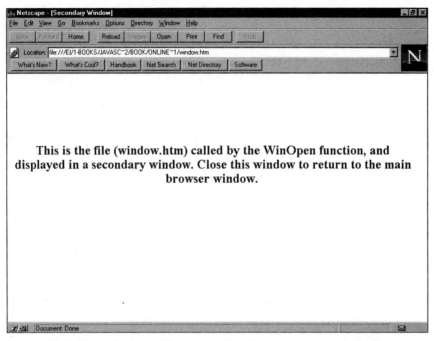

Figure 14-1: *If you don't specify any window features, you get them all.*

But look at the following example. In this example, we've added the "location" feature. Now we get a completely different window. Because we've specified one feature, JavaScript assumes all the others should be turned off; all we get this time is a window with the location bar.

Example 14.3

```
<SCRIPT LANGUAGE="JAVASCRIPT">
<!--
function WinOpen() {
    open("window.htm","Window1","location");
}
//-->
</SCRIPT>
```

Mix and match as you wish. What you want will depend on what you want the window to achieve. For instance, you may want the location bar, so the users can see the URL or enter another one.

You quite likely will want to size the window (at present you can't position the window, only size it, which is a serious limitation, though presumably one that will be fixed in later versions of JavaScript). You may want to provide a toolbar, but no other controls. Here's an example:

Example 14.4

```
<SCRIPT LANGUAGE="JAVASCRIPT">
<!--
function WinOpen() {
    open("window.htm","Window1","location,resize,height=250,→
width=450,toolbar, scrollbars");
}
//-->
</SCRIPT>
```

In this example you'll get a window that is 250 pixels high and 450 wide, with a location bar and toolbar, which is resizable. Notice that all the features appear within the same quotation marks, and that there are no spaces between them—features appearing after a space won't work. This is why this window doesn't have scroll bars, even though the word scrollbars appears at the end of the features.

THE PROBLEM WITH LINKS

It would be nice to be able to open these secondary windows using links rather than buttons. Indeed, you can open secondary windows using links, but there are problems with doing so. In the following example, we created two links to a page using the same function that was created in the previous example (with the scrollbars feature taken out), and the same onclick instruction that we used in the button. The first link doesn't refer to an HTML file in the normal way, though—it uses the onclick instruction to do so, but there's nothing in the HREF= attribute. The second link uses both the onclick instruction and the normal URL attribute:

Example 14.5

```
<A HREF="" onclick="WinOpen()">Open Secondary Window</A><BR>
<A HREF="window.htm" onclick="WinOpen()">Open Secondary
Window</A>
```

In both cases clicking on the link will open the secondary window (the same one we saw in the earlier example, because we're using the same function, WinOpen.). What's interesting, though, is what happens to the browser window below. If you are using one of the Netscape 2.0 browsers (or Netscape Navigator 3.0 beta 3), clicking on the first link displays a directory listing (as shown in Figure 14-2). In other browsers clicking on such a link would do nothing. This is a feature of the Netscape browsers that is not shared by most other browsers, so it's difficult to say what the new non-Netscape browsers will do when they're released; they may do the ideal thing, which would be to open the secondary window but do nothing to the original window.

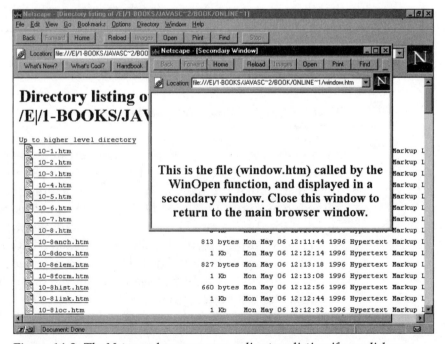

Figure 14-2: *The Netscape browsers open a directory listing if you click on a link with nothing in HREF=.*

In the second case, the one in which we have entered a filename in the HREF= attribute, the browser will open the same document in both windows; again, not quite what we wanted. Also, there are reports that doing this sort of thing may crash some browser versions on some operating systems (though the reports may be misidentifying the problem). Thus opening windows from links in this manner is a bit of a problem and, for the moment at least, to be avoided.

CLOSING SECONDARY WINDOWS

The user can always close a window using the normal window controls—by clicking on the X button in the top right corner in Windows 95, for instance. But it's a good idea to include a Close button if this is a temporary window—a window that you expect to be opened, read, and then closed. Create a button like this:

Example 14.6

```
<FORM>
<input type="button" Value="Close this Window"
onclick="self.close()">
</FORM>
```

Again, notice that we are using self.close(), not close(), as you must be specific in an event handler. If we had the close() method in a function being called from the onclick event handler, though, we could use click().

WRITING TO THE WINDOW

We've just seen how you can open a window and place the contents of a specified Web page into that window. There's something else you can do, though—you can write from your script to the new window. Take a look at this:

Example 14.7

```
function OpenWindow() {
    Win1 =
open("window.htm","SecWin","scrollbars=yes,width=350,height=230");
    var sText = "<BODY>This is some text<P></BODY>"
    Win1.document.write("<H2>Secondary window</H2><HR><P>" +→
sText)
}
function CloseWindow() {
    Win1.close()
}
```

In the HEAD we've created a function called OpenWindow( ). This uses the open method to create a new window; notice that this time we have a window name (Win1=) because we plan to use it later. You'll notice that we've specified window.htm to be placed into the window, as before. But as you'll see, this will be ignored, because we're going to write to the window using document.write( ) instead. (You don't have to specify an .HTM document. Simple enter open("", etc.)

After opening the window we declare a variable (sText), and place a string into it. You can see that the string includes some HTML tags. Finally, we use the document.write method to write something to this window. We have to name the window we want to write to, so we use Win1.document.write. We write HTML tags, text, and the contents of the sText variable to the window.

The second function, CloseWindow( ), quite simply uses the Win1.close( ) method to close the window we created. This example Web page has two buttons, one to call the OpenWindow( ) function, and one to call the CloseWindow( ) function. You can see the result of clicking on the first button in Figure 14-3.

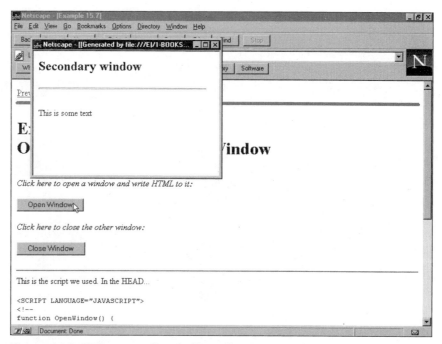

Figure 14-3: *We've created a window and written text to it.*

Now, try this. Click on the Open Window button in the original window. Click several times. If you have your browser window maximized, nothing appears to happen. But switch back to the window and you'll see that you've been writing to the window again. The window was already open, so it didn't open again. Yet the text you were writing *was* sent to the window. We'll see how to deal with that little problem in a moment.

WRITING TO ONE WINDOW FROM ANOTHER

Now that you have a window open, how can you write to it from the first window? Earlier we discussed how secondary windows are commonly used when you want to have two windows open at the same time, such as a glossary list in one window and a glossary definition in the other. Clicking on a button in the glossary list window could then display a related topic in the secondary window. (I say button, not link, because of the link problem we've just discussed. In most hypertext systems a glossary list would usually contain a list of links. Currently in JavaScript you can't do that.)

Writing to the window is simple. You use the `document.write` method. In other words, rather than write directly to the `window` object, you must write to the `document` object that is a property of the `window` in which you want the text to appear. For example, we could do this:

```
function MoreText() {
    Win1.document.write("<P>Here's some <P>more text for→
you...and some more. Yes, and more, and yet more<BR>")
}
```

This function uses the `write` method to place text in the `Win1` window. We have to include `document`, because you can't really write to windows, you have to write to the documents inside them. Notice again that we can include HTML tags within the text we are sending.

PROBLEMS WRITING TO WINDOWS

Writing to other windows in this way is a little erratic. Make sure that you place an HTML `<BR>` tag at the end of the text you are sending or it won't be written in its entirety. (Some of it may be written some of the time—it's hard to predict what will be written.) Even if you place the text to be written in a variable, then use the variable name in the `document.write` method, you should still use a `<BR>` at the end of the text in the variable. Also, note that there's a better way to write to a document, as we'll see under "The Document Stream" later in this chapter.

WHERE'S THAT WINDOW?

Actually the example we showed you above is not a good way to write to a window. The problem is that if the window is not visible, the user won't see anything happen and may not realize the window has been written to.

But there's a new `window` method called `focus()`. This is not available in any of the Netscape 2.0 browsers, but was introduced in Netscape Navigator 3.0 beta 3. It's used to bring the specified window to the foreground, and we can employ this method to resolve the problem we had with the last example. In the following example, we've added a function that—when called from a button—writes more text to the window, but also brings that window to the front:

Example 14.8

```
function MoreText() {
     Win1.document.write("<P>Here's some <P>more text for→
you...and some more. Yes, and more, and yet more<BR>")
     Win1.focus()
}
```

We write to the window's document. Then, once the script's done that, it uses `Win1.focus()` to bring the window back to the forefront. It's a good idea to use the `focus()` method whenever you are doing something to another window to make sure that the user can see what's happening. Try it in the Online Companion and you'll see how it works.

By the way, although in this case each time we click on the button we *add* to the document. If we'd opened a Web page in the window first, writing to it again will clear the Web page and then write the text, as you will see in the following example:

Example 14.9

```
function OpenWindow() {
     Win1 = open("window.htm","SecWin","scrollbars=yes,→
width=350,height=230");
}
```

This time we've opened `window.htm` in the new window—we haven't written to it. Now, if you try this example in the Online Companion you'll see that when you click on the button that runs the `MoreText()` function, the Web page is removed, and the new text written. Why? In effect the `document.write` command is opening a new document stream (which we'll discuss a little later in this chapter). When you open a new stream, you automatically clear the current document from the window. Each subsequent `document.write` instruction is part of the current stream, so clicking on the button several times simply adds to the document, it doesn't clear it again.

TIP

You cannot write to the end of a Web page. Once a Web page has been written, it can't be modified without being rewritten.

THE DOCUMENT OBJECT

We're not only working with the `window` object now, but with the `document` object. So before we go any further, let's take a look at the `document` object. These are the available properties:

Property	Description
alinkColor	The color of the text used in the document to display an active link—a link that the user has clicked on, but has not yet released with the mouse button (the HTML ALINK attribute).
anchor	Each anchor in the document (the <NAME= tags) is a property of the document, though each anchor has its own properties, so they are also objects.
anchors	This is an array (we learned about arrays in Chapter 10, "Objects, Properties & Methods") that lists all the anchor objects in the document.
bgColor	The color of the document background (the BGCOLOR attribute).

cookie	A piece of text related to the page stored in the cookie.txt file. (We talked about cookies in Chapter 13, "Advanced Topics.")
fgColor	The color of the document's text (the TEXT attribute).
form	Each form (the <FORM> tags) in the object is a property of the object. Again, though, as each form contains its own properties, each form is also an object.
forms	This is an array that lists all the form objects in the document.
lastModified	The date that the document was last modified (based on the host computer's date setting).
linkColor	The color of the text used in this document to display a link to a document that the user has not yet viewed (the LINK attribute).
link	Each link (the <A HREF= tags) in the form is a property and—as with each form and anchor—an object.
links	This is an array that lists all the link objects in the document.
location	The complete (absolute) URL of the document.
referrer	The URL of the document containing a link that the user clicked on to get to this document. If the user didn't get to this document via a link, this is empty.
title	The text between the document's <TITLE> and </TITLE> tags .
vlinkColor	The color of the text used in this document to display a link to a document that the user has already viewed (the VLINK attribute).

DOCUMENT METHODS

Now, here are the document object's methods:

Method	Property
clear	Clears the contents of the specified document.
close	Closes the document stream (we'll get to that next).
open	Opens the document stream.
write	Writes text to the document.
writeln	Writes text to the document, and ends with a newline character.

THE DOCUMENT STREAM

What's all this about the document stream? Well, using the document stream provides a better, more formal way to write to documents than the manner we've looked at so far. Previously we simply wrote straight to the document in the window. If you do that and there's no document in the window, then a document is automatically opened. In other words, you can open a blank window—simply don't specify a Web page or use `document.write` to put anything in it. Later, if you use `document.write` to send text to the document, a new document is automatically opened inside that window.

A better way to do this is to create a document "stream" using the `document.open()` method. In the following example we've modified an earlier example to use this more formal method:

Example14.10

```
function MoreText() {
    Win1.focus()
    Win1.document.open()
    Win1.document.write("Some guy hit my fender the other→
day, and I said unto him, \"Be fruitful, and multiply.\" But→
not in those words.<P>Woody Allen")
    }
```

Here's what we've done. First, we've used `Win1.focus()` to bring the window to the front (remember, this won't work on Netscape 2.0 browsers, only in Netscape Navigator 3.0 beta 3 or later). Then we used `Win1.document.open()` to open the document stream. That means "here comes a document." Unlike in the earlier examples, the original text (written with `document.write` in an earlier function) is cleared from the window, because when you open a stream, you clear the document. Next we use the `Win1.document.write` method to write the text.

Now, go to the Online Companion and try this. You'll probably find that the end of the text is missing. Remember the problem we had earlier, with missing text? Well, here's a quick fix for that:

Example 14.11

```
function MoreText() {
    Win1.focus()
    Win1.document.open()
    Win1.document.write("Some guy hit my fender the other→
day, and I said unto him, \"Be fruitful, and multiply.\"→
But not in those words.<P>Woody Allen")
    Win1.document.close()
}
```

Same function, except that we've added the `Win1.document.close()` method. This closes the document stream; you'll find that all the text will appear in the document—there'll be nothing missing.

MORE ABOUT THE DOCUMENT STREAM

When you open a document stream, the document is automatically a text document. But the open() method actually allows you to specify what type of document you want, like this: `open("mimetype")`. You can use `text/html`, `text/plain`, `image/gif`, `image/jpeg`, `image/x-bitmap`, or any plug-in that Netscape Navigator supports. Because we haven't specified anything in our examples, JavaScript assumes (rightly) that we want `text/html`.

Here's another thing to notice, by the way. If you click on this button over and over, the text is not added to the bottom of the document. Rather, the document is cleared each time, and the text rewritten. In fact that's the case in both this and the previous example. That's because the `document.open()` method closes the previous document stream, even if the previous stream did not use a `document.close()` statement.

TIP

Remember when, in an earlier example, we wrote to a window containing a Web page, without using `document.open()`? Even so, the Web page was cleared, right? That's because once a Web page's been written, its document stream is closed.

THE CLEAR() & WRITELN() METHODS

Let's look at the last two methods, `clear()` and `writeln()`. The `clear()` method, not surprisingly, clears the contents of a document. In our next Online Companion example we have a document that automatically opens a second window and writes to that window. Now, in theory you can use this to clear the window:

```
function ClearWindow()      {
    Win1.focus()
    Win1.document.clear()
    Win1.document.close()
}
```

Actually at the time of writing, `clear()` wasn't working well. You may have to click on the button calling this function twice to get the window to clear.

Still, there's a way around the problem. You can do this (as we did in our example):

Example 14.12

```
function ClearWindow()      {
    Win1.focus()
    Win1.document.open()
```

```
Win1.document.write()
Win1.document.close()
}
```

This uses the `document.write()` method, but doesn't write anything. That's the same as clearing the document. (You might think that simply opening and then closing the document—without bothering to write—should be enough. However, this method also takes two clicks of the button.)

Finally, the `writeln` method; this is the same as the `document.write()` method, except that a new line character is placed at the end of the text that is written. This is ignored when writing HTML, unless the text is being placed between <PRE> and </PRE> or <XMP> and </XMP> tags.

PICTURES, TOO

We can even insert pictures into a document. In fact, you can write any text or HTML tags to the document. Here's an example:

Example 14.13

```
function OpenWindow() {
        Win1 = open("","SecWin","scrollbars=yes,width=600,→
height=350");
        Win1.document.open();
        Win1.document.write("<HEAD><TITLE>Image Document</
TITLE></HEAD><IMG SRC='http://www.vmedia.com/u/pkent/bell.→
gif' WIDTH=144 HEIGHT=119 ALT='Wait a few moments and the→
Bell will appear...'><P>You have to do this just right, or→
the picture doesn't appear. Make sure you use the full URL→
of the picture--a relative URL may not be good enough. You→
should also include the image size; although it probably→
makes no difference to Netscape 3.0, earlier browsers may→
```

```
choke if you <I>don't</I> include the image→
size.<BR><FORM><input type='button' value='Close Window'→
onclick='window.close()'></FORM>")
        Win1.document.close()
```

You can see the result of this in Figure 14-4. The image will be placed into the window at the top.

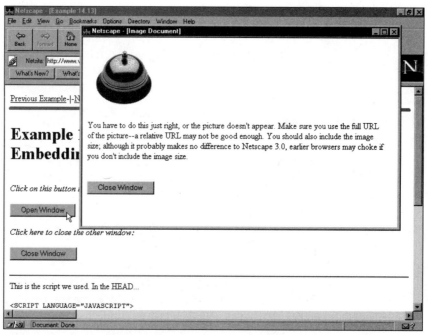

Figure 14-4: *You can even write picture <IMG> tags to your windows.*

To make sure this works, include an absolute URL to the image, not a relative URL; in other words, give the full URL, including the protocol (http://), the directory, and filename. If you use just the filename, you may find the image is not placed into the document, even if that file is in the same directory as the original HTML document. Also, use the `document.open()` and `document.close()` methods to make sure everything is written correctly.

CONTROLLING BACKGROUND COLORS

Have you seen all those color controls everyone's creating? They are actually very easy to build. You can create buttons in your documents that allow people to modify background colors. For example, if you have an unusual background color but have heard from some readers that they don't like it, you can give them the choice, like this:

Example 14.14

```
<FORM>
<INPUT TYPE="button" VALUE="Red"
onclick="document.bgColor='red'">
<INPUT TYPE="button" VALUE="White"
onclick="document.bgColor='white'">
<INPUT TYPE="button" VALUE="Blue"
onclick="document.bgColor='blue'">
<INPUT TYPE="button" VALUE="Green"
onclick="document.bgColor='green'">
<INPUT TYPE="button" VALUE="Blue (#0000FF)"
onclick="document.bgColor='#0000FF'">
</FORM>
```

TIP

Where do these colors come from? You can, if you prefer, use the color's hexadecimal values. (I'm sure you have the hexadecimal value for red, green, and blue on the tip of your tongue, don't you?) On the other hand, you can do what we did and use the color names built into JavaScript. See Appendix G, "Color Values" for a list of these names (and the corresponding hexadecimal values). Of course in most cases you won't need to refer to this list; simple type the name of the color and as long as it's nothing unusual, it's almost certainly in the list.

By the way, this

```
<INPUT TYPE="button" VALUE="Blue"
onclick="document.bgColor='blue'">
```

is just the same as this

```
<INPUT TYPE="button" VALUE="Blue"
onclick="document.bgColor='#0000FF'">
```

The hexadecimal number (0000FF) preceded by # is the equivalent of blue. Now you know that, you can forget about using hexadecimal values for colors; and if you want to see a color chart showing all the available colors, go to the Online Companion's Color Chart. (There's a link within this chapter's example links, or go directly to http://www.netscapepress.com/support/ javascript/colors.htm.)

YOUR SETTINGS OVERRIDE

The settings you make using the document object's properties: vlink, bgColor, fgColor, and so on, override both the document's HTML settings (the ones in the <BODY> tag, *and* the user's own preferences). Remember, users may choose to override <BODY> settings in General Preferences, but if you modify the settings using JavaScript, the script wins! Also, note that it doesn't matter where in the document you make these settings, the script still takes precedence. For instance, if you make the settings in a script above the <BODY> tag (so the <BODY> tag is read last), and the <BODY> tag has different settings, the scripts settings are still used.

CREATING "SLIDE SHOWS"

There are two window methods we haven't looked at yet that can be very useful: setTimeout and clearTimeout. The first is used to add a lag to script instructions. In other words, setTimeout tells the browser not to run the instruction until a certain time has passed. (If the user does something to move to another page before that time has passed, the instruction will not be executed.) The other method, clearTimeout, is used to stop the setTimeout method from working.

You use setTimeout like this:

```
setTimeout=("instruction", timedelay_in_milliseconds)
```

For instance, if you want to call function LetsMove() after five seconds, you would do this:

```
setTimeout=("LetsMove()", 5000)
```

Now, if you use the method in this manner, you won't be able to use clearTimeout to stop it. To do that, you need to provide an ID name that the clearTimeout method can refer to (after all you may have several timeouts working at once, so it has to know which one you want to stop). You create this ID by preceding the statement with the ID name, like this:

```
IDname=setTimeout=("instruction", timedelay_in_milliseconds)
```

So, in our example, you might do this:

```
move=setTimeout=("LetsMove()", 5000)
```

We've given the timeout the ID move, so later we can do this:

```
clearTimeout(move)
```

Here's an example that creates a little "slide show." The Web pages automatically change every five seconds:

Example 14.15

```
<SCRIPT LANGUAGE="JAVASCRIPT">
<!--
function LetsMove() {
    location='14-15A.htm'
}
//-->
</SCRIPT>
</HEAD>
<BODY onload="setTimeout('LetsMove()', 5000)">
```

The function LetsMove() is very simple; it uses the window.location property (we've used the shorthand location) to

load the file called 14-15A.htm. This function is run from the onload
event handler, which uses the setTimeout method. Note that we
have a 5000 millisecond (5 second) delay. (See Figure 14-5.)

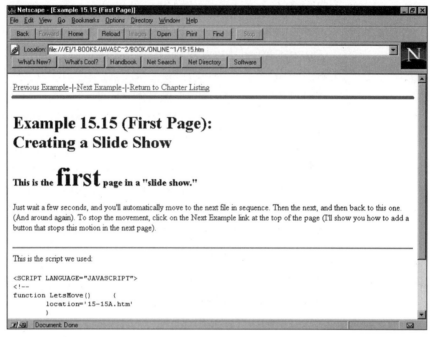

Figure 14-5: *setTimeout provides a very quick and easy way to create a slide show.*

TIP

*Although the setTimeout and clearTimeout methods are, strictly
speaking, window methods, you are not restricted to using them only
for window-related purposes. You can use these methods for any script
you wish.*

In this case there's no way to stop the event (except by moving to
another page before the delay is over). So let's see how to do so:

Example 14.16

```
<BODY onload="move=setTimeout('LetsMove()', 5000)">
```

We have the same function, but we've modified the event handler. We've simply placed `move=` before `setTimeout`. Now we can create this button, to stop the motion:

```
<INPUT TYPE="BUTTON" VALUE="Stop Movement"
onclick="clearTimeout(move)"><P>
```

This uses the `clearTimeout` method to refer to our timeout by its ID, `move`. By the way, if you create a little slide show like this, you may also want to add a button that allows the person to get started again—something like this:

```
<INPUT TYPE="BUTTON" VALUE="Next Page"
onclick="window.location='14-16A.htm'"><P>
```

This sets the `window.location` property to the name of the file you want to move to in sequence. When that file loads, a new timeout will begin, and the slide show will start up again.

WHERE DO YOU WANT TO GO?

Before we move on, let's look at a couple of little systems you can use to allow the user to make choices. First, we'll look at a selection box from which the user can choose. Then we'll look at how to add a Confirmation box to a link.

There are a variety of "image previewers" that JavaScript authors have used as examples, but you don't have to use them just for images. They allow users to make choices about what to load next, and where to load it. Whether to load a Web page, an image, a sound, an Adobe Acrobat PDF file, a Shockwave file, or anything else. You can use a system like this to load something into the current window, or open another window and load it there. Here's what we've done:

Example 14.17

```
<SCRIPT LANGUAGE="JAVASCRIPT">
<!--
function Dest(form) {
    var sGo
if (form.select1.selectedIndex == 0) sGo = "14-17a.htm";
```

```
if (form.select1.selectedIndex == 1) sGo = "14-17b.htm";
if (form.select1.selectedIndex == 2) sGo = "14-17c.htm";
if (form.select1.selectedIndex == 3) sGo = "14-17d.htm";
if (form.select1.selectedIndex == 4) sGo = "14-17e.htm";
if (form.select1.selectedIndex == 5) sGo = "14-17f.htm";
if (form.select1.selectedIndex == 6) sGo = "14-17g.htm";
if (form.select1.selectedIndex == 7) sGo = "14-17h.htm";
if (form.select1.selectedIndex == 8) sGo = "14-17i.htm";
if (form.select1.selectedIndex == 9) sGo = "14-17j.htm";
    form.select1.blur()   ;
    Win1=open(sGo,"Window1","width=400,height=200") ;
    Win1.focus()
}
//-->
</SCRIPT>
```

The function Dest takes information from the selection box
(which we'll see in a moment). It declares a variable called sGo, and
then uses a series of if statements to determine what to place in
that variable, depending on what's been selected in the selection
box. For instance, if the seventh item has been clicked on, it places
15-17g.htm into the variable.

Next, it uses the blur() method to remove focus from the selection
box. This is simply a little trick to avoid a problem that may occasion-
ally occur with this selection box. You see, we've used the onchange
event handler in the selection box, which causes a small problem. If
we *don't* use the blur() method, when the user reloads the page after
clicking on the selection box, the onchange event runs again. As the
page is reloading, though, the function we've created wouldn't be able
to find out what's selected—because nothing has been selected. So it
would open a blank window (actually your system might lock). By
using the blur() method we've moved focus from the selection box; if
the user reloads, the onchange event won't run.

Next, we open a window. Note that we are placing the text from
the sGo variable into the parameters, so whatever filename is in sGo
is the file that will be loaded into the window.

Finally, we used Win1.focus() again, to bring the window to the
front. That's just in case someone clicks on several of the items in
the selection box without closing the new window first.

Now, here's our selection box:

```
<form>
<select name="select1" size=4 onchange="Dest(this.form)">
<option>The White Room
<option>The Red Room
<option>The Green Room
<option>The Purple Room
<option>The Gray Room
<option>The Brown Room
<option>The Yellow Room
<option>The Blue Room
<option>The Crimson Room
<option>The Olive Room
</select>
</form>
```

When the user clicks on an item, the onchange event handler calls the Dest function, passing information from the form to the function. You can see the system in action in Figure 14-6.

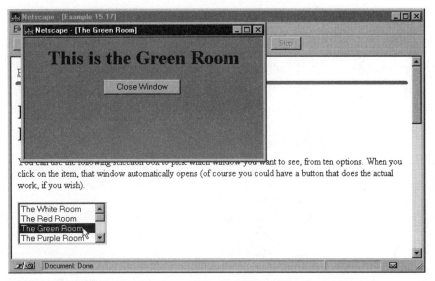

Figure 14-6: *This is a very simple way to allow the user to make a choice.*

This is a really simple way to let the user select what to do. Of course you can use it in many ways; you might incorporate it with a button, so the window does not open until the button's clicked. You don't have to open another window; you could use `window.location` to load another document into the current window. You could use it to run any script you want.

CONFIRMATION BOXES ON LINKS

The most recent release of JavaScript (Netscape Navigator 3.0 beta 4) has an improvement to the `onclick` event handler. You can now add a Confirmation box to the link to make the user confirm that he really wants to use the link. You can do it like this:

```
<A HREF = "URL"   onclick="return confirm('Your Text→
Here')">Your Text Here</a>
```

You might try this:

Example 14.18

```
<A HREF = "adult.htm"   onclick="return confirm('Remember,→
this page is for adults only. If you are under 18 or living→
in an area where such images are illegal, please do not→
continue. Click on Cancel to stop the transfer, or OK to go→
to the page.')">The Naughty Bits</a>
```

When the user clicks on the link, the Confirmation box opens (see Figure 14-7). If the user clicks on Cancel, the link operation will not work. Only if the user clicks on OK will the referenced page be transferred.

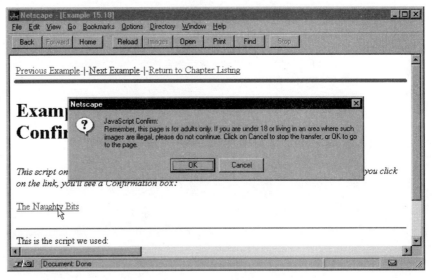

Figure 14-7: *A new feature lets you confirm Web page transfers.*

MOVING ON

Manipulating windows and documents is perhaps one of the most important and useful features of JavaScript and it's basic to virtually all JavaScript applications. These days many documents have frames, so you need to understand how to work with them. Each frame within a window is a property of that window. It's also an object in its own right—a window object, too! So let's move on to the next chapter, and figure out how to work with frames.

CHAPTER 15

Using JavaScript With Frames

Even if you haven't used *frames* in your own Web documents, you are probably familiar with them by now. The frames feature is one that was introduced with the Netscape 2.0 browser family. It allows a Web author to split the browser window into smaller parts, each part called a frame (in other hypertext systems such frames are often known as *panes*).

As this is such a new feature, and most Web authors are currently not using it, let's start by quickly reviewing how frames are created using HTML tags. Then we'll come back to JavaScript and see how you can create scripts that will control the frames.

FRAME BASICS

Creating frames is quite simple. First, you create the main document, one containing the HTML tags that define how the browser should create the frames. This file will contain nothing else—it won't be displayed in the browser window, it's simply the instructions that create the frames. This file has no <BODY> tag. Instead it uses a <FRAMESET> and </FRAMESET> tag pair; and nested within that pair are <FRAME> tags that describe each individual frame and, perhaps, more sets of the <FRAMESET> </FRAMESET> tag pairs.

A <FRAMESET> </FRAMESET> tag pair is used to split the browser window into columns or rows, for instance:

```
<FRAMESET COLS="50%,50%">
<FRAMESET>
```

This means "split the window into two columns, each 50 percent of the original window size." Actually this is not enough; unless we tell the browser what to put into each frame, we'll get a blank window. So we add <FRAME> tags:

Example 15.1

```
<FRAMESET COLS="50%,50%">
<FRAME SRC="15-1A.HTM">
<FRAME SRC="15-1B.HTM">
<FRAMESET>
```

You can see the result of this in Figure 15-1, and in the Online Companion. The first file, 15-1A.HTM is placed in the first column (the leftmost column), while 15-1B.HTM is placed in the second.

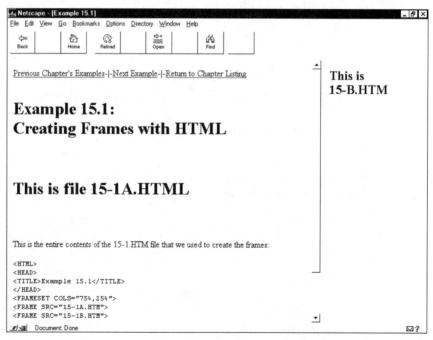

Figure 15-1: *Creating frames in HTML is quick and easy. This took four lines to create.*

Remember, the contents of the first file does not appear in the Web browser. In fact, here is the entire contents of that file:

```
<HTML>
<HEAD>
<TITLE>Example 15.1</TITLE>
</HEAD>
<FRAMESET COLS="75%,25%">
<FRAME SRC="15-1A.HTM">
<FRAME SRC="15-1B.HTM">
</FRAMESET>
</HTML>
```

The file does two things: it creates the frames, and it provides its <TITLE> to the browser. That's it. Don't bother putting any text in the document, as it won't appear in the browser. The only visible text will be the text from the two files in the SRC= attributes.

Now, here's a slightly more complicated frame setup. This time we have a nested <FRAMESET>:

Example 15.2

```
<HTML>
<HEAD>
<TITLE>Example 15.2</TITLE>
</HEAD>
<FRAMESET COLS="75%,25%">
    <FRAME SRC="15-2A.HTM">
    <FRAMESET ROWS="50%,50%">
      <FRAME SRC="15-2B.HTM">
      <FRAME SRC="15-2C.HTM">
    </FRAMESET>
</FRAMESET>
</HTML>
```

First we split the window into two columns, as before. Then we specified the document, 15-2A.HTM, that should go in the first frame (the leftmost). Then we nested another frameset; this time we are creating two rows. Where do these rows go? Well, we already filled the first column, so these rows go in the second column. Next we specify which documents go in those rows; 15-2B.HTM will go in the top row (because it appears first), then 15-2C.HTM will go in the bottom row.

Notice that you specify what goes where by its line position. You work from left to right when working with columns, and top to bottom when working with rows. Think of it like this: when you enter a <FRAMESET> tag you are stating how many positions there will be within the frameset ("50%,50%" means two positions, each taking up 50 percent of the space available; "40%,20%,40%" means three positions of different sizes, and so on). Immediately after the <FRAMESET> tag you begin filling the positions; in each position you must specify either another frameset, or a frame (<FRAME>). The first <FRAMESET> or <FRAME> tag defines the first position (leftmost or top), the second defines the second position, and so on.

TIP

As with JavaScript, it's a good idea to indent lines when creating frames, so you can quickly see how frames and framesets are nested below other framesets.

There are a variety of things you can do with frames by entering attributes into the <FRAME> tag.

Frame Property	Description
NAME="window_name"	Assigns a name to the frame so it can be targeted by links in other documents (normally frames in the same document) using the TARGET= attribute.
MARGINWIDTH="value"	This allows you to control the size of the left and right frame margins.
MARGINHEIGHT="value"	Controls the size of the upper and lower frame margins.
SCROLLING="yes|no|auto"	Adds a scroll bar to the window (by default you get a scroll bar if it's needed).
NORESIZE	Stops the user from changing frame sizes; by default the user can change the frame sizes (by dragging the margins).

GETTING OUT OF FRAMES

If you have a normal link within a frame and you click on the link you load the referenced document into that frame. What if you want to break out of the frame system, and load a document into the entire window? There are a couple of ways to do this, using the TARGET= attribute of the anchor tag. You can use either of these methods:

```
<A HREF="15-1.htm" TARGET="_top">Previous Example</A>
<A HREF="15-1.htm" TARGET="_parent">Previous Example</A>
```

In the first case, TARGET="_top", all the frames in the window are replaced with the targeted document (in this example, with 15-1.htm). In the second case, all the frames in the frameset holding the document that contains this link are replaced with the referenced document. If this is a nested frameset, then the parent frameset is unaffected. On the other hand, if there's only one frameset in the window, _top and _parent are, in effect, the same thing.

There's much more to learn about creating frames, but that's all we're going to cover here. If you want to learn more about frames, go to http://home.netscape.com/assist/net_sites/frames.html, or go the Netscape site at http://home.netscape.com and search for the word *frames*.

FRAMES ARE OBJECTS

As far as JavaScript is concerned, each frame in a frameset is an object. In addition, each frame is a property of the window object (or of another frame object). Frame objects can be used in virtually the same way as window objects (see Chapter 14, "Controlling Windows & Documents With JavaScript), with a few exceptions. You can think of a frame as a "subwindow," with fewer properties than a true window property (in particular, the defaultStatus, history, opener, and status properties all belong to the parent). Here, then, are the frame properties:

Frame Property	Description
document	The currently displayed document. (This property is also an object in its own right.)
frame	A subframe—a frame within the current frame.
frames array	An array that lists the child frames within this frame. (The parent window object also has a frames array.)
length	The number of frames within this frame.
name	The frame's name (the NAME attribute in the <FRAME> tag).
parent	A synonym for the parent window that contains this frame.
self	A synonym for the current frame.
window	A synonym for the current frame.

As for methods, frame objects have the same methods as window objects: `clearTimeout()` and `setTimeout()`. As we saw in Chapter 14, `clearTimeout()` is used to cancel `setTimeout()` or to stop it from working. The `setTimeout` method waits a specified number of milliseconds, then runs the instructions in its parentheses. You can review these in Chapter 14.

THE FRAMES ARRAY

The `window` object has another frame-related property, the `frames` array. Actually the array may also be a property of a `frame` object, if that `frame` object contains subframes. The array is a list of frames and, as with other arrays, allows you to refer to a `frame` using an index number: [0] for the first frame, [1] for the second, and so on.

REFERRING TO FRAMES

You can refer to a particular frame by name—if it has one, or by reference to the parent and the array index of that frame. For example, let's say you are writing a script that will appear inside the first frame (parent.frames[0]), and you want to refer to the third frame. You can call this parent.frames[2]; in other words, the third frame of the parent. (Remember, programmers count from 0! The first frame is 0, the second is 1, the third frame is 2, and so on.)

Let's assume that the third frame was named frame2 (using the tag <FRAME NAME="frame2">). You could then refer to this as parent.frame2.

For instance, we've created the following frames:

Example 15.3

```
<FRAMESET COLS="40%,20%,20%,20%">
<FRAME SRC=15-3a.htm NAME="frame1">
<FRAME SRC=15-3b.htm NAME="frame2">
<FRAME SRC=15-3c.htm NAME="frame3">
<FRAME SRC=15-3d.htm NAME="frame4">
</FRAMESET>
```

TIP

You can see in the <FRAME> tags that we've counted from 1 up. These are the frame names—you can call them whatever you want. The frames *array, though, will count from 0 up, without asking you what you prefer!*

As you can see, we have four frames within the frameset, each holding a different document. Notice that each <FRAME> tag has a NAME= attribute; we've given each of the frames a name. You can see what this looks like in Figure 15-2.

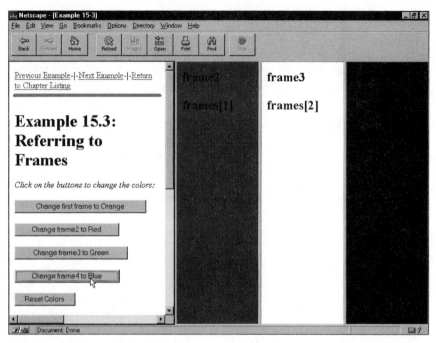

Figure 15-2: *Here are our four frames. You can use the buttons to change the colors.*

The first document, in the first frame, contains a number of buttons. (We won't bother looking at the other three documents, as they contain no JavaScript. They are little more than placeholders.) Here are the buttons we used:

```
<FORM>
<INPUT TYPE="button" VALUE="Change first frame to Orange"
onclick="parent.frames[0].document.bgColor='orange'"><P>
<INPUT TYPE="button" VALUE="Change frame2 to Red"
onclick="parent.frames[1].document.bgColor='red'"><P>
<INPUT TYPE="button" VALUE="Change frame3 to Green"
onclick="parent.frame3.document.bgColor='green'"><P>
<INPUT TYPE="button" VALUE="Change frame4 to Blue"
onclick="top.frames[3].document.bgColor='blue'"><P>
<INPUT TYPE="button" VALUE="Reset Colors" onclick="reset()">
</FORM>
```

The first three buttons change the background colors of the documents in the frames. We have referred to the frames in two different ways, however:

```
onClick="top.frames[3].document.bgColor='blue'"
```

This means, "when the user clicks on the button, change the background color (bgColor) in the document in the fourth frame in the frames array held by the top window to blue." Remember, we're using the frames array and counting from 0, so 3 is actually the fourth frame. Here's another way you can refer to a frame:

```
onClick="parent.frame3.document.bgColor='green'"
```

This time we are modifying frame3. This is the name we gave to the third frame in the third <FRAME> tag. The last button calls the reset( ) function:

```
function reset()    {
    self.document.bgColor="white"
    top.frames[1].document.bgColor="white"
    top.frames[2].document.bgColor="white"
    top.frames[3].document.bgColor="white"
}
```

This function changes all the colors back to white again. Notice that this time we used self.document.bgColor to change the color in the first frame. As the button is in the first frame, it's quicker to refer to the frame as self. We could also have used window.document.bgColor or current.document.bgColor. In fact, we could have just used document.bgColor, as we're referring here to the current window. Although they are optional, you may want to use self or current to make your scripts a little easier to read.

WHAT ABOUT TOP?

But how about top.document.bgColor? Couldn't we use that to set the background color of the first document? Well, no, because top refers to the window containing the frameset. There is no document in top; top contains frames which contain documents, but top itself cannot hold a document. It holds the framesets, which hold their documents, but top doesn't have its own document.

To demonstrate this, try the following example, in which we have three buttons that address `top`:

Example 15.4

```
<FORM>
<INPUT TYPE="button" VALUE="Change top frame to Orange"
onclick="top.document.bgColor='orange'"><P>
<INPUT TYPE="button" VALUE="Change Status Bar"→
onclick="top.status='Ah ha, you've just changed the status
bar.'"><P>
 <INPUT TYPE="button" VALUE="Change Status Bar:→
top.frames[2].status=" onclick="top.frames[2].status='And→
again.'">
</FORM>
```

The first button can't do anything. The `top` window has no viewable document, so it can't change the color; `top` is not the same as `self` or `window`. The second button *will* work, however. The `top` window has a status bar, so `top.status=` will work. However, so would `top.frames[2].status=` (see the last button); changing the status property of any frame changes the status bar message. (We're using `status`, which is a temporary status-bar message; it will disappear when you move the mouse pointer away from the button.)

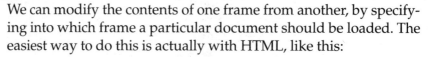

CHANGING A FRAME'S CONTENTS

We can modify the contents of one frame from another, by specifying into which frame a particular document should be loaded. The easiest way to do this is actually with HTML, like this:

```
<A HREF="15-5b.htm" TARGET="frame2">Change Frame2</A>
```

You simply name the frame using the `TARGET=` attribute. When the user clicks on this link, the document named `15-5b.htm` is loaded into `frame2`. For instance, here's an example in the Online Companion:

Example 15.5

```
<A HREF="15-5b.htm" TARGET="frame2">Change frame2</A><BR>
<A HREF="15-5b.htm" TARGET="frame3">Change frame3</A><BR>
<A HREF="15-5b.htm" TARGET="frame4">Change frame4</A><BR>
```

Click on each link, and you'll see the text in the appropriate frame change (see Figure 15-3).

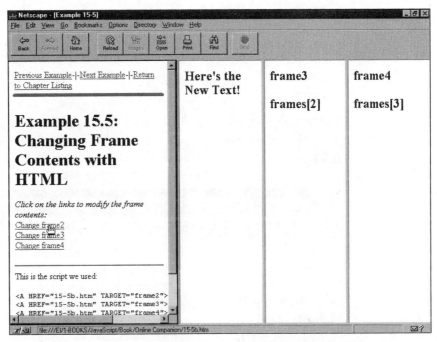

Figure 15-3: *The easiest way to change contents is by using HTML.*

But we can also write to a frame using JavaScript in much the same way that you can write to windows (see Chapter 14, "Controlling Windows & Documents With JavaScript"). For instance, take a look at this script:

Example 15.6

```
<SCRIPT LANGUAGE="JAVASCRIPT">
<!--
function new1()     {
    parent.frame2.document.write("<P>Here's some more text→
for you...and some more. Yes, and more, and yet more<BR>")
    }
function new2()     {
```

```
    parent.frame3.document.write("Making predictions is very→
difficult, especially about the future.<BR>")
    }
function new3()    {
    parent.frame4.document.write("Um...what else can I say?→
Oh, I know, I'll omit the line break and see what happens.")
    }
//-->
</SCRIPT>
```

The Online Companion example has three buttons to run these three functions. You can see in Figure 15-4 what happens when you use them.

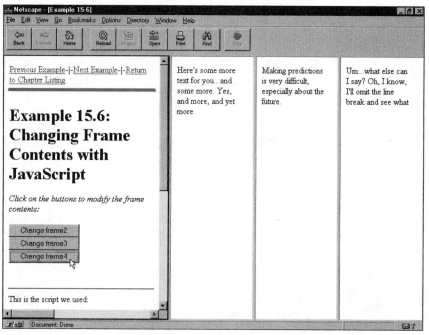

Figure 15-4: *You can write from one frame to another using* `document.write`.

Notice that there's part of the last document missing. Remember the problem with writing documents (see Chapter 14)? In the last function we forgot the <BR> tag, so some of the text was not written.

Of course we should really be using the more formal method for writing these things, like this:

Example 15.7

```
function new1()    {
    parent.frame2.document.open()
    parent.frame2.document.write("<P>Here's some more text→
for you...and some more. Yes, and more, and yet more<BR>")→
parent.frame2.document.close()
    }
function new2()    {
    parent.frame3.document.open()
    parent.frame3.document.write("Making predictions is very→
difficult, especially about the future.<BR>")→
parent.frame3.document.close()
    }
function new3()    {
    parent.frame4.document.open()
    parent.frame4.document.write("Um...what else can I say?
Oh, I know, I'll omit the line break and see what→
happens.") parent.frame4.document.close()
    }
```

This time we used document.open() and document.close(), and the text was written to the frames correctly.

CALLING FUNCTIONS IN OTHER FRAMES

You can also call functions that are inside documents in other frames. For instance, in our next example, we have placed the same functions in the first frame. But we now have a document in the fourth frame with buttons to call those functions:

Example 15.8

```
<FORM>
<INPUT TYPE="BUTTON" VALUE="Change frame2"
onclick="parent.frame1.new1()"><BR>
<INPUT TYPE="BUTTON" VALUE="Change frame3"
onclick="parent.frame1.new2()"><BR>
<INPUT TYPE="BUTTON" VALUE="Change frame4"
onclick="parent.frame1.new3()"><BR>
</FORM>
```

You can see this in action in Figure 15-5. As you can see, we are calling the same functions, but we have to tell the `onclick` event handler *where* the functions are: `parent.frame1`.

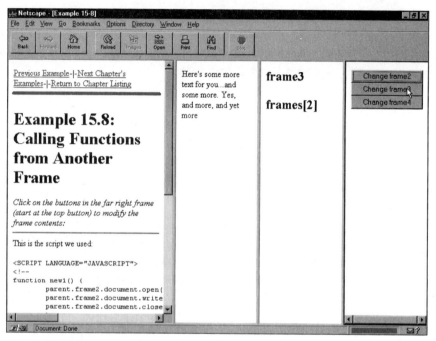

Figure 15-5: *This example uses buttons in the right-most frame to call functions in the left-most frame's document.*

MOVING ON

Working with frames is really quite straightforward; it's just like working with other windows, except that those "windows" are all together within the same "body." In fact, as we mentioned before, `frame` objects are really almost the same as `window` objects.

The next thing we're going to look at is working with forms. This is one of the most important uses for JavaScript. You can get Java-Script to do things for you on the user's computer that before would have required the use of a CGI script on the server. For instance, you can use JavaScript to search for information held in arrays within your document. You can also use them to verify that the user is entering the correct information into the form's text elements.

CHAPTER 16

Forms & JavaScript

We've already worked with forms quite a bit throughout this book. What we haven't done, however, is look closely at how we are passing information from a form to a script. In order to do that we need to understand the way that forms fit into the object hierarchy, so we'll begin by going over that quickly.

FORM OBJECTS

A form object is a property of the document object. There's also a forms array—another property of the document object. As you already know, the forms array is essentially a list of forms within the document that allows you to refer to a form by index number; forms[0] is the first form in the document, forms[1] is the second, and so on. (By first we mean closest to the top, of course. We count from the top down.)

Form objects have their own properties, of course:

Object	Property
action	A string that contains the destination URL for a form submission.
button	A button in a form, created using the <INPUT TYPE="BUTTON"> tag. A property of the document object. (This property is also an object in its own right.)
checkbox	A checkbox, created using the <INPUT TYPE="CHECKBOX"> tag. A property of the document object. (This property is also an object in its own right.)
elements array	An array that lists form elements in the order in which they appear in the form.
encoding	The MIME encoding of the form.
hidden	A hidden (<INPUT TYPE="HIDDEN">) element in a form. A property of the form object. (This property is also an object in its own right.)
length	The number of elements in the form
method	How data inputted in a form is sent to the server; the METHOD= attribute in a <FORM> tag.
radio	A radio button set (<INPUT TYPE="RADIO">) in a form. A property of the form object. (This property is also an object in its own right.)
reset	A reset button (<INPUT TYPE="RESET">) in a form. A property of the form object. (This property is also an object in its own right.)
select	A selection box (<SELECT>) in a form. A property of the form object. (This property is also an object in its own right.)
submit	A submit button (<INPUT TYPE="SUBMIT">) in a form. A property of the form object. (This property is also an object in its own right.)
target	The name of the window that displays responses after a form has been submitted.

text	A text element in a form (<INPUT TYPE="TEXT">). A property of the form object. (This property is also an object in its own right.)
textarea	A textarea element (<TEXTAREA>) in a form. A property of the form object. (This property is also an object in its own right.)

As you can see, a number of these properties are objects them-selves; each element within a form is an object, for instance.

Forms have one method: submit( ). This submits the form. It's the equivalent of clicking on the Submit button. In effect, it pro-vides a way for your scripts to "click" the Submit button. Forms also have one event handler, onsubmit. Although this event handler operates when the user clicks on the submit button, the event han-dler is actually placed within the <FORM> tag (not within the <INPUT TYPE="SUBMIT"> tag). We saw an example of this event handler in use in Chapter 12, "JavaScript Events—When Are Actions Carried Out?"

Note, however, that the elements within the form have event handlers, too:

Element	Handler
button (<INPUT TYPE="BUTTON">)	onclick
checkbox (<INPUT TYPE="CHECKBOX">)	onclick
hidden element (<INPUT TYPE="HIDDEN">)	none
radio (<INPUT TYPE="RADIO">)	onclick
reset button (<INPUT TYPE="RESET">)	onclick
selection list (<SELECT>)	onblur, onchange, onfocus
submit button (<INPUT TYPE="SUBMIT">)	onclick
text box (<INPUT TYPE="TEXT">)	onblur, onchange, onfocus, onselect
textarea (<TEXTAREA>)	onblur, onchange, onfocus, onselect

Passing Information From Forms

By now you've probably got the idea of how to address something using the object hierarchy, and working with forms is no different. If you want to refer to an element in the form, you can use the element name, or you can use the `elements` array. To refer to a form, you can use the `form` name or the `forms` array. For instance, you might refer to a `form` element like this:

    document.form1.radio1

or like this:

    document.forms[0].radio1

or like this:

    document.forms[0].elements[0]

One thing we haven't really discussed yet is how information is passed from a form to a function. Actually we've done this a lot throughout the book's examples, but we need to come back and explain exactly how that information is passed from forms.

For instance, take a look at this form:

Example 16.1

```
<FORM>
<input type="text" size="30"><P>
<input type="button" value="What Did You Type"
onclick="What(this.form)">
</FORM>
```

A simple form with a text box and a button. Note that we haven't named either element—we'll use the element's array to refer to them. When the user clicks on the button, the `onclick` event handler calls the `What()` function. Notice that in the parentheses we typed `this.form`, which means "pass a reference concerning this form to the function named `What()`." The function can then use the reference to retrieve the information it needs from the form. You can see it in action in Figure 16-1.

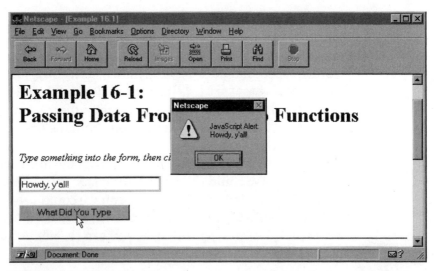

Figure 16-1: *Clicking on the button passes the text from the form to a function, which is then displayed in an Alert box.*

Now, as in most of the examples in this book, we've created functions something like this:

```
function functionname(form)]
```

What does `form` mean? Does it mean "this information is coming from a form?"; "treat this information in a special manner reserved for forms?"; "warning, this stuff comes from a `form` object?" Actually it means nothing so complicated. It's simply a name. In fact, here's the function we used in the Online Companion example:

```
function What(gertrude)    {
    alert(gertrude.elements[0].value)
}
```

What's `gertrude`? Just a name like any other—such as `form`. The text within the parentheses is simply a name. It means, in this case, this function is being passed some information, and we're going to refer to that information as `gertrude`." In most of our scripts we use the word `form` because it's simple and descriptive, but we want you to understand that there's nothing magic about `form`.

So what does this function do? It opens an Alert box and displays the value held by the `elements[0]` object—the first element in the form. That element is a text box, so the `value` is whatever you've typed into the box. Remember, gertrude is just a name; so `gertrude.elements[0].value` means "look at the information that was passed to this function—information that we are going to refer to as `gertrude`—look for information about the first element, and grab the `value`."

Incidentally, although we haven't given the form a name, we could have. We could call it `fred`, for instance (`<FORM NAME="fred">`). Still, that doesn't mean we could use `fred.elements[0].value`. Nor could we have used `forms[0].elements[0].value`, as you can see in this example:

Example 16.2

```
function What1(gertrude)   {
    alert(fred.elements[0].value)
}
function What2(gertrude)   {
    alert(forms[0].elements[0].value)
}
function What3(gertrude)   {
    alert(gertrude.elements[0].value)
}
```

We put three buttons in our Online Companion example to call these three functions. They do not refer to the objects quite correctly because we are not using `gertrude`, and nor do they use the full object hierarchy—`document.` is missing (we'll look at this next). You may get an error depending on your browser. If you click on the first button to call `What1()`, you may get an error message saying *fred is not defined*. Click on the second button to call `What2()`, and you may see *forms is not defined*. Only the third button works consistently, because we are referring to the form using the correct name—the one we put in parentheses, `gertrude`. So although all these methods of referring to the form may work on your browser, the first two are not, strictly speaking, correct, and should be avoided.

You Don't Need to Pass a Reference

But you don't need to pass a reference at all. You can simply refer to the form and its elements by the full name, adding the `document.` part. For example:

Example 16.3

```
function What1()    {
    alert(document.fred.elements[0].value)
}
function What2()    {
    alert(document.forms[0].elements[0].value)
}
```

As you can see, this time we are not passing information—there's nothing in the parentheses. In fact, take a look at these buttons:

```
<FORM NAME="fred">
<input type="text" size="30"><P>
<input type="button" value="document.fred.elements[0].value"
onclick="What1()"><P>
<input type="button"
value="document.forms[0].elements[0].value"
onclick="What2()"><P>
</FORM>
```

Notice that we called the function, but haven't placed anything in parentheses. So why do we bother passing `this.form` sometimes, if we really don't need to pass the reference? Well, it can make it easier by allowing us to type less. We can write a single function that is called from more than one form, each form passing the relevant information—using `this.form`—to the function.

In some cases this isn't appropriate, though; for example, if the function is operating on several forms at once, or operating on a different form from the one it's called from even, you may want to use the full element names.

PASSING INFORMATION BETWEEN FORMS

Let's see an example of how we might pass information from one form to another:

Example 16.4

```
function Pass()     {
    document.joe.elements[0].value =→
document.fred.elements[0].value
    }
```

Then we have these buttons:

```
<FORM NAME="fred">
<input type="text" size="30"><P>
</FORM>
<I>Now click on this button in the second form:</I>
<FORM>
<input type="button" value="Pass the Text" onclick="Pass()">
</FORM>
<I>You'll see the text in the third form:</I>
<FORM NAME="joe">
<input type="text" size="30"><P>
</FORM>
```

We've actually got three separate forms here. Type something into the first form, fred; click on the button, and the text is passed to joe, as you can see in Figure 16-2. Really very simple.

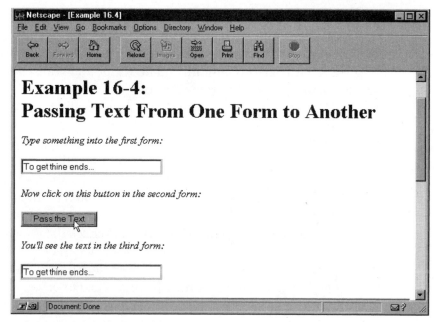

Figure 16-2: *Clicking on the button passes the text from the first text box to the second.*

Using simple scripts such as this, plus all the various techniques we've seen earlier in this book, you can see how to manipulate the data in forms. You can take data from one form, carry out calculations, pass it back to the same form or another form, and so on.

FORM VALIDATION

One big issue when working with forms is form validation. How can you be sure that what the user typed in makes sense? Until JavaScript, there was only one way to know—the user would submit the data, then a script at the server would check it to see if it was okay. If it wasn't, a document would be sent to the user's browser saying that the form is incorrectly filled out.

That system is a nuisance, for a few reasons. First, it takes up server resources—wouldn't it be better to make sure that the form was okay *before* the server dealt with it. Also, it's irritating to the user. He clicks on Submit, and he waits, and waits, and waits. Then he's told that he has screwed up.

With JavaScript you can create simple validation scripts for each field, then run the scripts before the data from the form is submitted. You could validate the form when the user moves from one element to another (using `onblur`), or when the user clicks on the Submit button (by using `onsubmit` in the `<FORM>` tag). If the form validation fails—and returns false to `onsubmit`—then the data is not sent back to the server.

Also, you can use form validation to check data that will be used by the scripts themselves. As we'll see in Chapter 18, "The Area Code Application," our Area Code program does everything internally— there's no communication with the server. However, we use validation to make sure that the user is entering information that is valid.

How do we validate data, then? Well, you've already seen the basic components. We take data from a form element—usually a text box—and pass it to a function. The function then checks that the data is valid (that it is within a range of valid ranges), and, based on what it finds, performs an action. For example, you may wish to check that a user types a number and not letters, which would be meaningless in a calculation and may cause an error. The function could then display an Alert, warning the user that the data is incorrect.

CHECKING A NUMBER

We're going to look at the input in a text box, check that the number is within a certain range (100 to 200 inclusive), and then decide what to do; either display an Alert box telling the user that he input the wrong number, or pass the number to another form. We've used the same `Pass()` function—well, with a few additions.

Example 16.5

```
function Pass()     {
var nCheck = document.fred.elements[0].value
        if (nCheck >= 100)          {
                if (nCheck >=201) {
                        alert("You entered a number that's too→
high. You must enter a number within the range of 100 to→
200 inclusive.")
                }
                else {
                        document.joe.elements[0].value =→
document.fred.elements[0].value
                }
        }
        else {
                alert("You entered a number that's too low.→
You must enter a number within the range of 100 to 200→
inclusive.")
                }
}
```

We used the same buttons in our Online Companion for this example as in the previous example: the button called Pass(). So what does Pass() do? Well, we started by taking the value typed into the text box and placing it in a variable calls nCheck. Next we started an if statement. The first line looks at the value in nCheck. It checks to see if the value is greater than or equal to 100. If it is, the number may be okay—it's above the lower limit, after all. So if the number is 100 or more, we move to the next line, which checks to see if it's 201 or more. If it is, then it's out of bounds—it's supposed to be 100, 200, or anything in-between. So if this line evaluates to true, we carry out the next instruction, which is to display an Alert box (see Figure 16-3).

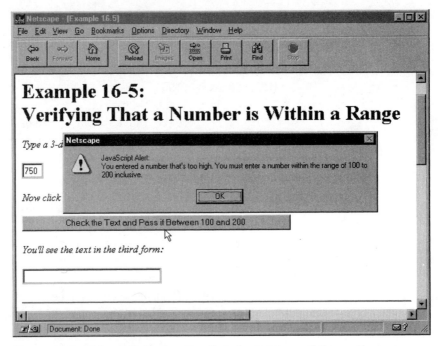

Figure 16-3: *We've called a function that checked to see if the number was okay—but it was too high.*

If the line evaluates to `false`, though, it means the number is okay, so we carry out the `else` clause:
`document.joe.elements[0].value = document.fred.elements[0].value.`

This, of course, takes the value and passes it to the other text box, as we saw earlier.

And the final `else` clause? That's related to the first `if` statement, of course, and is used if the number is less than 100. It displays an Alert box with a different message.

All quite simple—except there's a problem. Try typing non-numeric characters into that text box, and then click on the button. You'll get an error message.

Is It a Number?

Well, we'd better check to see if the text is numeric. If it's not, this script crashes. So here's a new version:

Example 16.6

```
function Pass()     {
var sCheck = document.fred.elements[0].value
nCheck = parseInt(sCheck, 10)
    if (nCheck <=99 || nCheck == 0)       {
        alert("This is not a 3-digit number.")
        }
    else {
        if (nCheck >= 100)           {
                if (nCheck >=201) {
                        alert("You entered a number that's→
too high. You must enter a number within the range of 100→
to 200 inclusive.")
                }
                else {
                        document.joe.elements[0].value = nCheck
                }
        }
    }
}
```

We started this script a little differently. This time we placed the text into sCheck (rather than nCheck). Strictly speaking the stuff coming from the text box is text, not a number (text boxes contain text strings, remember). Then we added nCheck = parseInt(sCheck). Now, you'll remember parseInt() from Chapter 7, "More on Functions." This function looks at the value in the parentheses, and tries to extract a number from it. In our example, parseInt is evaluating sCheck, which is whatever the user typed into the text box (the 10 simply means "try to extract a number in base 10 from the string"). And we're passing the value to another variable, nCheck. Now, if it can't extract a number, it passes 0. If the user types a few numbers followed by non-numeric characters, it throws those characters away and keeps the numbers; and if the user types non-numeric characters followed by numbers, it throws it all away. For example:

```
12egty = 12
12 = 12
agj12 = 0
```

So we end up with a number, or maybe 0. Then we check the result. The if statement looks at the number to see if it's less than or equal to 99—as it will be if the user has not typed three digits. It also checks to see if the number is equal to 0. If parseInt is unable to extract a number from sCheck, it will set nCheck to 0.

So we need to check to see what nCheck holds. If it holds 99 or less, or if it holds 0, we see the Alert box. Otherwise (if it's 100 or more), we move on to the else statement. Why are we checking to see if it's less than 99, *and* if it holds 0? Isn't 0 less than 99? Well, yes it is, but unless we did it this way the script simply wouldn't work correctly. If the user types letters instead of a number, parseInt appears to pass 0 (if you added alert(nCheck) at this point in the script the Alert box would display 0), but it's not a true 0. The script apparently won't recognize the contents of nCheck as being less than 99. It will, however, recognize that nCheck contains 0. Weird, but true.

Now, the else clause holds the rest of the function that we've already seen, with one exception. We changed this:

```
document.joe.elements[0].value =→
document.fred.elements[0].value
```

to this:

```
document.joe.elements[0].value = nCheck
```

Why did we make this change? Well, assume, for instance, that the user typed in 213khk;jh. The parseInt() function would evaluate this to 213, which is a valid number within our range. Then, using the old script, we would copy the text from the first text box

(213khk;jh) into the second text box. Instead, we've copied the text from nCheck, the evaluated number, into the check box. So we decided that if the user typed three numbers followed by garbage, we would accept the numbers.

How Long Is It?

Another condition you may want to check is length: how long is the text that the user has typed? In fact it may be a good idea to check the number of characters typed in the example we've just seen. Here's how you could do that:

Example 16.7

```
function Length()   {
var sCheck = document.fred.elements[0].value
    if (sCheck.length > 3) {
        alert("You have typed too many characters")
    }
    else {
    Pass()
        }
}
```

We've added a new function (the other one was getting a bit long and complicated); and we changed the button to call this function instead of Pass().

We declared a variable called sCheck again, and gave it the contents of the text box. Then we have a simple if statement to check the number of characters in sCheck; sCheck.length > 3 is checking the length property of the sCheck object (remember, a string variable is a string object). If it's greater than 3 characters, an Alert box is opened. If it's not, the else() clause calls Pass() and we continue checking the number.

Of course with a very slight modification, we can check to make sure that the number's neither too long, nor too short.

Example 16.8

```
function Length()  {
var sCheck = document.fred.elements[0].value
    if (sCheck.length > 3 || sCheck.length < 3) {
      alert("You must type 3 characters: no more, no less")
    }
    else {
    Pass()
        }
    }
```

The if (sCheck.length > 3 || sCheck.length < 3) bit checks to see if the string is greater than three characters, or less than three characters.

MOVING ON

We'll come back to form validation later, in Chapter 18, "The Area Code Application." In that chapter you'll see an example of validation integrated into an actual application.

For now, though, we're going to move on to the next chapter, "Communicating With the User," where you can learn more about how to send messages to the user.

CHAPTER 17

Communicating With the User

JavaScript allows you to create interactive Web pages—rather than simply providing static information that the user reads or views. Your pages can ask the user to take an active role, to "make things happen." So communicating with the user is an important part of working with JavaScript. We've already seen many examples of how you can communicate with the user, from using the Alert box to putting messages into the status bar. In this chapter we want to put it all together and see how these different methods can be employed.

First, here are a number of different ways that you can communicate with the user:

- The Alert box—shows the user a message.

- The Confirm dialog box—shows a message, and asks the user to make a two-option choice.

- The Prompt dialog box—shows a message, asks the user to make a two-option choice and, if choosing the OK option, asks the user to type information.

- Mix and match—by using a mix of different boxes, you can make more complicated decision "trees."

- Default status-bar messages—display a message in the status bar.

- Status-bar messages—display a message in the status bar that only appears under specific circumstances (when the user points at a link, or makes a choice in a Prompt or Confirm box, for instance).

- Write information to text boxes and textareas.

- Open secondary windows and display messages.

We've already seen many of these individual components in action (we've used the Alert box dozens of times, for instance), but let's take a look at a few ways that you might communicate with your readers.

INCORPORATING USER INFORMATION

You can collect information from users in a couple of ways: they can type the information into forms, or into a Prompt dialog box. Once you have the information stored in variables or simply held in the form itself, you can use it any way you want. For instance, you might have a user fill information into a form, then click on a button at the bottom of the page to open a new document and incorporate the information that was typed into the form in a new document. In fact, let's see how that might be done. We created this form in which the user types information:

Example 17.1

```
<FORM>
First Name: <input type="text" size="30"><BR>
Last Name: <input type="text" size="30"><BR>
Address: <input type="text" size="30"><BR>
City: <input type="text" size="30"><BR>
State/Province/Region: <input type="text" size="30"><BR>
Zip/Postal Code: <input type="text" size="30"><BR>
Country: <input type="text" size="30"><BR>
<input type="button" value="Next Page"
onclick="Use(this.form)">
</FORM>
```

As you can see, there are a number of text boxes, plus a button. The button uses an onclick event handler to call the Use( ) function. Here is that function:

```
function Use(form) {
    var sFname = form.elements[0].value
    var sLname = form.elements[1].value
    var sAddr = form.elements[2].value
    var sCity = form.elements[3].value
    var sState = form.elements[4].value
    var sZip = form.elements[5].value
    var sCou= form.elements[6].value
    if (confirm("Let's just check that we got the right→
information, shall we? Your name is " + sFname + " " +→
sLname + ". Your address is " + sAddr + ", " + sCity + ", "→
+ sState + ", " + sZip + ", " + sCou + ". Is that all→
correct?"))
    {
        alert("We've open an alert box if you→ click on OK,→
but you could do anything you want, such as move to another→
page using→ location='url'.")
    }
}
```

This is really quite simple. We've taken the information typed by the user and placed that information into variables. Then we've displayed a Confirm dialog box that shows the user what he typed and asks for confirmation, as you can see in Figure 17-1. If the user clicks on OK, the Alert box opens. We could do anything at this point, though, such as move to another page or call another function that uses the data.

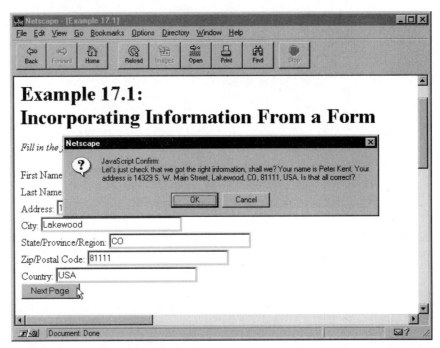

Figure 17-1: *We are communicating with the user; we've taken the user's words and asked the user to confirm that they are correct.*

USING THE PROMPT BOX

Another way to collect information is with the Prompt dialog box. Rather than giving the user a form to fill in, you can ask the user a series of questions, one by one, as in the following example:

Example 17.2

```
<SCRIPT LANGUAGE="JAVASCRIPT">
<!--
var sFname = prompt("What is your first name?","")
var sLname = prompt("What is your last name?","")
```

```
var sAddr = prompt("What is your street address?","")
var sCity = prompt("What is your city?","")
var sState = prompt("What is your state, province, or→
region?","")
var sZip = prompt("What is your zip or postal code?","")
var sCou= prompt("What is your country?","")
//-->
</SCRIPT>
```

We put this script in the HEAD of the document, so it runs before the document is loaded. We're going to write this information to the document itself. So we couldn't put this script in a function and call it with the onload event handler, as that would run the script after the document has loaded. Notice the prompt( ) method. We are taking the value from the Prompt dialog box and placing it in a variable. We now have two things in parentheses: the text that will appear in the Prompt dialog box as a question followed by "", which means "don't use a default value in the text box." (Take this out and you'll see undefined in the text box.)

Next we have this in the BODY of the document:

```
Now we've collected all that information, we can write it to
the document if we wish:<P>
<SCRIPT LANGUAGE="JAVASCRIPT">
<!-
document.write("Let's just check that we got the right→
information, shall we? Your name is "
+ sFname + " " + sLname + ". Your address is " + sAddr→
+ ", " + sCity + ", " + sState + ", " + sZip + ", " + sCou→
+ ". Is that all correct?")
//-->
</SCRIPT>
```

We're simply writing all variable contents to the document using document.write; you can see the result in Figure 17-2.

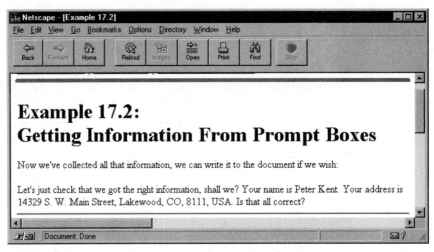

Figure 17-2: *This time we collected information from the user via Prompt dialog boxes, then used the information in the document.*

STATUS BAR MESSAGES

There are three forms of status bar messages. First, there's the type that we are all used to and which we have no control over: those inserted by the browser. When you point at a link, or load a Web page, the browser displays information in the status bar. It may be the URL of the link you are pointing at, or information about the progress of the document transfer.

Then there's something called the *default* status-bar message. This is a JavaScript feature that lets you set a message that will be displayed at any time that something else is not being displayed there. It's set using the `windows.defaultStatus` property.

Finally, there's a *temporary* status-bar message (also known as a *transient* or *priority* status-bar message). This is set using the `windows.status` property, and is a message that will appear for a short time—while the user points at a link, for instance.

DEFAULTSTATUS

We'll begin by setting the `defaultStatus` property. You can set this at any time: when the user loads the page, when the user clicks on a button to carry out some JavaScript operation, and so on. For instance, try something like this:

Example 17.3

```
defaultStatus = "Hello, how ya'll doing?"
```

TIP

After a document has finished loading, you'll see the `Document: Done` *message in the status bar. Often the defaultStatus message does not replace this* `Document: Done` *message until you move the mouse.*

In our Online Companion example we put this script in the HEAD. This message will appear as soon as the browser reads the HEAD—before it's even had a chance to load the remainder of the document. Of course you could also put this into the `onload` event handler, but then the message won't appear until after the document has loaded; or, you can combine both like this:

Example 17.4

```
<SCRIPT LANGUAGE="JAVASCRIPT">
<!--
defaultStatus = "Hold on, we're loading..."
//-->
</SCRIPT>
</HEAD>
<BODY onload="defaultStatus = 'Hello, how ya\'ll doing?'">
```

This displays *Hold on, we're loading…* when the document begins loading; then the *Hello, how ya'll doing?* message after it's finished. Of course if the page loads very quickly, you may never see the first message.

You can change the `defaultStatus` message at any time, in different ways. You could, for instance, change it when the user enters information into a form element, like this:

Example 17.5

```
<FORM>
Type something, then press Tab: <INPUT TYPE="TEXT" SIZE="30"
onblur="self.defaultStatus='Here\'s what you typed: ' +→
document.forms[0].elements[0].value"><P>
<INPUT TYPE="TEXT" SIZE="30">
</FORM>
```

We are using an `onblur` event handler here to set the `defaultStatus` value. Notice a couple of things. First, we haven't used simply `defaultStatus`, but `self.defaultStatus`. You may remember that when you refer to something in the object hierarchy from an event handler, you must include the `window` part (actually in this case we used `self`, which is a synonym for "current window").

We've also taken the information typed into the text box, along with some extra text (*Here\'s what you typed:*), and passed that to the status bar.

You can change the `defaultStatus` any way you want. Here are a couple more ways you can change it:

Example 17.6

```
<FORM>
<INPUT TYPE="BUTTON" VALUE="Change"
onclick="self.defaultStatus='Let\'s change the status→
message from this button!'">
</FORM>
<A HREF="nowhere" onmouseover="self.defaultStatus='Now from→
this link!'; return true">Or just point at this link (which→
doesn't go anywhere) to change the status message.</A>
```

This time we used an `onclick` event handler on a button to change the `defaultStatus`, and an `onmouseover` on the link. Notice anything strange about the link? First, we included `; return true` at the end of the message that we want to display. In theory you need this bit to make the `onmouseover` event handler work with `defaultStatus`. It works *without* this bit on some browsers, but it's safer to leave it in just in case it really is required for some other browsers.

Also, when you use this example in the Online Companion you'll find that it doesn't appear to work at first—you point at the link and you see the URL, not the message we are trying to set. It's not until you move the mouse away from the link that the status-bar message appears. Remember, we are setting `defaultStatus`, which is the message that appears when the browser doesn't want to display anything else. So when it wants to display the URL, you won't see the original message. Which brings us to the `status` message.

> **TIP**
>
> *How do you "cancel" a* `defaultStatus` *message? Simply write a blank* `defaultStatus` *message.*

WORKING WITH STATUS

The status message overrides other messages, but it is only temporary. It's commonly used to display a message when the user points at a link, like this:

Example 17.7

```
<A HREF="nowhere" onmouseover="self.status='This link takes→
you to ... '; return true">Point at the link to see another→
message.</A>
```

This is easy to do; simply use `onmouseover`, remembering to include `; return true` at the end (you definitely must include this in the case of the `status` property).

As we've discussed earlier, these status messages set on links can be a bit of a nuisance. You see a lot of it, because many people operate under the theory that "if you can, you should, and it's fun doing new stuff anyway." Think carefully, though, before you do it, and consider whether the benefits outweigh the possible irritation. And take a look at Chapter 12, "JavaScript Events—When Are Actions Carried Out?" for an example of when it really does make sense to put a message over the link, that is, to mask the link (see "onMouseOver").

Can we change `status` from elsewhere. Well, yes, but it rarely makes sense, because the message is temporary. For instance, you could put it on a button, like this:

Example 17.8

```
<FORM>
<INPUT TYPE="BUTTON" VALUE="Try to Change Status Bar"
onclick="self.status='You\'ll see this message until you→
move the mouse from the button.'">
</FORM>
```

You'll find when you click on the button, the new message appears and then, when you move the mouse, it disappears. Remember, it's only temporary.

> **TIP**
>
> *You can see an example of a more advanced status bar message—one that moves along the status bar—in Chapter 19, "Ready-to-Use Scripts."*

WRITING TO THE CURRENT PAGE

You'll remember that you can't write to the current page. Once the source HTML document has been loaded, trying to write to it won't add text to the display; instead the document will be cleared and a *new* document written. (In some browsers a bug may stop the new text from being written, but the old text will be cleared.) For instance, if we try this:

Example 17.9

```
function Rewrite() {
    document.open()
    document.write("Write this to the document<BR>")
    document.close()
}
//-->
```

What happens if we call this from within the document? The document is cleared, and the new text written to the document (click on Reload to come back).

There is a simple way around this problem, though—a way to write to a document without losing it. Write to a textarea. For instance, if you want to send messages to the user in some way without losing the document that the user is reading, you could write them to the text area. Try this, for instance:

Example 17.10

```
<FORM>
First Name: <input type="text" size="30"><BR>
Last Name: <input type="text" size="30"
onfocus="elements[7].value = s1 "><BR>
Address: <input type="text" size="30"
onfocus="elements[7].value = s2 "><BR>
City: <input type="text" size="30" onfocus="elements[7].value
= s3 "><BR>
State/Province/Region: <input type="text" size="30"
onfocus="elements[7].value = s4 "><BR>
Zip/Postal Code: <input type="text" size="30"
onfocus="elements[7].value = s5 "><BR>
Country: <input type="text" size="30"
onfocus="elements[7].value = s6 "><P>
<B>See the instructions here:</B><BR>
<TEXTAREA COLS="40" ROWS="2">Type your first name in the
text box.</TEXTAREA>
</FORM>
```

We created a form similar to one we saw earlier in this chapter. This time, though, we have a textarea at the bottom; we'll use this to display information about each field. Notice that we have the text *Type your first name in the text box* in the textarea to begin— we're using this script to move focus to the first text box when we load the file:

```
document.forms[0].elements[0].focus()
```

So the text in the textarea refers to the first text box. Then, we have a series of onfocus event handlers, such as this:

```
onFocus="elements[7].value = s4 "
```

In this case we are placing the contents of variable s4 into the 8th element within the current form, when the user moves focus to this text box. Here are the variables we are using (we defined them in the HEAD):

```
var s1 = "Type your last name here."
var s2 = "Type your street address."
var s3 = "Your city name, please."
var s4 = "Yes, yes, you know—state, province, etc."
var s5 = "Okay, zip or postal code."
var s6 = "Yep, now your country."
```

So each onfocus displays a different message within the textarea—each message related to the text box that focus is moving to—as you can see in Figure 17-3.

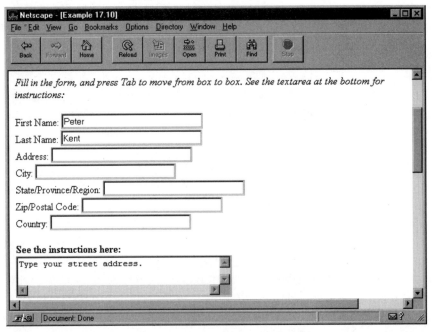

Figure 17-3: *Writing to the textarea provides a very simple way to communicate with a user.*

Writing to the textarea provides a very simple way to communicate with the user. This is a simple example, but you can get fancy and send messages to the user related to operations carried out by the JavaScript. You can use this system to carry out calculations and display the result, for instance.

> **TIP**
>
> *We used a textarea in this example, but we could just as easily have used a text box, instead. The textarea has the advantage of providing more space. However, remember that there's a problem with the line breaks that must be placed in long messages. (See Chapter 11, "More About Built-in Objects," to find out how to set the line breaks so that the correct break is used regardless of the browser being used to view the document. We'll be looking at this again in the following chapter, too.)*

MOVING ON

Tired of theory yet? Want to put it all into action? That's what we will be doing in the next couple of chapters.

In the next chapter, we'll examine the area-code program that we created. This lets you search for information about a particular area code in the North American Dialing Plan. You can search by area code, city, or region (state, province, or island nation in the Caribbean). You'll see how the skills you've learned so far can create actual JavaScript applications.

CHAPTER 18

The Area Code Application

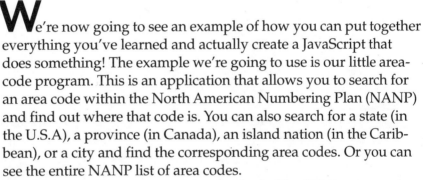

We're now going to see an example of how you can put together everything you've learned and actually create a JavaScript that does something! The example we're going to use is our little area-code program. This is an application that allows you to search for an area code within the North American Numbering Plan (NANP) and find out where that code is. You can also search for a state (in the U.S.A), a province (in Canada), an island nation (in the Caribbean), or a city and find the corresponding area codes. Or you can see the entire NANP list of area codes.

In Figure 18-1 you can see what this looks like. Why not go to the Online Companion and try it out. It's very simple. Type an area code into the Search Text box and click on Search. Or click on an option button, then type the appropriate text into the Search Text box and click on Search. The result of the search will be seen in the text area at the bottom of the page. You can also click on the Display ALL Area Codes option button to display the entire list in the text area.

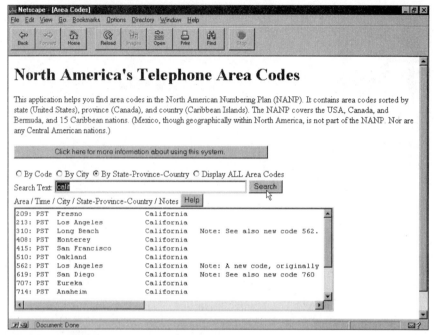

Figure 18-1: *The Area Code program in action.*

WHY THE AREA CODE APPLICATION?

JavaScript gives you a way to make your Web pages interactive. Computer systems consist of code that provides functional behavior, but by itself this is not enough to be of any real use. The bit that you also need in order to have a program that actually *does* something is *data*.

There are many JavaScript examples on the Web that demonstrate function but where you have to provide the data. For example there are calculator examples. You provide the data by typing it in. Examples that require you to key in all of the data each time tend to be just that, examples and not of any real use. We wanted to give you a real world example of a JavaScript application that someone might actually want to use for a reason other than to find out how JavaScript works. So we needed data.

The Area Code application has all the data it needs stored in arrays within the code. This may not be the most elegant way to input data into a program but it suits our purposes because it is simple. And it's a real-world application. Right now we're talking with a record company about putting a simple JavaScript "database" on the Web, one that would allow users to search for a band's concert dates and locations. The Area Code application is ideally suited to that kind of purpose.

WHERE'S THE DATA?

Where is all this information stored? Well, you'll remember from Chapter 9, "Building Arrays," that we can store information such as this area-code stuff in an array, and that's just what we did. In fact we began by creating an array object like this:

```
function makeArray(n) {
    this.length = n
    return this
}
```

You'll remember that this is how you start creating an array (yes, there's now a built-in Array object, but at the time of writing very few people had the browser required to use that object—Navigator 3.0 beta 3 or later—so we are using the earlier method for creating objects.) Once we've created the array object class, we can create the actual arrays—the instances—themselves, like this:

```
var cde = new makeArray(187)
var area = new makeArray(187)
var cit = new makeArray(187)
var tz = new makeArray(187)
var no = new makeArray(187)
```

> ### TIP
>
> *We've used a lot of comment lines within the script to make the script easier to read. You can see the script in its entirety by opening the Area Code application and viewing the source. You can find this application in the Online Companion (http://www.netscapepress.com/support/ javascript, or go directly to http://www.netscapepress.com/support/ javascript/areacode.htm).*

We now have five arrays:

- cde   The area codes
- area   The area each code represents (state, province, island,etc.)
- cit   The city names
- tz   The time zone
- no   The notes related to that area code.

Then we had to place the information into the arrays, like this:

```
area[1]="Alabama";cde[1]=205;tz[1]="CST ";cit[1]="Birmingham→
";no[1]="See also the new code 334."
area[2]="Alabama";cde[2]=334;tz[2]="CST ";cit[2]="Montgomery→
";no[2]="A new code; originally within the 205 area."
area[3]="Alaska";cde[3]=907;tz[3]="-09 ";cit[3]="Anchorage→
";no[3]=""
area[4]="Alberta";cde[4]=403;tz[4]="MST ";cit[4]="Edmonton→
";no[4]=""
area[5]="Antigua";cde[5]=268;tz[5]="-04 ";cit[5]="St. Johns→
";no[5]="A new code,
originally within the 809 area. The old code may be used until
March 31 1997."
```

> ### TIP
>
> *It's very important to make sure that you get the array numbers correct, or you will mess up the program. For instance, if you mistype a number— for example, 19 instead of 119—you will place the information into the wrong array position, perhaps writing over something else.*

As we showed you in Chapter 9, "Building Arrays," we placed each array one after another on the same line for each index number (187 index positions). For example, take a look at this:

```
area[5]="Antigua";cde[5]=268;tz[5]="-04 ";cit[5]="St. Johns→
";no[5]="A new code, originally within the 809 area. The old→
code may be used until March 31 1997."
```

We start by placing the word Antigua into position 5 in the area array. The number 268 goes into position 5 in the cde array; -04 goes into position 5 in the tz array; St. Johns goes into position 5 in the cit array; and the note at the end goes into position 5 in the no array. Notice that we separated each of these with a ;.

Now, you don't have to place all of these on the same line. You could do all of the area array, then do all of the cde array, and so on with each array in a separate block. We like to have all the arrays together, so we can quickly enter information for each area code at one time, and can quickly see all the information in one place. However, in some cases we weren't able to use this method, and had to move some of the array assignments down.

You see, we ran into a size limitation. At present (Navigator 3.0 beta) JavaScript has, under some circumstances, a 255-character limitation on a line, and a number of our lines exceeded this limit. Look at this line:

```
area[6]="Arizona";cde[6]=520;tz[6]="MST";cit[6]="Tuscon→
";no[6]="A new code, originally within the 602 area. The old→
code has expired for much of Arizona. In Tuscon it expires→
on Dec 31 1996, in Flagstaff, Prescott, Yuma it expires on→
June 30 1996."
```

JavaScript just didn't like this. The entire line was too long. Luckily there's a quick fix. We simply removed the ; before the no[6], and moved the no[6] assignment down onto another line, like this:

```
area[6]="Arizona";cde[6]=520;tz[6]="MST";cit[6]="Tuscon";

no[6]="A new code, originally within the 602 area. The old→
code has expired for much of Arizona. In Tuscon it expires→
on Dec 31 1996, in Flagstaff, Prescott, Yuma it expires on→
June 30 1996."
```

Now it works fine. We had a slightly more complicated problem with this entry:

```
area[30]="Caribbean";cde[30]=809 ;tz[30]="CCT";cit[30]="→
";no[30]="These are the countries currently covered by this→
code (with their new codes if changing soon): Anguilla,→
Bahamas (242), Barbados (246), Bequla, British Virgin→
Islands, Cayman Islands, Dominica, Dominican Republic,→
Jamaica, Montserrat (664), Mustique, Nevis, Palm Island, St.→
Kitts, St. Lucia (758), St. Vincent, Trinidad and Tobago,→
Union Island, US Virgin Islands"→
```

Not only is the entire line too long, but the note itself is too long to be assigned to a variable in one block. So we simply did this:

```
var ex1="A code covering a number of Caribbean nations. This→
is gradually being split into smaller areas. See also new→
codes 242, 246, 268, 284, 441, 473, 664, 787, 869, 758, 868."

var ex2="These are the countries currently covered by this→
code (with their new codes if changing soon): Anguilla,→
Bahamas (242), Barbados (246), Bequla, British Virgin→
Islands, Cayman Islands, Dominica, Dominican Republic,→
Jamaica, Montserrat (664), Mustique, Nevis, Palm Island"→

var ex3=", St. Kitts, St. Lucia (758), St. Vincent, Trinidad→
and Tobago, Union Island, US Virgin Islands"

area[30]="Caribbean";cde[30]=809 ;tz[30]="CCT";cit[30]="→
";no[30]=ex1 + ex2 + ex3
```

First we declared three variables, ex1, ex2, and ex3, and split the note into those variables. Then we concatenated these on the last line when we assigned them to no[30].

That's how we put the data into the script, and there's quite a bit of it—almost 190 entries, with 5 arrays, so it's almost 950 array assignments. It's often easier to work with this sort of data in a good word processor, and then copy it to your HTML editor later. A good word processor will have the sort of text-management tools that can really speed things up with lists like this; really good search and replace tools, the ability to copy and paste columns, and so on.

The Form

Now let's see the form we created:

```
<FORM NAME="form1">
<INPUT TYPE="BUTTON" VALUE="Click here for more information→
about using this system." onclick="Info()"><P>
<INPUT TYPE="radio" NAME="radSearchType"CHECKED VALUE =
"CODE"onclick="ClearAll(this.form);">By Code
<INPUT TYPE="radio" NAME="radSearchType"  VALUE = "CITY"
onclick="ClearAll(this.form);">By City
<INPUT TYPE="radio" NAME="radSearchType"   VALUE = "STATE"
onclick="ClearAll(this.form);">By State-Province-Country
<INPUT TYPE="radio" NAME="radSearchType"   VALUE = "ALL"
onclick="ShowAll(form)">Display ALL Area Codes
<BR> Search Text:
<INPUT TYPE="text" NAME="txtSearch" SIZE=50>
<INPUT TYPE="button" VALUE="Search"
onclick="SearchType(this.form)">
<BR>
Area / Time / City / State-Province-Country / Notes <INPUT
TYPE="button" VALUE="Help" onclick="Help()">
<BR>
<TEXTAREA NAME="txtResults" ROWS=10 COLS=73></TEXTAREA>
</FORM>
```

You can see the form created by this in Figure 18-2. We start with a large button that calls the Info( ) function. This function opens a new window and displays information about using the system. (We'll show you this and the other functions as we go through the script.)

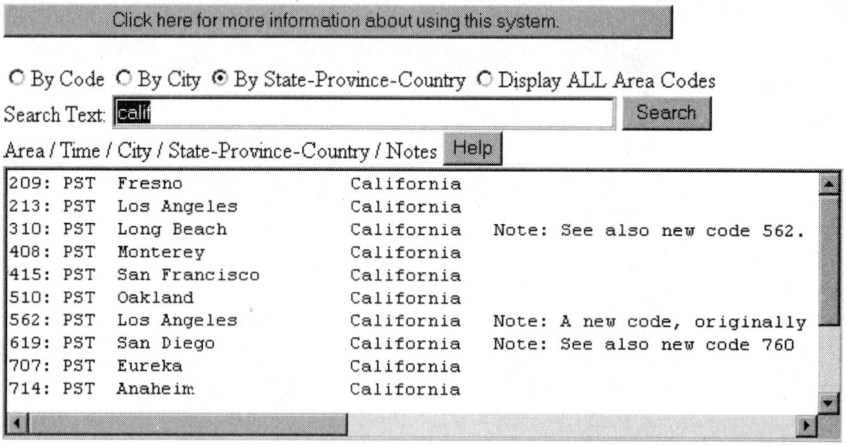

Figure 18-2: *The form we created for the Area Code application.*

Next we have several option buttons. These are used to determine how the data is searched: by code, city, or state-province-country. There's also a button that displays the entire list of entries. Now, the first three of these buttons call the ClearAll( ) function; this function is used to clear the contents of the textarea at the bottom of the page, to move focus to the Search Text box, and to select the contents of that box.

The last option button is a little different. It calls the ShowAll( ) function which clears the contents of the textarea, displays a Confirm box which asks if you want to continue, and writes all the information from the arrays into the textarea.

Then we have the txtSearch text box—this is where the user types the text to be searched for—and a button that the user clicks on to call the SearchType( ) function. This function determines which type of search should be carried out and calls the appropriate function to do so.

Next we have the Help button. This calls the Help( ) function, another one used to open an information window. Finally, we have a large textarea at the bottom of the form, the txtResults element. This is where the results of the search are placed.

SETTING FOCUS ON THE FORM

After the form, we have this script:

```
<SCRIPT LANGUAGE="JavaScript">
<!--
    //set the focus to the txtSearch box:
    document.form2.txtSearch.focus()
    document.form2.txtSearch.select()
//-->
</SCRIPT>
```

This simply sets the focus on the txtSearch box once the form has been loaded. In other words, the cursor is placed in the txtSearch box; .The expression document.form2.txtSearch.focus() indicates that we wish to use the focus() method on the txtSearch element of the form named form2.txt, in the document. You'll also notice that we used the select() method in addition to focus(). That's so if there's any text in the text box when the document is loaded (for example, if the user does a search, then comes back later to do another), then that text will be highlighted. All the user has to do is type and the existing text is replaced.

TIP

If you create a "database" program like this, be careful not to run into an inherent size limitation. While JavaScript itself doesn't have a built-in script-size limitation, Windows 3.1 does. You should avoid producing a Web page anywhere near 64K because, thanks to the way that Windows handles memory, Windows 3.1 browsers may have problems with the JavaScript.

THE FUNCTIONS

Now let's take a look at the functions that actually make this application work. (We've already seen the makeArray() function, so we won't revisit that one.) We placed all the functions in the HEAD of the document—not necessarily in the order that they are run, since the order of their definitions doesn't matter. We have these functions:

Function	Definition
info()	Opens a window that contains information about the program. Called from the large button at the top of the form.
Help()	Opens a window that explains the information returned. Called from the Help button.
ClearAll()	Clears the contents of the textarea, moves focus back to the text box, and highlights the text in the text box.
ShowAll()	Writes all the area code information to the textarea. Called when the user clicks on the Show ALL Area Codes option button.
AddText()	Grabs information from the arrays, and passes it back to the calling function. Called by the ShowAll(), CodeSearch(), CitySearch(), and StateSearch() functions.
SearchType()	Checks to see which option button the user clicked on, and then calls the appropriate function (CodeSearch(), CitySearch(), or StateSearch()). Called when the user clicks on the Search button.
CodeSearch()	Searches for a particular area code. Called by the SearchType() function, if the By Code option button is selected.
ValidateAreaCode()	Called by the CodeSearch() function to determine whether the user typed a three-digit number.
CitySearch()	Searches for a particular city. Called by the SearchType() function, if the By City option button is selected.
StateSearch()	Searches for a particular state, province, or island nation. Called by the SearchType() function, if the By State-Province-Country option button is selected.

You can see how these functions are linked together. For example, clicking on the Search button calls SearchType(), which may call CodeSearch(), which calls both AddText() and ValidateAreaCode(). Let's see how each of these functions works.

INFO() & HELP()—VIEWING INFORMATION WINDOWS

When you click on the large button labeled Click here for more information about using this system, the info() function is called. Here's the info() function:

```
function Info()      {
     WinInfo = open("area1.htm","Info","menubar,scrollbars,→
toolbar,height=350,width=600")
}
```

This is a simple little function. It opens a window and loads the area1.htm file into that window. The window has a menubar, scroll bars, and toolbar.

The Help button is similar; it calls the Help() function:

```
function Help()      {
     WinInfo2 = open("area2.htm","Info2","height=400,→
width=600,scrollbars")
}
```

This time we loaded area2.htm. This window has only scroll bars. We added a menubar and toolbar to the first window (WinInfo) because we have a link in area1.htm that takes people to the Bellcore Web site, to find more information about the North American Numbering Plan. The second window (WinInfo2) is intended to be opened, read, and closed, so we have fewer components.

By the way, we checked both windows in VGA mode, to make sure that the windows wouldn't be too large in a low resolution video mode. Unfortunately that makes them smaller than they could be in a higher resolution—but that's just one of the tradeoffs you have to make now and then. (We could have chosen to have the windows maximized, full size. But you risk confusing users when you do that, as they may not realize that a new window has opened and the old one is below the current one. We wanted the user to be able to see the old window below.)

CLEARALL()—CLEAR THE TEXTAREA

When you click on one of the first three option buttons, the textarea is cleared and the text in the Search Text box is highlighted. This is done by calling the `ClearAll()` function:

```
function ClearAll(form) {
    form.txtResults.value = ""
    form.txtSearch.focus()
    form.txtSearch.select()
}
```

First we set the value held in `form.txtResults`—in other words, "the value in the `txtResults` element in the `form`." Which form? Notice that the word `form` appears in parentheses after `ClearAll`. If you look at the option buttons in the form, you'll see that `this.form` is being passed to the function. The form is identifying itself, so the function knows which form to work with. We're setting the value in the textarea to `""`; in other words, we're putting an empty string into the textarea, so it's cleared.

Next we use the `focus()` and `select()` methods, as we saw a moment ago, to place the cursor inside the text box and highlight any text that might be left over from an earlier search.

SHOWALL()—DISPLAY ALL THE ENTRIES

The `ShowAll()` function is called from the last option button:

```
<INPUT TYPE="radio" NAME="radSearchType"    VALUE = "ALL"
    onclick="ShowAll(form)">Display ALL Area Codes
```

This function gets the entire area-code list and places it into the textarea. Here's how:

```
function ShowAll(form)      {
    var sText = ""
    form.txtResults.value = ""
    if (!confirm("Displaying all of the area codes may take→
```

```
twenty seconds or more (and you won't see any \"busy\"→
indicator while retrieving the information). Do you wish to→
continue?")) {
                //if user clicks on cancel we do this:
                form.radSearchType[0].checked = true
                form.txtSearch.focus()
                form.txtSearch.select()
                return
        }
        //if user clicks on OK we do this:
        for (var i = 1; i <= area.length; i++) {
                sText = AddText(sText, i)
        }
        form.txtResults.value = sText
        form.txtSearch.focus()
        form.txtSearch.select()
}
```

We begin by declaring a variable, sText. Then we use same
form.txtResults.value = "" instruction (that we've just seen in
ClearAll()), to clear the contents of the textarea.

Next we have an if statement. We begin the statement by displaying a Confirm box with a message that warns the user that it
will take a while to display all the information. Currently
JavaScript has no way to display a "busy" or "at work" indicator.
Displaying all the area codes may take 20 seconds or more; therefore, we thought we should warn people what was happening.
Without the Confirm box, it appears as if nothing is happening after the textarea has been cleared. (Unfortunately there are some
browser bugs at work here; with some browsers, on some systems,
it may take a *very* long time.)

What happens if the user clicks on the Cancel button? Well, notice that we have !confirm; this means if confirm is not true, carry
out the following instructions (the instructions in the { }). You'll remember that if the user clicks on OK, confirm returns true. So if the
user clicks on Cancel (if confirm is not true), then we run the instructions in the { }:

```
form.radSearchType[0].checked = true
```

```
form.txtSearch.focus()
form.txtSearch.select()
return
```

The first line uses the checked property, which is a property of a form element. The radSearchType element is the set of radio buttons in our form. We've used the radio object; radSearchType is the name of our radio object, and radSearchType[0] means "the first radio button in the set." And as we are setting the property to true, it means that we are selecting the first radio button. In other words, if the user decides not to go ahead and display the entire list of area codes, we reset the form, selecting the By Code radio button again. Then we use the focus() and select() methods, which we've seen before, to move focus to the Search Text box and highlight any text that's there. Then the return statement exits this function.

What happens if the user clicks on OK? We do this:

```
//if user clicks on OK we do this:
for (var i = 1; i <= area.length; i++) {
        sText = AddText(sText, i)
}
form.txtResults.value = sText
form.txtSearch.focus()
form.txtSearch.select()
}
```

We have a for loop here. We declare a variable named i, and initialize it with the value 1. That represents the first value ([1]) in our arrays. (Remember from Chapter 6, "Conditionals & Loops—Making Decisions & Controlling Scripts," this is the *initial expression*, and we are initializing counter i.) Next the *conditional expression* is evaluated: i<=area.length. This means, "as long as the value held by variable i is the same or less than the length property of the area array is 1 or greater." The length property of the array object is the number of index positions in the array. Remember when we created the array object? We did this:

```
function makeArray(n) {
    this.length = n
}
```

That means "the length property of this object is equal to n." Where does n come from? It's passed to the makeArray object in parentheses. Then, when we created the instance of the area array object, we did this:

```
var area = new makeArray(187)
```

We are passing the number 187 to the makeArray object, so the length of the area array is 187. Now, back to the ShowAll() function. You can now see that i <= area.length means, "if the counter i contains the number 187 or less, continue. If it contains 188, stop."

We are beginning with the value 1, of course, so the for loop now continues and runs the code between the { } brackets, as shown in this piece:

```
sText = AddText(sText, i)
```

We are taking the value returned by the AddText() function to the sText variable. We'll look at AddText() in a moment; this function is used to grab the information from the arrays. In parentheses, we pass this function the current value held by sText, along with the value in the counter i. AddText() then grabs the information from that array position (if the counter i holds 15, for instance, it grabs the information from position 15), adds that information to the information it was given by sText, then returns the information back to the sText variable. So sText is collecting each array entry, one by one. When this part of the code has run, the for loop then runs the *update expression:*

```
i++
```

This increments the value in i. So we begin with 1, then after the first loop we go to 2, then after the second loop we go to 3, and so on, all the way to 188 when the loop stops running because i will no longer be less than or equal to area.length. At that point we run the rest of the instructions:

```
form.txtResults.value = sText
form.txtSearch.focus()
form.txtSearch.select()
```

First we set the value property of txtResults (the textarea); we place the contents of sText into the box. Then we use the focus()

and select() methods to move focus to the Search Text box and highlight the text in the box.

That's it. Let's take a look at AddText() to see how it managed to grab the information for us.

AddText()—Grabbing Information From the Arrays

This function is called by the ShowAll(), CodeSearch(), CitySearch(), and StateSearch() functions. It's the heart of the application—the function that actually grabs the information from the arrays and hands it back to the functions so they can display it in the textarea.

```
function AddText(sText, i) {
    sText = sText + cde[i] + ": " + tz[i] + " " + cit[i] + "→
" + area[i]
    if ( no[i] != "" )      {
        sText = sText + "   Note: " + no[i] + nl
    }
    else     {
        sText = sText + nl
    }
    return sText
}
```

When a function calls AddText(), it passes two items: the contents of the sText and i variables. As we just saw, sText is the variable containing the information that will be placed in the textarea, while i is a counter. (The other functions that call AddText() work in a similar way to the ShowAll() function we've just seen.)

AddText() begins by assigning several things to the sText variable. First, it assigns sText—that's right, it assigns itself. We want to keep the information that's already in sText, and in the same position, so sText = sText is the same as saying "keep the current contents." Then we add the value held by cde[i]; this is the cde array (the array holding the area codes). We are looking in array position i; remember, i is being passed to AddText(), so the other function is telling AddText() which array position to look in.

Then we add a colon and a space (:), followed by the data in the same position from the tz array (time zone). Then we add a space, followed by the information from the cit array (city), then a space followed by the information from the same position in the area array (the state, province, or island nation).

Next we have an if statement. We want to know if there's something in the no array, the notes. So we do this:

```
if ( no[i] != "" )    {
```

This means, "if the item in the no array at position i is not equal to "", run the instructions after the { bracket." If it's not equal to "", that means there *is* something in the no array at that position. So what do we do if there is? This:

```
sText = sText + "    Note: " + no[i] + nl
```

We assign sText to itself again, then add several spaces and Note:, followed by another space and the value from the no array. Finally we add nl. This is a variable that contains the characters required to create a line break at the end of all this information, so when we write to the textarea all the information is not written to one long line. (Instead, each area-code's information appears on its own line.) So where does the value in nl come from? Well, the value required depends on the browser you are using, so we set the value in nl when the browser first opens the document. We'll look at that later in this chapter, in "The Line Break Problem."

What do we do if there *isn't* anything in the no array at that position? We have this instruction:

```
sText = sText + nl
```

Again, we assign sText to sText, then add the nl variable's value.

Finally, when the if statement has finished, what happens? We have this line:

```
return sText
```

We return the value held by sText to the function that called AddText(). Remember the following from the ShowAll() function:

```
sText = AddText(sText, i)
```

The value returned by AddText( )—the sText variable with the additional information—is returned to ShowAll( ) and placed back into the sText variable.

So you can see that in this way a function can request information from particular array positions (or, in the case of ShowAll( ), all the array positions), and AddText( ) will add the information one position at a time.

Searching the Arrays

We've now seen how the Display ALL Area Codes option button works. Now let's see how we can search for specific entries. We can search for a particular area code, city, or region (state, province, country). We do this by clicking on the appropriate option button, and then clicking on the Search button. So let's see what the Search button does:

```
<INPUT TYPE="button" VALUE="Search" onclick="SearchType→
(this.form)">
```

As you can see, when you click on the Search button, the onclick event handler calls the SearchType( ) function, and passes the information from this.form to that function. So we'll begin there, by seeing what SearchType( ) does.

SearchType()—Which Search Do You Want?

We used the SearchType( ) function to look at the option buttons and figure out what type of search the user wants, and then call that search. This function is called when the user clicks on the Search button. Here's how we did it:

```
function SearchType(form) {
    //Clear the textarea box:
    form.txtResults.value = ""

    if (form.radSearchType[0].checked) {
        CodeSearch(form)
            return
```

```
        }
    if (form.radSearchType[1].checked) {
        CitySearch(form)
          return

    }
    if (form.radSearchType[2].checked) {
        StateSearch(form)
          return

    }

}
```

We've actually begun by clearing the contents of the textarea; you've seen form.txtResults.value = "" a number of times already. Then we use a series of nested if statements to decide which type of search to carry out: if (form.radSearchType[0].checked){ means "look at the checked property for the radSearchType radio button in position 0—the first button." If the radio button is selected, then the value held by checked is true, so the if statement continues and runs the instructions after the { brace. The first instruction is CodeSearch(form), which means "call the CodeSearch( ) function and pass the contents of the form to that function." The next instruction, return, exits the function.

If the radio button is not selected, checked contains false—so the if statement moves on, and runs the next if statement. We have two more if statements: the first looking at radio button [1] (the second one), and the other looking at button [2] (the third one). If button [1] is selected (so checked is true), then the script calls the CitySearch( ) function. If button [2] is selected, it calls StateSearch( ).

And that's all there is to SearchType( ). Once it's made its decision, we move to the selected function and carry out the search.

CODESEARCH()—SEARCHING FOR AN AREA CODE

The CodeSearch( ) function is called by the SearchType( ) function, if the By Code radio (option) button is selected. Here's the function:

```
function CodeSearch(form) {
  var bFound = false
```

```
var nCode = 0
var sText = ""
var sSearch = form.txtSearch.value

    if (ValidateAreaCode(sSearch)) {
        nCode = sSearch
        for (var i = 1; i <= cde.length; i++) {
            if (nCode == cde[i]) {
                bFound = true
                break
            }
        }
        if (bFound) {
            sText = AddText(sText, i)
                form.txtResults.value = sText
        }
        else {
                alert("Area code not found");
        }
    }
    form.txtSearch.focus()
    form.txtSearch.select()
}
```

We begin by declaring several variables: bFound, nCode, sText, and sSearch. We've assigned various values to these variables: bFound is set to false, nCode is 0, sText is an empty string, and sSearch takes the value from form.txtSearch.value—the information that the user typed into the Search Text box.

Next we have an if statement. This begins by using the ValidateAreaCode() function, which looks at the area code that the user typed and checks it to make sure that it's okay. (Notice that we pass the value from sSearch to the function.) We'll look at this function in a moment, but for now all you need to know is that it returns true if the area code is okay, and false if it is not.

If the area code is valid, the next statement takes the value in sSearch (the area code the user typed) and places it into nCode. Then we have a for loop that will run its instructions if the value in cde.length (the number of items in the cde array) is less than or equal to the value in counter i; as before, we're going to go through each array position, starting at 1. If i *is* less than or equal to cde.length, the if statement runs. This compares the value in nCode (the value the user typed), with the value in the cde array at position i (position 1, then 2, and so on). When the two values match—that is, when we've found the area code that the user typed in—true is assigned to the bFound variable; then use the break keyword, which stops the loop from continuing. Otherwise, as long as nCode does not equal the value in cde at that position, the i++ incremental expression runs, increasing the value in i and trying again. So in this way the function examines the cde array entries, stopping when it finds the area code that the user typed.

When the for loop ends—when break runs, or when we get all the way to the end of the array and i exceeds the cde.length value—we move to the next if statement. This examines bFound. Remember, if we found a matching area code, bFound contains true, in which case we do this:

```
sText = AddText(sText, i)
form.txtResults.value = sText
```

We call the AddText( ) function in the same way that we called the ShowAll( ) function. AddText( ) grabs the information from the arrays in position i and returns them to the sText variable. Then we write the contents of sText to the txtResults textarea.

What happens if bFound is false? We set bFound to false when we initialized it, and if we didn't find a match then it's still false. Well, we use this else statement:

```
else {
     alert("Area code not found");
}
```

This opens an Alert box and tells the user that the area code was not found. Finally, whatever the outcome of the search, we end the CodeSearch( ) function with the usual:

```
form.txtSearch.focus()
form.txtSearch.select()
```

We move focus to the Search Text box and highlight the text.

VALIDATEAREACODE()—IS THE AREA CODE OKAY?

The ValidateAreaCode() function is called by the CodeSearch()
function. It's used to examine the information typed into the Search
Text box, and to make sure that it is valid—that is, that it's a three-
digit number. Here's the script:

```javascript
function ValidateAreaCode(sText) {
    //Make sure it is a number:
    for (var i = 0; i < sText.length; i++) {
        var sChar = sText.substring(i, i + 1)
        if (sChar < "0" || sChar > "9") {
            alert("Not a valid number. Enter an area code")
            return false
        }
    }
    //Check to see if the number is less than 100 or more than 999
    i = parseInt(sText, 10)
        if (i < 100 || i > 999) {
            alert("Area code should be a 3-digit number")
            return false
        }
        //Validation passed:
        return true
}
```

First, notice that CodeSearch() passed sText to this function. The
sText variable contains the text that the user typed into the Search
Text box (the text that we want to look at). We begin with a for
loop. We set the counter i to 0. Then we use the conditional expression i < sText.length. This means continue if the value held by i
is less than the length of the sText variable. If the user types a 3-
digit number, as he should, then when i increments to 3 (from 0 to
1, 2, 3—0 represents the first digit, 1 the second, 2 the third, so 3
would be the fourth, which we don't want), the loop stops. Next
we declare a variable called sChar, and use the substring() method
on the sText variable. The substring() method is a string-object
method that is used to grab a character (or several characters) from
a string. substring(i, i + 1) means grab the text starting at position i in the string, and finishing at position i + 1. In other words,

"grab one character, the character at position i." (You have to give substring( ) an ending position, which is actually the position immediately after the last character you want to grab, thus i + 1.) This character is then placed into the sChar variable.

Next we have an if statement nested within the for loop. This takes value in sChar and examines it. sChar < "0" || sChar > "9" means that if the value held by sChar is less then 0 or greater than 9, continue. In other words, if the character contains anything but a digit from 0 to 9 (for example, if the user typed a letter or some other character), the if statement displays the Alert box; then, when the user clicks on OK, returns false to the CodeSearch( ) function, telling that function that the text the user typed is invalid.

If the character is not less than 0 or more than 9, then it must be valid, so the loop goes around again and checks the next character. When it's checked all the characters (when i has incremented above the sText.length value), the script moves on to the next part:

```
    //Check to see if the number is less than 100 or more
than 999
i = parseInt(sText, 10)
    if (i < 100 || i > 999) {
        alert("Area code should be a 3-digit number")
        return false
    }
    //Validation passed:
    return true

}
```

This takes the value from sText and uses parseInt to extract a number from it, placing that number into the variable i. (We use parseInt to make sure we've got a number; if the user typed text instead of a number, parseInt will return 0.) Then we use an if statement to check to see if the value held by i is less than 100 (99 or less, in which case it's a two-digit number or less), or greater than 999 (1000 or more, in which case it's a four-digit number or more). If it is, then the Alert box is displayed informing the user, and the function returns false to the CodeSearch( ) function, telling that function that the text the user typed is invalid. If it's not, then we continue to the end of the script and return true to the CodeSearch( ) function, telling that function that the text the user typed is valid.

CITYSEARCH()—SEARCHING FOR A CITY

The CitySearch( ) function is called by the SearchType( ) function, if the By City radio (option) button is selected. Here's the function:

```
function CitySearch(form) {
  var bFound = false
  var sSearch = form.txtSearch.value
  var sCity
  var sText = ""
  var nStringLength = sSearch.length

  if (nStringLength == 0){
      form.txtSearch.focus()
        return
  }
  sSearch = sSearch.toLowerCase()
  for (var i = 1; i <= cit.length; i++) {
      sCity = cit[i]
    //get the city name to the same length of string
      sCity = sCity.substring(0,nStringLength);
      sCity = sCity.toLowerCase()
      if (sSearch == sCity) {
        bFound = true;
              sText = AddText(sText, i)
      }
  }
  if (bFound) {
    form.txtResults.value = sText
  }
  else {
      alert("No Cities exist which match your search text")
  }
  form.txtSearch.focus()
  form.txtSearch.select()

}
```

We start by declaring five variables: bFound (false); sSearch (containing the value from the txtSearch text box—that is, the value typed by the user); sCity (we placed nothing in here); sText (an empty string); and nStringLength (the value from the length property of the sSearch string object—that is, the number of characters that the user typed).

Next we use a quick if statement to see if we should bother to continue. If nStringLength is equal to 0—that is, if the user didn't type anything into the Search text box—all we do is move the focus back to the Search text box and stop. return means "exit out of the function and go back to where the function was called." In other words, don't go any further in this function.

However, if the user did type something into the text box, we continue to the next part of the script. First, we change the text that the user typed to lowercase, using the toLowerCase( ) method. sSearch = sSearch.toLowerCase( ) means "convert the text in sSearch to lowercase, then put it back into the sSearch variable."

Then we use a for loop; as long as the value in counter i is less than or equal to the cit.length value (the number of items in the cit array), the loop continues. What does the loop do? Well, it starts by copying the contents of the cit array, at position I, into variable sCity. Then it cuts this value down to size, using the substring( ) method (which we just looked at, in the ValidateAreaCode( ) function). sCity = sCity.substring(0,nStringLength) means "grab all the text starting as the first position in the sCity variable, and ending at the nStringLength position, and copy it into the sCity variable." Remember, nStringLength is the length of the text that the user typed into the Search text box.

Next we take that text and convert it to lowercase using the toLowerCase( ) method. Now both strings—the text we've found in the array, and the text that the user typed into the text box—are the same size and both lowercase. So it's an easy matter to compare the two:

```
    if (sSearch == sCity) {
      bFound = true;
            sText = AddText(sText, i)
  }
```

The if statement looks at the two strings, sSearch and sCity. If they are exactly the same, it sets bFound to equal true and then uses the AddText() function that we reviewed earlier to add the text for that city into the sText variable. If the two don't match, nothing happens; bFound is not set to true (so it remains unchanged—remember, we initialized bFound as false), and we don't use the AddText() function. Either way the the code is now at the end of the loop and it returns to the top (it increments the counter i in the for line). The script loops around adding cities to the sText variable.

Once the loop has finished going around (when i = cit.length), we move on to the next part of the script:

```
if (bFound) {
    form.txtResults.value = sText
}
```

Here we look at bFound, and decide what to do. If bFound contains true, then that means at least one match was found and we copy the contents of sText to the txtResults textarea. If it contains false, we use the else clause:

```
else {
        alert("No Cities exist which match your search→
text")
    }
```

This displays an Alert box which tells the user that there's no match. Finally, whatever the result of the search, we do the usual thing:

```
form.txtSearch.focus()
form.txtSearch.select()
```

We move focus to txtSearch and highlight the text.

STATESEARCH()—SEARCHING FOR A REGION

The StateSearch( ) function is called by the SearchType( ) function, if the By State-Province-Country radio (option) button is selected. Here's the function:

```
function StateSearch(form) {
  var bFound = false
  var sSearch = form.txtSearch.value
  var sState
  var sText = ""
  var nStringLength = sSearch.length

    if (nStringLength == 0){
        form.txtSearch.focus()
        return
    }
    sSearch = sSearch.toLowerCase()
    for (var i = 1; i <= area.length; i++) {
            sState = area[i]
        //get the state name to the same length of string
            sState = sState.substring(0,nStringLength);
            sState = sState.toLowerCase()
            if (sSearch == sState) {
              bFound = true;
                      sText = AddText(sText, i)
// only use the following if the State data is entered into→
the arrays in alphabetical order
            }
          else {
              if (sSearch < sState) {
              //State is in alphabetical order so if we are here,
              //we have gone past where the search string would
              //have been in the list. No need to look further.
                break;
              }
          }
    }
    if (bFound) {
        form.txtResults.value = sText
```

```
          }
          else    {
                  alert("No states, provinces, or island nations exist→
          which match your search text");
          }
          form.txtSearch.focus()
          form.txtSearch.select()
      }
```

This is very similar to the `CitySearch()` function that we just looked at, with a few differences, starting here:

```
      else {
          if (sSearch < sState)
          //State is in alphabetical order so if we are her
          //we have gone past where the search string would
          //have been in the list. No need to look further.
          break;
          }
      }
```

As you see, we entered the information into our arrays in alphabetical order by state/province/island-nation order. So we can add a little bit of code that speeds up a search slightly. This code stops the search as soon as it's passed the point at which it makes sense to search. For example, if you are searching for Utah, once the script gets to Vermont it stops, because V comes after U. Of course this is only good if you have everything in alphabetical order— which is why we didn't do this for the `CitySearch()` function.

This extra bit of code simply adds an `else` clause. If `sSearch` does not equal `sState`, the `else` clause looks at it and uses the following `if` statement (we've removed the comment lines):

```
          if (sSearch < sState) {
      break;
          }
```

This means "if sSearch is less than sState, then use the break command." The sSearch variable contains the text the user typed, and sState contains the contents of the area array at the current position. So if sSearch is (alphabetically speaking) less than sState, we've gone past the position at which the text we are looking for could be. The break command will break out of the for loop.

THE LINE BREAK PROBLEM

There's a small problem with line breaks in JavaScript. The way you create a line break varies depending on which browser has loaded the document containing your JavaScript. Windows browsers use one method, UNIX and Macintosh browsers use another method. In our example we wanted to put a line break at the end of each line of data written to the textarea. In a Windows browser, we must use \r\n at the end of a line to push the next line down. In Macintosh browsers we have to use \r, and with UNIX browsers we have to use \n. That's tricky. How can we write two scripts and get the browser to pick one? Well, we saw how to do this in Chapter 11, "More About Objects," and we've used the same method we saw there. Right at the top of the HTML document we used this script:

```
//Set up the newline characters to be used in the textarea
box - this depends on which platform
//the browser is running on
var nl=null
    if (navigator.appVersion.lastIndexOf('Win') != -1) {
        nl = "\r\n"
    }
    else    {
        if (navigator.appVersion.lastIndexOf('Mac') != -→
1)   {
            nl = "\r"
        }
            else {
                nl = "\n"
            }
    }
```

We declared a variable called nl. Now we have an if statement. The statement uses the lastIndexOf method to see if Win is in the string. If it is, the method returns some number, indicating where in the string Win is found. If it isn't in the string, it returns −1. Then we compare this result to −1. The != −1 piece means, "not equal to −1." So if it's not equal (if Win *is* in the string), the next line is executed—and we place \r\n into the nl variable. If the letters Win don't appear in the string, though, we get −1, so the else line is executed and we use a nested if statement to see if the letters Mac are in the string. If they are we place \r into nl. If they aren't, we move on and place \n into the variable (if it's not a Windows or Macintosh computer, it must be UNIX). As we saw earlier in this chapter, later in our script we use nl to place the correct characters into the strings when we write to the textarea (using the text from the AddText( ) function).

MOVING ON

Was that a lot of work? You've learned everything you need to know to create a script like the one we've just looked at—but something may have occurred to you: creating big JavaScripts can take a lot of time. Still, there are other ways to go about creating JavaScripts. You can borrow bits of code from real JavaScript programmers, people who've probably been programming for years and have the experience and skills that helps them throw together scripts in half the time it would take a new programmer.

In the next chapter we're going to look at where you can find JavaScript code "libraries" from which you can borrow. In many cases you can quickly copy a script, drop it into your Web page, and customize just one or two things to get it to work for you.

CHAPTER 19

Ready-to-Use Scripts

If you've never programmed anything before JavaScript, you've learned something by now. Programming JavaScript is no simple task. (That's why programmers get paid so much. Programming is a skill that takes a lot of learning and just the right type of person!) You may have decided that you'll never build anything large or complicated in JavaScript, although you've also learned how to do lots of little things to spruce up your pages.

If building large or complicated scripts is not your thing, there's something else you can do; you can take other people's JavaScripts, modify them, and drop them into your pages. Now, I'm not suggesting that you steal anyone's work—you don't have to. There are plenty of JavaScript programmers quite willing to provide JavaScripts to the public. And that's the subject of this chapter, how you can find the JavaScripts you need and import them into your own pages.

Of course you've got to know *what* to modify in a script. Often the authors will include comments pointing out the bits you must change. But even if they don't, if you've read the rest of the book you should be able to identify the different parts of a JavaScript, figure out how it works, and modify just the bits that need to change.

FINDING JAVASCRIPTS

In Appendix H, "Finding More Information," we've listed all sorts of JavaScript resources. (You can also find this appendix in the Online Companion, so you don't need to type all those URLs.) Spend a little time moving around these sites and you'll run into all sorts of useful samples. You'll notice that many authors have given permission to the public to use these scripts. Read the permission statements, however, as there may be some restrictions. (For example you can use them for personal pages, but not for commercial sites. Some have simply been placed into the public domain, which means that you can do anything with them that you like.)

There are also sites that have actual libraries of JavaScripts from which you can grab pieces. Try these sites:

JavaScript 411
http://www.freqgrafx.com/411/
Among other things, this site has a Snippet Library.

The JavaScript Library at the JavaScript Index
http://www.c2.org/~andreww/javascript/lib/
The JavaScript Index maintains a library of JavaScript source code.

JavaScript: Simple Little Things To Add To Your Pages
http://tanega.com/java/java.html
A lot of simple things that you can add to your pages. (We've looked at most of the things the author of this page has described, but check to see if he's added more.)

JavaScript Sweden, JavaScript Source Codes
http://www.ostrabo.uddevalla.se/dis/javascript/source.html
A library of scripts you can copy into your pages.

The JavaScript Archive
http://planetx.bloomu.edu/~mpscho/jsarchive/
A couple of calculators, a script used to test browsers to see if they work with JavaScript, and more.

JavaScript Applets
http://www.oz.net/~alden/javascript/jsintro.html
Currently a small collection, though unusual stuff; a Blackjack
game, for instance, and a compound-interest calculator.

Timothy's JavaScript Page
http://www.essex1.com/people/timothy/index.html
A small collection of interesting scripts.

You may find more libraries listed at the JavaScript Index (at
http://www.c2.org/~andreww/javascript/collections.html).
You'll find lots of scripts in these libraries, and many more at individual programmer's sites. You'll find different types of banners,
games, calculators, color-changing utilities, clocks and timers, and
more. Before you take a script, however, check to see if you can use
it. If the site gives explicit permission, then fine, use it. If not, you'd
better contact the author first.

 ## ADDING A CLOCK

Want to add a clock to your Web page? Here's how. Go to the Snippet Library at JavaScript 411 (http://www.freqgrafx.com/411/
library.html), and find the link to the Clock page (or go directly to
http://www.freqgrafx.com/411/clock.html). You'll find the page
shown in Figure 19-1. You can see the digital clock in the text box
near the bottom of the page. This clock is actually taken from the
Netscape Communications documentation.

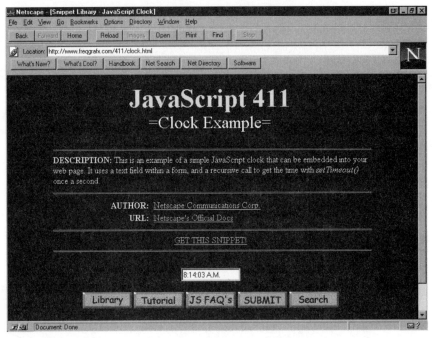

Figure 19-1: *The Clock snippet from JavaScript 411.*

Notice the *GET THIS SNIPPET!* link above this clock. Click on the link and Netscape loads the clock.js file. When it opens, you'll notice that the very first tag in the page is `<XMP>`; the `<XMP>` `</XMP>` tag pair tells the browser to display everything between the tags—without interpreting the HTML tags—so you can see the entire script (see Figure 19-2). We used the `<XMP>` tags in the Online Companion to display the scripts used in our pages.

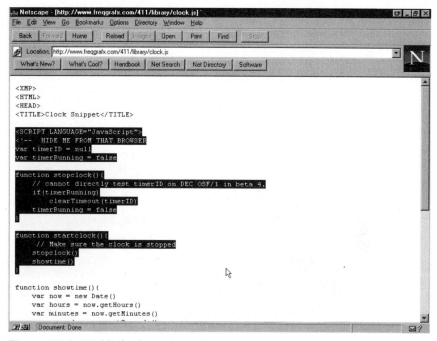

```
<XMP>
<HTML>
<HEAD>
<TITLE>Clock Snippet</TITLE>

<SCRIPT LANGUAGE="JavaScript">
<!-- HIDE ME FROM THAT BROWSER
var timerID = null
var timerRunning = false

function stopclock(){
    // cannot directly test timerID on DEC OSF/1 in beta 4.
    if(timerRunning)
        clearTimeout(timerID)
    timerRunning = false
}

function startclock(){
    // Make sure the clock is stopped
    stopclock()
    showtime()
}

function showtime(){
    var now = new Date()
    var hours = now.getHours()
    var minutes = now.getMinutes()
```

Figure 19-2: *Highlight the script and copy it.*

Now highlight the script; you'll have to take the script from the top—the code that does the actual work—plus the form in the BODY of the document that is used to create the text box that holds the clock. You'll also notice that there's an `onload` instruction in the `<BODY>` tag; you'll need that too, of course.

Example 19.1

Now simply paste all this into your Web document. This is a very simple example, because there's really nothing to change. Drop the entire first script into the HEAD of your document, modify the `<BODY>` tag (to show `<BODY onload="startclock()">`, with the current script), and then drop the `<FORM>` into the body of your page just where you want it. Open the document in your browser and you've got a clock!

SCROLLING STATUS-BAR MESSAGES

The last example was very simple, because there was nothing to change. You don't even have to look closely at the script, you simply drop it into the right place. Let's look at another example, though, one that takes a little more thought.

Take a look at the scrolling status-bar message in the same library at http://www.freqgrafx.com/411/scroller.html. (While it may be confusing, these messages have become known to many as *scrollbars* or *scrollers*, so if you see these terms used in JavaScript sites they are often referring to status-bar messages—not window scroll bars.) You can see this page in Figure 19-3.

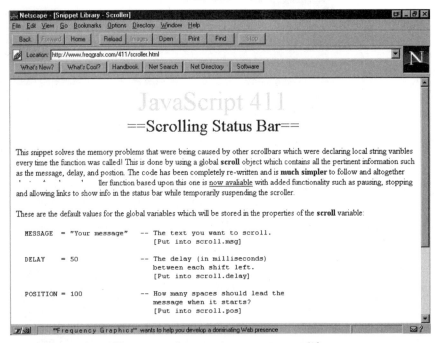

Figure 19-3: *A scrolling status-bar message you can modify.*

In this case you can see that the author has actually provided instructions, telling you what you'll need to change. There's the MESSAGE, the DELAY, and the POSITION. Click on the Get This Code Snippet link to open the code. This time you'll have to be a bit more selective about what you take. First, you'll see that the author has included the following comment at the top:

```
/*
Copyright (C) 1996  Frequency Graphics   All Rights Reserved.
   Feel free to reuse this code snippet
   provided this header remains intact
```

In other words, this code snippet is not in the public domain. It doesn't belong to you, although the author is giving you permission to use it as long as the copyright header remains with the code. So make sure that you include this header with the script you copy.

You'll also notice that there's nothing in the BODY of the document that you need. Everything is in the script in the HEAD, and in the <BODY> tag which looks like this:

```
<body onload="scroller()">
```

So the script in the HEAD creates a `scroller()` function, which is called by the `onload` instruction in the <BODY> tag. In other words, as soon as the browser has finished loading the document, it starts the status-bar message.

So, modify the <BODY> tag in your Web document, and copy the entire script from the snippet's HEAD into the HEAD of your Web document. Then save the document and take a look in your browser. There it is, your Web page with the **Frequency Graphics** *wants to help you create a dominating Web presence* scrolling message. Now you know it's working and all you need to do is make it display your message, at the rate you want it displayed.

The first step, then, is to substitute your message. That's easy enough; just search for ** or for **F r e q u (you'll notice that the scrolling message has spaces between each letter in F r e q u e n c y G r a p h i c s.) You'll find several lines like this:

```
var MESSAGE  = "**F r e q u e n c y   G r a p h i c s**"
                + "  wants to help you develop"
                + " a dominating Web presence"
```

Replace this with your own text. You can do one long line if you wish, like this:

```
var MESSAGE = "*^*^*SLUG FEST*^*^* You want slugs, we got→
'em. The best slug site in Cyberspace!"
```

However, there's a bug in early versions of Netscape (Version 3.0 beta 4 and earlier) in which very long lines of text—255 characters or more—may cause errors. So you can break it up, like the original script:

Example 19.2

```
var MESSAGE = "*^*^*SLUG FEST*^*^*"
        + " You want slugs, we got 'em."
        + " The best slug site in Cyberspace!!!"
```

Make sure that your text has quotation marks around it, of course.

Now save your file, reload it into the browser, and see what it looks like now. Your message will scroll along the bottom in place of Frequency Graphics' message.

Next, let's change the delay. This controls how quickly the message moves across the status bar. The instructions in the Snippet Library said that you need to change the DELAY = setting, so search for the word DELAY. You'll find it in a couple of places, but you need to find where the DELAY variable is declared:

```
var DELAY    = 50
```

Change this value. For instance, replace 50 with 200. Save the file, reload in the browser, and see what happens. It's now much slower. Experiment with different values until you have the one you think works best.

Finally, we can change the starting position—the point at which the message first appears on the status bar. The instructions said that this is controlled through the POSITION = setting, so look around for POSITION. Again, you'll find the word POSITION several places in this script, but you are looking for where the variable is declared (close to where the DELAY variable is declared, actually):

```
var POSITION = 100
```

Substitute some other value for 100; try 50, for instance. Save and reload, and see what it does. If the value's too small, the message scrolls too quickly to be read, because it will start all the way over at the left side of the scroll bar. The larger the value, the more to the right the message begins. If it's too large, though, the message won't appear for a few seconds, as it's starting "off" the status bar. In fact this is a good way to make the message appear a few moments after the page has loaded, rather than right away.

TIP

The JavaScript 411 Snippet Library contains other more advanced scrolling status-bar message examples, which give you more control over the messages.

DON'T STEAL, BORROW

Although you can't simply take someone's script without permission and drop it straight into your pages, there's nothing to stop you from "borrowing" a script and seeing how it works. In the same way that writers and poets read the works of the great authors and poets to see how they did it, you should examine the JavaScripts you like. Copy a script from the source document to your hard disk, then play with it to see how it works. You'll then see how you can do similar things in your own scripts.

To do this, of course, you'll need to understand JavaScript, even if you are no master of the art. You'll need to understand what we've studied in the first part of this book, all about functions, variables, objects, and so on. Once you know that stuff, though, you'll be able to read scripts and understand them and learn.

MOVING ON

Well, that's it. If you've made it this far you've got a good grounding in JavaScript. You won't be a JavaScript guru, but you will understand the basics: enough to add many types of scripts to your Web pages, to read and understand other people's scripts, and to continue with your JavaScript education.

The rest of this book contains a variety of reference materials. You'll find summaries of JavaScript's objects, properties, and event handlers, list of reserved words, and the colors you can use. You'll also find a reference table showing the different symbols used by JavaScript, to help you understand the scripts you find on the Web.

Most important, there's an appendix providing information about finding more information. Your education is not over, after all. There's plenty more to learn! You can also find this appendix in our Online Companion at http://www.netscapepress.com/support/javascript/.

Finally, we've included a script index. This is a list of scripts, sorted by purpose. Look in this list for the sorts of things that we've covered in this book, and for each one you'll find the page containing the script and the Online Companion example script number.

The Appendices

The following appendices are not intended as a substitute for the Netscape JavaScript documentation (also known as the JavaScript Authoring Guide). Rather, we've placed them here to help you see how everything fits together. You can also find a summary of each object, property, and method. You can look up something, figure out if it is what you need, and then refer to the full documentation for the complete details. There's way too much information in the JavaScript documentation to squeeze into this book—and it changes constantly—so you want to make sure that you have the latest version of the documentation.

See Appendix H, "Finding More Information," for information about where to get the JavaScript documentation. (It's free, and available in several formats.) See, for example, http:// home.netscape.com/eng/mozilla/2.0/handbook/javascript/ index.html.

Appendix A

About the Online Companion

Included on the Online Companion for the *Official Netscape JavaScript Book* is a complete listing of the scripts in the book. Please visit the site at http://www.netscapepress.com/support/javascript/ to find a complete index of the scripts. Don't waste time typing in the scripts. Copy them directly from the Online Companion.

Netscapepress.com features a catalog of other Netscape Press titles, technical support information, and news about the Internet.

Also found at http://www.netscapepress.com/ is *Navigate!*, the official electronic publication of Netscape Press. Netscape Press is a joint effort between Ventana and Netscape Communications Corp., and serves as the publishing arm of Netscape. *Navigate!* is a monthly online publication that offers a wide range of articles and reviews aimed at Netscape users. *Navigate!* features interviews with industry icons and experts, as well as articles excerpted from upcoming Netscape Press titles.

Appendix B

The JavaScript Objects & Arrays

This appendix lists the various JavaScript objects and arrays. For each one you will find associated properties, methods, and event handlers with a short description of what each one does. We've also noted the parent object of each. You may also want to refer to the hypertext Object Hierarchy page in the Online Companion (http://www.netscapepress.com/support/javascript/10-9.htm to get an idea of how the objects are related to each other.

Remember, by the way, that we are treating all objects that are descendants of another objects as *properties* of that object. See the note concerning this in Chapter 10, "Objects, Properties & Methods."

ANCHOR

An HTML anchor, created using the <A NAME=> tag. It can be targeted by a link. If the anchor includes the HREF= attribute, it is also a link object.

The anchor object is a property of the document object. It has no properties, methods, or event handlers.

ANCHORS ARRAY

The anchors array is a property of the document object, and is a list of all the anchor objects in a document. If an anchor is also a link, then it appears in *both* the anchors and the links arrays.

PROPERTIES

length   The number of anchors in the document.

ARRAY

The array object is a new one, introduced with Netscape Navigator 3.0, beta 3), so it won't work with Netscape 2.0. It's a built-in object—not a property of another object.

PROPERTIES

length   The number of values held in the array.

BUTTON

This is a property of a `form` object. It's created using the `<INPUT TYPE="BUTTON">` tag.

PROPERTIES

name   The NAME= attribute in the HTML tag.
Value   The VALUE= attribute in the HTML tag.

METHODS

click   Simulates a mouse click on a button.

EVENT HANDLERS

onclick

CHECKBOX

This is a property of a `form` object. It is created using the `<INPUT TYPE="CHECKBOX">` tag.

PROPERTIES

checked	The selection state of the checkbox.
defaultChecked	The tags CHECKED= attribute.
name	The tag's NAME= attribute.
value	The tag's VALUE= attribute.

METHODS

click	Simulates a mouse click on a button.

EVENT HANDLERS

onclick

DATE

A built-in object—not a property of another object. Allows you to carry out a variety of procedures using dates and times.

METHODS

getDate()	Looks in the Date object and returns the day of the month.
getDay()	Returns the day of the week.
getHours()	Returns the hours.
getMinutes()	Returns the minutes.
getMonth()	Returns the month.
getSeconds()	Returns the seconds.
getTime()	Returns the complete time.
getTimeZoneoffset()	Returns the time-zone offset (the number of hours difference between Greenwich Mean Time and the time zone set in the computer running the script).
getYear()	Returns the year.
parse()	Returns the number of milliseconds in the Date

string since January 1, 1970 00:00:00. (The Date object stores times and dates in the form of milliseconds since this date.) Note, however, that this method is not currently working correctly.

setDate()	Changes the Date object's day of month.
setHours()	Changes the hours.
setMinutes()	Changes the minutes.
setMonth()	Changes the month.
setSeconds()	Changes the seconds.
setTime()	Changes the complete time.
setYear()	Changes the year.
toGMTString()	Converts the Date object's date (a numeric value) to a string in GMT time, returning for example, Weds, 15 June 1997 14:02:02 GMT (the exact format varies depending on the operating system that the computer is running).
toLocaleString()	Converts the Date object's date (a numeric value) to a string, using the particular date format the computer is configured to use.
UTC()	Use Date UTC(year, month, day, hrs, min, sec) to return that date in the form of the number of milliseconds since January 1, 1970 00:00:00. (The hrs, min, and sec are optional.)

DOCUMENT

A property of the window and frames objects; the document displayed in the window or in the frame.

PROPERTIES

alinkColor	The color of an active link (ALINK).
anchor	An HTML anchor, created using the <A NAME=> tag. (This property is also an object in its own right.)

anchors array	An array listing the document anchor objects (<A NAME=>). (This property is also an object in its own right.)
bgColor	The document's background color (BGCOLOR).
cookie	A piece of information stored in the cookie.txt file. A property of the document object.
fgColor	The document's text color (the TEXT attribute in the <BODY> tag).
form	A form (<FORM>) in a document. (This property is also an object in its own right.)
forms array	An array listing the form objects in the order in which they appear in the document. (This property is also an object in its own right.)
lastModified	The date the document was last changed.
linkColor	The color of the document's links, the LINK attribute in the <BODY> tag (links to documents that the user has not yet viewed).
link	An <A HREF=> tag in the document. (This property is also an object in its own right.)
links array	An array of the link objects in a document, in the order in which they appear. (This property is also an object in its own right.)
location	The URL of the currently displayed document. You can't change the document.location (as that's the location of the document currently displayed). You can, however, change window.location (replacing the current document with another). While window.location *is* also an object in its own right, document.location is *not*.
referrer	The URL of the document containing the link that the user clicked on to get to the current document.
title	The document's title (<TITLE>).
vlinkColor	The text color of links pointing to documents that the user has viewed. The VLINK attribute of the <BODY> tag.

METHODS

clear	Clears the contents of the specified document.
close	Closes the document stream.
open	Opens the document stream.
write	Writes text to the document.
writeln	Writes text to the document, and ends with a newline character.

ELEMENTS ARRAY

A property of the form object. An array listing the elements in a form.

PROPERTIES

length	The number of elements in the form.

FORM

A property of the document object. A form within the document.

PROPERTIES

action	A string containing the destination URL for a form submission.
button	A button in a form, created using the <INPUT TYPE="BUTTON"> tag. (This property is also an object in its own right.)
checkbox	A checkbox, created using the <INPUT TYPE="CHECKBOX"> tag. (This property is also an object in its own right.)
elements array	An array listing form elements in the order in which they appear in the form. (This property is also an object in its own right.)
encoding	The MIME encoding of the form.

hidden	A hidden (<INPUT TYPE="HIDDEN">) element in a form. A property of the form object. (This property is also an object in its own right.)
length	The number of elements in the form.
method	How data input into a form is sent to the server; the METHOD attribute in a <FORM> tag.
radio	A radio button set (<INPUT TYPE="RADIO">) in a form.(This property is also an object in its own right.)
reset	A reset button (<INPUT TYPE="RESET">) in a form. (This property is also an object in its own right.)
select	A selection box (<SELECT>) in a form. (This property is also an object in its own right.)
submit	A submit button (<INPUT TYPE="SUBMIT">) in a form. (This property is also an object in its own right.)
target	The name of the window that displays re-sponses after a form has been submitted.
text	A text element in a form (<INPUT TYPE="TEXT">). (This property is also an object in its own right.)
textarea	A textarea element (<TEXTAREA>) in a form. (This property is also an object in its own right.)

METHODS

submit	Submits a form (the same as using the Submit button).

EVENT HANDLERS

onsubmit

FORMS ARRAY

A property of the document object. An array that lists the forms in the document.

PROPERTIES

length   The number of forms in the document.

FRAME

A property of the window object. A frame within the window. A frame object functions in the same way as a window object, with a few exceptions.

PROPERTIES

frames array	An array listing the child frames within this frame. (This property is also an object in its own right.)
length	The number of frames within this frame.
name	The frame's name (the NAME attribute in the <FRAME> tag).
parent	A synonym for the parent window containing this frame.
self	A synonym for the current frame.
window	A synonym for the current frame.

METHODS

clearTimeout()	Used to stop the setTimeout method from working.
setTimeout()	Waits a specified number of milliseconds, then runs the instructions.

FRAMES ARRAY

A property of both the window and frame objects. Lists the frames within the window or within the frame.

PROPERTIES

Length	The number of frames within the window or frame object.

HIDDEN

A property of a form object. A hidden (<INPUT TYPE="HIDDEN">) element in a form.

PROPERTIES

name	The name (the NAME attribute) in the tag.
value	The VALUE= attribute in the tag.

HISTORY

A property of the window object. The window's history list.

PROPERTIES

Length	The number of items in the history list.

METHODS

back	Loads the previous document in the history list.
forward	Loads the next document in the history list.
go	Loads a document in the history list, specified by its position in the list.

IMAGE

A property of the document object. An image embedded into a document with the <IMG> tag. This is a new object, introduced with Netscape Navigator 3.0 beta 3).

PROPERTIES

border	The <IMG> tag's BORDER attribute.
complete	A boolean value which indicates whether the browser has completely loaded the image.
height	The HEIGHT attribute.
hspace	The HSPACE attribute.
lowsrc	The LOWSRC attribute.
src	The SRC attribute.
vspace	The VSPACE attribute.
width	The WIDTH attribute.

EVENT HANDLERS

onload

onerror

onabort

IMAGES ARRAY

A property of the document object. A list of all the images in the document.

PROPERTIES

length	The number of images in the document.

LINK

A property of the document object. An <A HREF=> tag in the document.

PROPERTIES

hash	A string beginning with a hash mark (#) that specifies an anchor within the URL.
host	The host name part of the URL which includes a colon and the port number.
hostname	The same as the host property, except that the colon and port number are not included.
href	The entire URL.
pathname	The directory path portion of a URL.
port	The :port portion of a URL.
protocol	The URL type (http:, ftp:, gopher:, and so on).
search	Part of the URL beginning with a ? that specifies search information.
target	The window that displays the content of the referenced document when the user clicks on a link (the TARGET attribute).

EVENT HANDLERS

onclick

onmouseover

LINKS ARRAY

A property of the document object. A list of all the links in the document.

PROPERTIES

length	The number of links in the document.

LOCATION

A property of the document object. The full URL of the document. Do not confuse this with the window.location property, which can be used to load a new document. The window.location property is not an object in its own right. Also, while window.location can be modified by a script, document.location cannot.

PROPERTIES

hash	A string beginning with a hash mark (#) that specifies an anchor within the URL.
host	The host name part of the URL which includes a colon and the port number.
hostname	The same as the host property, except that the colon and port number are not included.
href	The entire URL.
pathname	The directory path portion of a URL.
port	The :port portion of a URL.
protocol	The URL type (http:, ftp:, gopher:, and so on).
search	Part of the URL beginning with a ? that specifies search information.
target	The window that displays the content of the referenced document when the user clicks on a link (the TARGET attribute).

MATH

This is not a property of another object; it's a built-in object. Math contains mathematical constants and functions.

PROPERTIES

E	Euler's constant and the base of natural logarithms (approximately 2.718).
LN2	The natural logarithm of two (approximately 0.693).

LN10	The natural logarithm of ten (approximately 2.302).
LOG2E	The base 2 logarithm of e (approximately 1.442).
LOG10E	The base 10 logarithm of e (approximately 0.434).
PI	The value of pi (approximately 3.14159).
SQRT1_2	The square root of one-half (one over the square root of two approximately 0.707).
SQRT2	The square root of two (approximately 1.414).

METHODS

abs()	Returns a number's absolute value (its "distance from zero"; for instance, both 2 and -2 have absolute values of 2).
acos()	Returns the arc cosine of a number (in radians).
asin()	Returns the arc sine of a number (in radians).
atan()	Returns the arc tangent of a number (in radians).
ceil()	Returns the integer equal to or immediately above a number (ceil(-22.22) would return 22; ceil(22.22) would return 23; ceil(22) would return 22).
cos()	Returns the cosine of a number (in radians).
exp()	Returns e^{number}.
floor()	The opposite of ceil. (ceil(-22.22) would return 22; ceil(22.22) would return 22; ceil(22) would return 22).
log()	Returns the natural logarithm (base e) of a number.
max()	Returns the greater of two numbers.
min()	Returns the lesser of two numbers.
pow()	Returns $base^{exponent}$.
random()	Returns a pseudo-random number between zero and one. (This method only works on UNIX

versions of Netscape Navigator.)

round()	Returns a number which is rounded to the nearest integer.
sin()	Returns the sine of a number (in radians).
sqrt()	Returns the square root of a number.
tan()	Returns the tangent of a number.

NAVIGATOR

This is not a property of another object; it is a built-in object. Information about the browser that has loaded the document.

PROPERTIES

appCodeName	The browser's code name (*Mozilla*, for instance).
appName	The browser's name.
appVersion	The browser's version number.
userAgent	The user-agent header text sent from the client to the server.

METHODS

javaEnabled	This method is currently not in JavaScript, but will probably be added soon. It will check to see if the browser is a JavaScript-compatible browser and, if so, whether JavaScript has been enabled.

OPTIONS ARRAY

A property of a `select` object. A list of all the options (`<OPTION>`) within the selection box.

PROPERTIES

defaultSelected	The default selection in the selection list.

index	The index position of an option in the selection list.
length	The number of options (<OPTIONS>) in the selection list.
name	The name (the NAME attribute) of the selection list.
selected	A boolean value which indicates the selection state of an option <OPTION> in the selection list.
selectedIndex	The index (position) of the selected <OPTION> in the selection list.
text	The text after an <OPTION> tag in the selection list.
value	The VALUE= attribute of the selection list.

PASSWORD

A property of a document object. A <INPUT TYPE="PASSWORD"> tag.

PROPERTIES

defaultValue	The default value of the password object (the VALUE= attribute).
name	The name (the NAME= attribute) of the object.
value	The current value held by the field. Initially it's the same as the VALUE= attribute (defaultValue), but if a script modifies the value held by the field value will change.

METHODS

focus	Moves focus from the field.
blur	Moves focus to the field.
select	Selects the input area.

RADIO

A property of a `form` object. A set of radio buttons (option buttons) in the `form` (`<INPUT TYPE="RADIO">`).

PROPERTIES

checked	The state of a checkbox or option button (radio button).
defaultChecked	The default state of a checkbox or option button (radio button).
length	The number of buttons in the set.
name	The name (the NAME= attribute) of the object.
value	The VALUE= attribute.

METHODS

click	Simulates a mouse click on a button.

EVENT HANDLERS
onclick

RESET

A property of a `form` object. A reset button (`<INPUT TYPE="RESET">`)

PROPERTIES

name	The name (the NAME= attribute) of the object.
value	The VALUE= attribute.

METHODS

click	Simulates a mouse click on a button.

EVENT HANDLERS
onclick

SELECT

A property of a form object. A selection box (<SELECT>).

PROPERTIES

length	The number of options (<OPTIONS>) in the selection list.
name	The name (the NAME attribute) of the selection list.
options	The number of options in the list.
selectedIndex	The index (position) of the selected <OPTION> in the selection list.
text	The text after an <OPTION> tag in the selection list.
value	The VALUE= attribute of the selection list.

METHODS

blur	Removes focus from the selection list.
focus	Moves focus to the selection list.

EVENT HANDLERS

onblur

onchange

onfocus

STRING

This is not a property of another object; it is a built-in object. A series of characters. Strings are entered into a script between quotation marks.

PROPERTIES

length	The number of characters in the string.

METHODS

anchor()	Used to turn the string into an HTML anchor tag (<A NAME=).
big()	Changes the text in the string to a big font (<BIG>).
blink()	Changes the text in the string to a blinking font (<BLINK>).
bold()	Changes the text in the string to a bold font (<B>).
charAt()	Finds the character in the string at a specified position.
fixed()	Changes the text in the string to a fixed-pitch font (<TT>).
fontcolor()	Changes the text in the string to a color (<FONT COLOR=>).
fontsize()	Changes the text in the string to a specified size (<FONTSIZE=>).
indexOf()	Used to search the string for a particular character, and returns the index position of that character.
italics()	Changes the text in the string to italics (<I>).
lastIndexOf()	Like indexOf, but searches backward to find the last occurrence of the character.
link()	Used to turn the string into an HTML link tag (<A HREF=).
small()	Changes the text in the string to a small font (<SMALL>).
strike()	Changes the text in the string to a strikethrough font (<STRIKE>).
sub()	Changes the text in the string to a subscript font (<SUB>).
substring()	Returns a portion of the string between specified positions within the string.
sup()	Changes the text in the string to a superscript font (<SUP>).
toLowerCase()	Changes the text in the string to lowercase.
toUpperCase()	Changes the text in the string to uppercase.

SUBMIT

A property of a form object. A submit button in the form (<INPUT TYPE="SUBMIT">).

PROPERTIES

name	The name (the NAME= attribute) of the object.
value	The VALUE= attribute.

METHODS

click	Simulates a mouse click on a button.

EVENT HANDLERS

onclick

TEXT

A property of a form object. A text field in the form (<INPUT TYPE="TEXT">).

PROPERTIES

defaultValue	The default value of the text object (the VALUE= attribute).
name	The name (the NAME= attribute) of the object.
value	The current value held by the field. Initially it's the same as the VALUE= attribute (defaultValue), but if a script modifies the value held by the field value will change.

METHODS

blur	Removes focus from the text box.
focus	Moves focus to the text box.
select	Selects the input area.

EVENT HANDLERS

onblur

onchange

onfocus

onselect

TEXTAREA

A property of a `form` object. A textarea field in the `form`
(`<TEXTAREA>`).

PROPERTIES

defaultValue	The default value of the textarea object (the VALUE= attribute).
name	The name (the NAME= attribute) of the object.
value	The current value held by the field. Initially it's the same as the VALUE= attribute (defaultValue), but if a script modifies the value held by the field value will change.

METHODS

blur	Removes focus from the textarea.
focus	Moves focus to the textarea.
select	Selects the input area.

EVENT HANDLERS

onblur

onchange

onfocus

onselect

WINDOW

This is not a property of another object; it is the top-level object. The browser window.

PROPERTIES

defaultStatus	The default status bar message.
document	The currently displayed document. (This property is also an object in its own right.)
frame	A frame (<FRAME>) within a window. (This property is also an object in its own right.)
frames array	An array listing the window's frame objects in the order in which they appear in the document. (This property is also an object in its own right.)
history	The window's history list. (This property is also an object in its own right.)
length	The number of frames in the window.
location	The full (absolute) URL of the document displayed by the window. (This property is also an object in its own right.)
	Don't confuse this with document.location, which is the URL of the currently displayed document. You can change window.location (replacing the current document with another), but you can't change the document.location (as that's the location of the document currently displayed).
name	The name assigned to the window when opened.
opener	Refers to the window in which a script used window.open to open the current window. This is a new property, introduced with Netscape Navigator 3.0 beta 3).
parent	A synonym for the window containing the current frame. A property of the frame and window objects.

self	A synonym for the current window or frame.
status	A message in the status bar.
top	A synonym for the top-most browser window containing the current frame.
window	A synonym for the current window or frame. The same as self.

METHODS

alert()	Opens an Alert message box.
clearTimeout()	Used to stop the setTimeout method from working.
close()	Closes the window.
confirm()	Opens a Confirm message box; the user has two choices, OK and Cancel—the method returns true if the user clicks on OK, false if on Cancel.
blur()	Moves the focus away from the specified window. (This is a new method, introduced in the Netscape Navigator 3.0 beta 3.)
focus()	Brings the specified window to the foreground. (Another new method.)
open()	Opens a new window.
prompt()	Opens a Prompt dialog box; the user can type into this box and the typed text is returned to the script.
setTimeout()	Waits a specified number of milliseconds, then runs the instructions.

EVENT HANDLERS

onload

onunload

Appendix C

JavaScript Properties

Properties are related to objects. Many properties work with multiple objects. This Appendix is a quick summary of the different properties available. It's a good idea to read through this list simply to get an idea of what's available to you.

The list tells you which object or objects may use each property. (See Appendix B, "The JavaScript Objects & Arrays" for more information about each object and its related properties, methods, and event handlers.) Remember, many properties are objects in their own right; they have their own properties. We've indicated which properties are also objects.

A quick word about what you'll find when you go looking for more information. The Netscape JavaScript Authoring Guide (see Appendix H, "Finding More Information," for the source of this documentation) has a properties table, but it doesn't list all the items that we have treated as properties. Remember that there are objects that are descendants of another object, yet which function independently of that object. As we discussed in Chapter 10, "Objects, Properties & Methods," for simplicity's sake we have chosen to treat all descendants of an object as properties. So while, for instance, it could be argued that an anchor object is not, strictly speaking, a property of the document object, it *is* a descendant of the document object. The distinction between a property of an object and an object that is a descendant of another object yet not a property of that object is not particularly important, so we regard the anchor as a property of the document object.

Of course a number of objects are not properties; Date, Math, Array, navigator, and string objects are "built-in" objects—objects that are available from anywhere because they are not related to other objects.

action	A string that contains the destination URL for a form submission. A property of the form object.
alinkColor	The color of an active link (ALINK). A property of the document object.
anchor	An HTML anchor, created using the <A NAME=> tag. A property of the document object. (This property is also an object in its own right.)
anchors array	An array which lists the document anchor objects (<A NAME=>). A property of the document object.
appCodeName	The browser's code name (*Mozilla*, for instance). A property of the navigator object.
appName	The browser's name. A property of the navigator object.
appVersion	The browser's version number. A property of the navigator object.
bgColor	The document's background color (BGCOLOR). A property of the document object.
border	The <IMG> tag's BORDER attribute. A property of the image object. This is a new property, introduced with Netscape Navigator 3.0 beta 3).
button	A button in a form, created using the <INPUT TYPE="BUTTON"> tag. A property of the form object. (This property is also an object in its own right.)
checkbox	A checkbox, created using the <INPUT TYPE="CHECKBOX"> tag. A property of the form object. (This property is also an object in its own right.)
checked	The state of a check box or option button (radio button). A property of the checkbox object and the radio object.

complete	A boolean value which indicates whether the browser has completely loaded an image. A property of the image object. This is a new property, introduced with (Navigator 3.0 beta 3).
cookie	A piece of information stored in the cookie.txt file. A property of the document object.
defaultChecked	The default state of a check box or option button (radio button). A property of the checkbox object and the radio object.
defaultSelected	The default selection in a selection list (<SELECT>). A property of the select object.
defaultStatus	The default status-bar message. A property of the window object.
defaultValue	The default value of a password, text, or textarea object (the VALUE= attribute). A property of the hidden, password, text, and textarea objects.
document	The currently displayed document. A property of the window and frame objects. (This property is also an object in its own right.)
E	Euler's constant and the base of natural logarithms (approximately 2.718). A property of the Math object.
elements array	An array that lists form elements in the order in which they appear in the form. A property of the form object.
encoding	The MIME encoding of the form. A property of the form object.
fgColor	The document's text color (the TEXT attribute in the <BODY> tag). A property of the document object.
form	A form (<FORM>) in a document. A property of the document object. (This property is also an object in its own right.)
forms array	An array that lists the form objects in the order in which they appear in the document. A property of the document object.
frame	A frame (<FRAME>) within a window. A property of the window object. (This property is also an object in its own right.)

frames array	An array that lists the window's frame objects in the order in which they appear in the document. A property of the window object.
hash	A string beginning with a hash mark (#) that specifies an anchor within the URL. A property of the location and link objects.
height	The HEIGHT attribute of an <IMG> tag. A property of the image object. This is a new operator, introduced with Netscape Navigator 3.0 beta 3).
hidden	A hidden (<INPUT TYPE="HIDDEN">) element in a form. A property of the form object. (This property is also an object in its own right.)
history	The window's history list. A property of the window object. (This property is also an object in its own right.)
host	The hostname part of the URL that, includes a colon and the port number. A property of the location and link objects.
hostname	The same as the host property, except that the colon and port number are not included. A property of the location and link objects.
href	The entire URL. A property of the location and link objects.
hspace	The HSPACE attribute of the <IMG> tag. A property of the image object. This is a new property, introduced with Netscape Navigator 3.0 beta 3).
image	An image embedded with the <IMG> tag. A property of the document object. (This property is also an object in its own right.) This is a new property, introduced with Netscape Navigator 3.0 beta 3).
images array	An array that lists the embedded image objects. A property of the document object.
index	The index position of an option in a selection list (<SELECT>). A property of the options array.
lastModified	The date the document was last changed. A property of the document object.

length	A number that is related to the object or array using the property, such as a number of elements in a form or the number of frames in a window. A property of the frame, history, radio, select, string, and window objects; and a property of the anchors, elements, forms, frames, links, options, and images arrays.
linkColor	The color of the document's links. The LINK attribute in the <BODY> tag (links to documents that the user has not yet viewed). A property of the document object.
link	An <A HREF=> tag in the document. A property of the document object. (This property is also an object in its own right.)
links array	An array of the link objects in a document, in the order in which they appear. A property of the document object.
LN2	The natural logarithm of 2 (approximately 0.693). A property of the Math object.
LN10	The natural logarithm of 10 (approximately 2.302). A property of the Math object.
location	The full (absolute) URL of the document displayed by the window. A property of the window object. (This property is also an object in its own right.)

Also, a property of the document object. The URL of the currently displayed document. Thus you can change window.location (replacing the current document with another), but you can't change the document.location (as that's the location of the document currently displayed). While window.location *is* also an object in its own right—document.location is *not*. |
LOG2E	The base 2 logarithm of e (approximately 1.442). A property of the Math object.
LOG10E	The base 10 logarithm of e (approximately 0.434). A property of the Math object.
lowsrc	The LOWSRC attribute of an <IMG> tag. A property of the image object. This is a new property, introduced with Netscape Navigator 3.0 beta 3).

method	How data input in a form is is sent to the server; the METHOD attribute in a <FORM> tag. A property of the form object.
name	The name (the NAME= attribute) of an object. A property of button, checkbox, frame, hidden, password, radio, reset, select, submit, text, and textarea objects, and the options array. For the window object, name is the name assigned to the window when opened.
opener	Refers to the window in which a script used window.open to open the current window. A property of the window object. This is a new property, introduced with Netscape Navigator 3.0 beta 3).
options array	An array of the options (<OPTION>) in a selection list (<SELECT>), in the order in which they appear. A property of the select object.
password	A password (<INPUT TYPE="PASSWORD") object in a form. A property of the form object. (This property is also an object in its own right.)
parent	A synonym for the window that contains the current frame. A property of the frame and window objects.
pathname	The directory path portion of a URL. A property of the link and location objects.
PI	The value of pi (approximately 3.14159). A property of the Math object.
port	The :port portion of a URL. A property of the link and location objects.
protocol	The URL type (http:, ftp:, gopher:, and so on). A property of the link and location objects.
radio	A radio button set (<INPUT TYPE="RADIO">) in a form. A property of the form object. (This property is also an object in its own right.)
referrer	The URL of the document that contains the link that the user clicked on to get to the current document. A property of the document object.

reset	A reset button (<INPUT TYPE="RESET">) in a form. A property of the form object. (This property is also an object in its own right.)
search	Part of the URL beginning with a ? that specifies search information. A property of the link and location objects.
select	A selection box (<SELECT>) in a form. A property of the form object. (This property is also an object in its own right.)
selected	A boolean value that indicates the selection state of an option <OPTION> in a selection list (<SELECT>). A property of the options array.
selectedIndex	The index (position) of the selected <OPTION> in a selection list (<SELECT>). A property of the select object and options array.
self	A synonym for the current window or frame. A property of the frame and window objects.
SQRT1_2	The square root of one-half (1 over the square root of 2, approximately 0.707). A property of the Math object.
SQRT2	The square root of two (approximately 1.414). A property of the Math object.
src	The SRC attribute of an of an <IMG> tag. A property of the image object. This is a new property, introduced with Netscape Navigator 3.0 beta 3).
status	A message in the status bar. A property of the window object.
submit	A submit button (<INPUT TYPE="SUBMIT">) in a form. A property of the form object. (This property is also an object in its own right.)
target	The name of the window that displays responses after a form has been submitted; or, the window that displays the content of the referenced document when the user clicks on a link (the TARGET attribute). A property of the form, link, and location objects.

text	The text after an <OPTION> tag in a selection list (<SELECT>). A property of the options array.
	Also, a text element in a form (<INPUT TYPE="TEXT">). A property of the form object. (This property is an object in its own right.)
textarea	A textarea element (<TEXTAREA>) in a form. A property of the form object. (This property is also an object in its own right.)
title	The document's title (<TITLE>). A property of the document object.
top	A synonym for the top-most browser window that contains the current frame. A property of the window object.
type	A form element's TYPE= attribute or tag name. A property of text, radio, checkbox, hidden, submit, reset, password, button, select, textarea, and image objects. This is a new property, introduced with Netscape Navigator 3.0 beta 3).
typeof	Returns a string that tells the type of its unevaluated operand. This is a new operator, introduced with Netscape Navigator 3.0 beta 3).
userAgent	The user-agent header text sent from the client to the server. A property of the navigator object.
value	The current value held by the related object. Initially it's the same as the VALUE= attribute (defaultValue), but if the user or a script modifies the value held by the object then value will change. A property of the button, checkbox, hidden, password, radio, reset, submit, text, and textarea objects and the options array.
vlinkColor	The text color of links pointing to documents that the user has viewed. The VLINK attribute of the <BODY> tag. A property of the document object.

vspace	The VSPACE attribute of an <IMG> tag. A property of the image object. This is a new property, introduced with Netscape Navigator 3.0 beta 3).
width	The WIDTH attribute of an <IMG> tag. A property of the image object. This is a new property, introduced with Netscape Navigator 3.0 beta 3).
window	A synonym for the current window or frame. The same as self.

Appendix D

The JavaScript Event Handlers

This appendix provides a summary of the event handlers that are available for use in JavaScript. Events are actions a user may take, such as clicking on a button or link, opening or closing a document, and moving focus to and from form elements. The event handlers are placed within HTML tags.

onabort—The JavaScript is executed if the user stops an image from loading (by clicking on the Stop button or loading another document, for instance). This works with the <IMG> tag, but it's a new event handler, introduced with Netscape Navigator 3.0 beta 3.

onblur—The JavaScript is executed when a particular form component loses focus, that is, when the component was selected (the cursor inside it, for instance) and the user moves focus to another component by clicking elsewhere or pressing Tab. The onblur event handler works with the selection list (<SELECT>), multi-line text-input (<TEXTAREA>), and text input (<INPUT TYPE="TEXT">) components.

onchange—The same as the onblur, with the exception that something must have been changed in the form components for the JavaScript to be run.

onclick—The JavaScript is executed when the user clicks on a button (`<INPUT TYPE="BUTTON">`), checkbox (`<INPUT TYPE="CHECKBOX">`), option (radio) button (`<INPUT TYPE="RADIO">`), a link (`<A HREF=>`), or a Reset (`<INPUT TYPE="RESET">`) or Submit (`<INPUT TYPE="SUBMIT">`) button.

onerror—The JavaScript is executed if an image could not be loaded. This event handler works with the `<IMG>` tag, but note that it's a new event handler, introduced with the Netscape Navigator 3.0 beta 3.

onfocus—Similar to the onblur, except that the focus is moving *to* the component, not away.

onload—The JavaScript is run when the page is loaded into the browser (specifically, once the browser has finished loading the page and any frames), or when an image is loaded into a document. Used within the `<BODY>`, `<FRAMESET>`, and `<IMG>` HTML tags. This event handler was added to the `<IMG>` tag with Netscape Navigator 3.0 beta 3.

onmouseover—The JavaScript executes when the user simply points at a link (`<A HREF=>`) with the mouse pointer.

onselect—The JavaScript is executed when the user selects text in a text (`<INPUT TYPE="TEXT">`) or textarea (`<TEXTAREA>`) form component.

onsubmit—The JavaScript is executed when the user submits a form. It's placed in the `<FORM>` tag, but runs when the user clicks on a submit button (the `<INPUT TYPE="SUBMIT">` tag).

onunload—The JavaScript is run when the user does something to load another page into the browser—forcing unload of the current page. Used within the `<BODY>` and `<FRAMESET>` HTML tags.

Appendix E

Reserved Words

The following words cannot be used when you are naming variables, functions, methods, or objects. Also, avoid the names of built-in objects, functions, and methods, such as, date, getdate, math, and sqrt. See Appendices B and C for a more exhaustive list. While you can sometimes use such names, you may run into a conflict.

abstract	false
boolean	final
break	finally
byte	float
case	for
catch	function
char	goto
class	if
const	implements
continue	import
default	in
do	instanceof
double	int
else	interface
extends	long

native

new

null

package

private

protected

public

return

short

static

super

switch

synchronized

this

throw

throws

transient

true

try

var

void

while

with

Appendix F

Symbol Reference

It can be tricky for a newcomer to programming to keep all those little symbols straight. So here's a quick-reference table that will help you quickly identify the different symbols you'll run across while viewing JavaScripts.

Note: bitwise operations listed below are not described in this book.

+	Addition/concatenation operator; adds two numerical values together, joins two strings together.
*	Multiplication operator; multiplies two values together.
/	Division operator; divides one value by another.
%	Modulus operator; divides one value by another, then drops the digits to the right of the decimal place.
–	Subtraction operator; subtracts one value from another, or changes a value to a negative value (unary negation).
++	Increment operator; increments a value (adds one to it).
—	Decrement operator; decrements a value (subtracts one from it).
!	Boolean NOT; tells you what value the variable *doesn't* contain. X = !Y would mean that if Y is true, X is set to false, and if Y is false X is set to true.
&&	Boolean AND; "ands" two variables together. X=Y && Z, means that X is only true if Y *and* Z are both true.

||	Boolean OR. X=Y || Z, means that X is true if Y *or* Z (or both or them) are true.
^	Boolean Exclusive OR. X = Y ^ Z, means that X is set to true if Y *or* Z are true—but not if both Y *and* Z are true.
&=	Boolean AND assignment. X &= Y means that X is set to true only if X *and* Y are both true before the expression is evaluated.
^=	Boolean Exclusive OR assignment. X ^= Y means that X is set to true if X *or* Y are true—but not both true—before the expression has been evaluated.
|=	Boolean OR assignment. X |= Y, means that X is set to true if either X *or* Y are true before the expression has been evaluated.
=	Assignment operator; assigns values to variables.
+=	Addition assignment; adds the variables together, and modifies the variable on the left side.
-=	Subtraction assignment; subtracts the variable on the left from the one on the right, and modifies the variable on the left.
*=	Multiplication assignment; multiplies the variables together, then modifies the variable on the left.
/=	Division assignment; divides the variable on the left by the one on the right, then modifies the one on the left.
%=	Modulus assignment; divides the variable on the left by the one on the right, discards the digits to the right of the decimal place, and modifies the variable on the left.
<	Conditional operator. Less than.
<=	Conditional operator. Less than or equal to.
>	Conditional operator. Greater than.
>=	Conditional operator. Greater than or equal to.
==	Conditional operator. Equal to.
!=	Conditional operator. Not equal to.

?:	Shorthand if statement operator, or ternary operator (? is used in combination with :, as in variable = (condition) ? value1 : value2).
" "	Double-quotation marks—enclose string literals, and instructions in event handlers.
' '	Single-quotation marks—enclose string literals when the statement is already enclosed in double-quotation marks.
;	Separates individual statements within a function.
.	Divides up parts of object property or method name, e.g.: document.write
,	Separates parameters and features within feature list.
()	Enclose parameters (arguments) after function name, and set operator precedence.
[]	Encloses item position number in array.
{ }	Enclose blocks of script within statements, functions, and loops.
~	Bitwise complement.
<<=	Bitwise left shift assignment.
&	Bitwise operator, And.
<<	Bitwise operator, left shift.
|	Bitwise operator, Or.
>>	Bitwise operator, right shift.
^	Bitwise operator, Xor.
>>>	Bitwise operator, zero-fill right shift.
>>=	Bitwise right shift assignment.
>>>=	Bitwise zero fill right shift assignment.
<!— //—>	HTML comment tags, used in JavaScripts to hide scripts from non-JavaScript browsers; everything between the symbols is ignored by non-JavaScript browsers.

//	JavaScript comment line; everything to the right of the symbol is assumed to be a comment and ignored.
/* */	JavaScript comment block; everything between the asterisks is assumed to be a comment and ignored.

Appendix G

JavaScript Colors

Several properties and methods require that you specify a color. You can do this by either entering the hexadecimal representation of the color, or by entering the color names.

Colors are used by these properties: `alinkColor`, `bgColor`, `fgColor`, `linkColor`, and `vlinkColor`.

Colors are used by this method: `fontcolor`.

In Netscape Navigator 2.0, and perhaps in some other browsers, you can also use these color names in the HTML tags, such as `<BODY BGCOLOR="bisque">`, and `<FONT COLOR="colorname">Text</font>`.

Listed below are the colors you can use. We've also shown each color's red, green, and blue hexadecimal values. To see what these colors actually look like, see our Color page in the Online Companion, at http://www.netscapepress.com/support/javascript/colors.htm.

Color	Red	Green	Blue
aliceblue	F0	F8	FF
antiquewhite	FA	EB	D7
aqua	00	FF	FF
aquamarine	7F	FF	D4
azure	F0	FF	FF
beige	F5	F5	DC
bisque	FF	E4	C4
black	00	00	00
blanchedalmond	FF	EB	CD

blue	00	00	FF
blueviolet	8A	2B	E2
brown	A5	2A	2A
burlywood	DE	B8	87
cadetblue	5F	9E	A0
chartreuse	7F	FF	00
chocolate	D2	69	1E
coral	FF	7F	50
cornflowerblue	64	95	ED
cornsilk	FF	F8	DC
crimson	DC	14	3C
cyan	00	FF	FF
darkblue	00	00	8B
darkcyan	00	8B	8B
darkgoldenrod	B8	86	0B
darkgray	A9	A9	A9
darkgreen	00	64	00
darkkhaki	BD	B7	6B
darkmagenta	8B	00	8B
darkolivegreen	55	6B	2F
darkorange	FF	8C	00
darkorchid	99	32	CC
darkred	8B	00	00
darksalmon	E9	96	7A
darkseagreen	8F	BC	8F
darkslateblue	48	3D	8B
darkslategray	2F	4F	4F
darkturquoise	00	CE	D1
darkviolet	94	00	D3
deeppink	FF	14	93
deepskyblue	00	BF	FF
dimgray	69	69	69
dodgerblue	1E	90	FF
firebrick	B2	22	22
floralwhite	FF	FA	F0
forestgreen	22	8B	22
fuchsia	FF	00	FF
gainsboro	DC	DC	DC
ghostwhite	F8	F8	FF

gold	FF	D7	00
goldenrod	DA	A5	20
gray	80	80	80
green	00	80	00
greenyellow	AD	FF	2F
honeydew	F0	FF	F0
hotpink	FF	69	B4
indianred	CD	5C	5C
indigo	4B	00	82
ivory	FF	FF	F0
khaki	F0	E6	8C
lavender	E6	E6	FA
lavenderblush	FF	F0	F5
lawngreen	7C	FC	00
lemonchiffon	FF	FA	CD
lightblue	AD	D8	E6
lightcoral	F0	80	80
lightcyan	E0	FF	FF
lightgoldenrodyellow	FA	FA	D2
lightgreen	90	EE	90
lightgrey	D3	D3	D3
lightpink	FF	B6	C1
lightsalmon	FF	A0	7A
lightseagreen	20	B2	AA
lightskyblue	87	CE	FA
lightslategray	77	88	99
lightsteelblue	B0	C4	DE
lightyellow	FF	FF	E0
lime	00	FF	00
limegreen	32	CD	32
linen	FA	F0	E6
magenta	FF	00	FF
maroon	80	00	00
mediumaquamarine	66	CD	AA
mediumblue	00	00	CD
mediumorchid	BA	55	D3
mediumpurple	93	70	DB
mediumseagreen	3C	B3	71
mediumslateblue	7B	68	EE

mediumspringgreen	00	FA	9A
mediumturquoise	48	D1	CC
mediumvioletred	C7	15	85
midnightblue	19	19	70
mintcream	F5	FF	FA
mistyrose	FF	E4	E1
moccasin	FF	E4	B5
navajowhite	FF	DE	AD
navy	00	00	80
oldlace	FD	F5	E6
olive	80	80	00
olivedrab	6B	8E	23
orange	FF	A5	00
orangered	FF	45	00
orchid	DA	70	D6
palegoldenrod	EE	E8	AA
palegreen	98	FB	98
paleturquoise	AF	EE	EE
palevioletred	DB	70	93
papayawhip	FF	EF	D5
peachpuff	FF	DA	B9
peru	CD	85	3F
pink	FF	C0	CB
plum	DD	A0	DD
powderblue	B0	E0	E6
purple	80	00	80
red	FF	00	00
rosybrown	BC	8F	8F
royalblue	41	69	E1
saddlebrown	8B	45	13
salmon	FA	80	72
sandybrown	F4	A4	60
seagreen	2E	8B	57
seashell	FF	F5	EE
sienna	A0	52	2D
silver	C0	C0	C0
skyblue	87	CE	EB
slateblue	6A	5A	CD
slategray	70	80	90

snow	FF	FA	FA
springgreen	00	FF	7F
steelblue	46	82	B4
tan	D2	B4	8C
teal	00	80	80
thistle	D8	BF	D8
tomato	FF	63	47
turquoise	40	E0	D0
violet	EE	82	EE
wheat	F5	DE	B3
white	FF	FF	FF
whitesmoke	F5	F5	F5
yellow	FF	FF	00
yellowgreen	9A	CD	32

Appendix H

Finding More Information

This appendix lists a variety of sources of JavaScript information. Note that this information is also available in the Online Companion, which you can reach at http://www.netscapepress.com/ support/ javascript/.

You'll find a Web page containing this information, and a bookmark file that you can download and import into your own bookmark system.

NETSCAPE'S JAVASCRIPT AUTHORING GUIDE

You must get a copy of Netscape's JavaScript Authoring Guide. It contains a wealth of information, all the funky little details you really need to work with the various objects, properties, methods, and so on.

You can currently find the documentation covering the Netscape 2.0 version of JavaScript at
http://www.netscape.com/eng/mozilla/2.0/handbook/ javascript/ or
http://home.netscape.com/eng/mozilla/Gold/handbook/ javascript/

Here's the documentation for Netscape 3.0 JavaScript:
http://home.netscape.com/eng/mozilla/3.0/handbook/ javascript/

You can also download the documentation from Netscape to your hard disk, though it's not always up to date. There's currently a link at the bottom of the Contents frame in the 2.0 version documentation, or try http://home.netscape.com/eng/mozilla/Gold/handbook/javascript/jsdoc.zip. The documentation is currently in ZIP format.

You can also find the Netscape documentation in a variety of other formats, though not always completely up to date:

JavaScript Authoring Guide in WinHelp Format
http://www.jchelp.com/javahelp/javahelp.htm
The Netscape documents placed into a Windows Help file.

JavaScript Authoring Guide in Adobe Acrobat (PDF)
http://www.ipst.com/docs.htm
This site has the authoring guide in Adobe Acrobat (PDF) format.

OTHER DOCUMENTATION

Here are some other documents that may be useful:

Introduction to JavaScript by Stefan Koch (was known as "Voodoo")
http://rummelplatz.uni-mannheim.de/~skoch/js/script.htm
This Danish site contains good tutorials, plus background info and useful links. It's also mirrored at the following US and Australian sites, respectively.
http://www.webconn.com/java/javascript/intro/
http://www.pride-web.com.au/pride/java_script/script.htm

Persistent Client State HTTP Cookies Preliminary Specifications
http://www.netscape.com/newsref/std/cookie_spec.html
Background information about working with cookies.

The JavaScript FAQ
http://www.freqgrafx.com/411/jsfaq.html
Frequently asked questions about JavaScript. Useful information on JavaScript bugs, too.

Web Interactivity: JavaScript, CGI facilitate Dynamic Web Pages
http://www.ostrabo.uddevalla.se/dis/javascript/man874p.html
A brief explanation of the differences between client-based
JavaScript and server-based Common Gateway Interface (CGI).

 ## JavaScript Libraries

Here are a few JavaScript libraries from which you can borrow
scripts (see Chapter 19, "Ready-to-Use Scripts").

JavaScript 411
http://www.freqgrafx.com/411/

The JavaScript Library at the JavaScript Index
http://www.c2.org/~andreww/javascript/lib/

JavaScript: Simple Little Things To Add To Your Pages
http://tanega.com/java/java.html

JavaScript Sweden, JavaScript Source Codes
http://www.ostrabo.uddevalla.se/dis/javascript/source.html

The JavaScript Archive
http://planetx.bloomu.edu/~mpscho/jsarchive/

JavaScript Applets
http://www.oz.net/~alden/javascript/jsintro.html

Timothy's JavaScript Page
http://www.essex1.com/people/timothy/index.html
You may find more libraries listed at the **JavaScript Index**
http://www.c2.org/~andreww/javascript/collections.html

 ## Resource Sites

These are currently the best JavaScript link sites:

Gamelan JavaScript List:
http://www.gamelan.com/noframe/Gamelan.javascript.html
Lots of JavaScript stuff. Gamelan has a Java list, too.

The JavaScript Index:
http://www.c2.org/~andreww/javascript/
Links to many JavaScript samples and resources.

Yahoo's JavaScript Category:
http://www.yahoo.com/Computers_and_Internet/Languages/
JavaScript/
Not as much stuff as the last two sites, but pretty good nonetheless.
Here are other JavaScript sites worth checking on. Not so many
links, but often good examples, tutorials, and so on:

Netscape's JavaScript Introduction page:
http://www.netscape.com/comprod/products/navigator/ver-
sion_2.0/script/
An introductory promotional page for JavaScript, with links to the
authoring guide and resources page.

Netscape's JavaScript Resources page:
http://www.netscape.com/comprod/products/navigator/ver-
sion_2.0/script/script_info/
A small list of links to example JavaScripts and JavaScript resources.

Unofficial JavaScript Resource Center:
http://www.intercom.net/user/mecha/java.html
Useful samples, loads of links.

LiveSoftware's JavaScript Resource Center:
http://jrc.livesoftware.com/
JavaScript examples, two newsgroups, and a chat room.

JavaScript 411:
http://www.freqgrafx.com/411/
Very useful site. It has a snippets library (take bits of JavaScript
code for your Web pages), the JavaScript FAQ, and tutorials.

JavaScript Sweden Site:
http://www.ostrabo.uddevalla.se/dis/javascript/
Another very useful site. Contains tutorials, library, and documentation, including a mirror of documentation from Netscape
Communications.

TeamJava's Home Page:
http://www.teamjava.com/
Java and JavaScript consultants, plus lots of links to JavaScript
stuff.

Eric's JavaScript Page
http://www.pass.wayne.edu/~eric/javascript/
A small JavaScript links page.

DISCUSSION GROUPS

The JavaScript Mailing List
There is an unofficial repository of information in the form of a
mailing list for people interested in JavaScript. For more information about the list or to view old messages point your Web browser
to http://www.obscure.org/javascript/
To join send e-mail to **majordomo@obscure.org** with this in the
body of the message: **subscribe javascript**.
To get a digest—a single message each day containing all the list's
messages pasted together—send e-mail to
majordomo@obscure.org with the following in the body of the
message: **subscribe javascript-digest.**

Java Message Exchange
http://porthos.phoenixat.com/~warreng/WWWBoard/
wwwboard.html
A Web-based discussion group.

Internet Relay Chat
The #javascript channel on Internet Relay Chat is used for
JavaScript discussions.

Netscape's JavaScript Newsgroup
This newsgroup is on the secnews.netscape.com secure newserver.
However, it's currently a private group, only available to members
of the Development Partners program (see http://
developer.netscape.com/index.html for more information).
snews://secnews.netscape.com/netscape.devs-javascript

Netscape's LiveWire Newsgroup

Netscape also has a LiveWire newsgroup; again, only for the Developers. snews://secnews.netscape.com/netscape.devs-livewire

Java Message Exchange

A Web-based discussion group: http://porthos.phoenixat.com/~warreng/WWWBoard/wwwboard.html

comp.lang.javascript Newsgroup

This newsgroup is available at many local news servers.

LiveSoftware's JavaScript Newsgroups

JavaScript Development Group: news://news.livesoftware.com/livesoftware.javascript.developer
JavaScript Examples Group: news://news.livesoftware.com/livesoftware.javascript.examples
Go to the LiveSoftware news server (news.livesoftware.com) to participate in these newsgroups. In Netscape, for instance, just type the full URL—news://news.livesoftware.com/livesoftware.javascript.examples, for instance—into the Location box and press Enter to open the Newsgroup window, connect to the server, and open the newsgroup. For more information, go to the LiveSoftware site: http://jrc.livesoftware.com/

LiveSoftware's JavaScript Chat Room

http://jrc.livesoftware.com/chat.html

For more information about JavaScript chat, newsgroups, and mailing lists, see the JavaScript Index: http://www.c2.org/~andreww/javascript/.

Appendix I

The Scripts We Used

You'll find loads of sample scripts scattered through this book. Many of them can be taken and pasted into your HTML pages (some may require modifications to make them work with your data).

This appendix contains a list of the scripts we've used. Go to the chapter and find the script, read the text, and if it's what you want you can either quickly type it into your HTML document, or go to the Online Companion (http://www.netscapepress.com/support/javascript/) and copy the text from our documents. There's no need to copy the whole source document (though you can do that if you wish)—all you need to do is copy the script from the "face" of the document itself. (Go take a look, you'll see what we mean).

Script Purpose	Example	Page
Adding numbers	5.1	88
Adding numbers	5.8	92
Alert box, opens when user clicks on Submit button, onsubmit	12.9	257
Alert box, opens when user points at link, onmouseover	12.5	252
Alert box, opens when user selects text, onselect (may not work)	12.6	254
Alert message box, opening	3.1	51

Script Purpose	Example	Page
Conditionals, else clause	6.4	111
Conditionals, Greater Than (>)	6.7	114
Conditionals, Greater Than or Equal To (>=)	6.8	115
Conditionals, if statements without brackets	6.5	111
Conditionals, nesting if statements	6.9	116
Conditionals, Not Equal To (!=)	6.6	113
Conditionals, the ? operator	6.12	121
Conditionals, the if statement	6.1	106
Confirmation box, adding to link	14.18	312
Date object methods	11.2	226
Date object, creating instances	11.1	224
Date; document-modified, inserted into page	2.1, 3.1	29, 51
Dividing numbers	5.4	89
Document stream, closing	14.11	301
Document stream, opening	14.10	300
else clause	6.4	111
escape	7.14	157
eval	7.11	151
focus()	14.8	297
Focus, changing to a window	14.8	297
for loops	6.13	122
for loops, mimicking with nested ifs	6.14	125
Form validation, onsubmit	12.8	255
Form validation, using onblur	12.1	243
Form validation, using onchange	12.2	246
Form validation, using onfocus	12.3	248
Form validation: see also the Area Code Application	Chapter 18	359–388
Form validation; making sure it's not too long	16.7	343
Form validation; checking that it's a number	16.6	341

Index

Don't Miss Your Connection!

Are you sure you have the latest software?
Want to stay up-to-date but don't know how?

Ventana Online helps Net surfers link up to the latest Internet innovations and keep up with popular Internet tools.

- **Save money by ordering electronically** from our complete, annotated online library.

- **Explore Ventana's** *Online Companions*™—regularly updated "cybersupplements" to our books, offering hyperlinked listings and current versions of related free software, shareware and other resources.

- **Visit the hottest sites on the Web!** Ventana's "Nifty Site of the Week" features the newest, most interesting and most innovative online resources.

So check in often to Ventana Online. We're just a URL away!
http://www.vmedia.com

Explore the Internet

Internet Business 500

$29.95, 488 pages, illustrated, part #: 287-9

This authoritative list of the most useful, most valuable
online resources for business is also the most current list,
linked to a regularly updated *Online Companion* on the
Internet. The companion CD-ROM features a hypertext
version of the entire book, linked to updates on Ventana
Online.

Walking the World Wide Web, Second Edition

$39.95, 800 pages, illustrated, part #: 298-4

More than 30% new, this book now features 500 listings
and an extensive index of servers, expanded and
arranged by subject. This groundbreaking bestseller
includes a CD-ROM enhanced with Ventana's exclusive
PerpetuWAVE technology; updated online components that
make it the richest resource available for Web travelers;
Netscape Navigator; and a hypertext version of the book.

Quicken 5 on the Internet

$24.95, 472 pages, illustrated, part #: 448-0

Get your finances under control with *Quicken 5 on the
Internet*. Quicken 5 helps make banker's hours a thing of
the past—by incorporating Internet access and linking you
directly to institutions that see a future in 24-hour services.
Quicken 5 on the Internet provides complete guidelines to
Quicken to aid your offline mastery and help you take
advantage of online opportunities.

HTML Publishing on the Internet for Windows
HTML Publishing on the Internet for Macintosh

$49.95, 512 pages, illustrated
Windows part #: 229-1, Macintosh part #: 228-3

Successful publishing for the Internet requires an understanding of "nonlinear" presentation as well as specialized software. Both are here. Learn how HTML builds the hot links that let readers choose their own paths—and how to use effective design to drive your message for them. The enclosed CD-ROM includes Netscape Navigator, HoTMetaL LITE, graphic viewer, templates conversion software and more!

The Web Server Book

$49.95, 680 pages, illustrated, part #: 234-8

The cornerstone of Internet publishing is a set of UNIX tools, which transform a computer into a "server" that can be accessed by networked "clients." This step-by-step in-depth guide to the tools also features a look at key issues—including content development, services and security. The companion CD-ROM contains Linux™, Netscape Navigator™, ready-to-run server software and more.

The Windows NT Web Server Book

$49.95, 680 pages, illustrated, part #: 342-5

A complete toolkit for providing services on the Internet using the Windows NT operating system. This how-to guide includes adding the necessary World Wide Web server software, comparison of the major Windows NT server packages for the Web, becoming a global product provider and more! The CD-ROM features Alibaba™ Lite (a fully licensed Web server), support programs, scripts, forms, utilities and demos.

 Books marked with this logo include a free Internet *Online Companion*™, featuring archives of free utilities plus a software archive and links to other Internet resources.

Web Pages Enhanced

Shockwave!

$49.95, 400 pages, illustrated, part #: 441-3

Breathe new life into your Web pages with Macromedia Shockwave. Ventana's *Shockwave!* teaches you how to enliven and animate your Web sites with online movies. Beginning with step-by-step exercises and examples, and ending with in-depth excursions into the use of Shockwave Lingo extensions, *Shockwave!* is a must-buy for both novices and experienced Director developers. Plus, tap into current Macromedia resources on the Internet with Ventana's *Online Companion*. The companion CD-ROM includes the Shockwave player plug-in, sample Director movies and tutorials, and much more!

Java Programming for the Internet

$49.95, 800 pages, illustrated, part #: 355-7

Create dynamic, interactive Internet applications with Java Programming for the Internet. Expand the scope of your online development with this comprehensive, step-by-step guide to creating Java applets. Includes four real-world, start-to-finish tutorials. The CD-ROM has all the programs, samples and applets from the book, plus shareware. Continual updates on Ventana's *Online Companion* will keep this information on the cutting edge.

Exploring Moving Worlds

$24.99, 288 pages, illustrated, part #: 467-7

Moving Worlds—a newly accepted standard that uses Java and JavaScript for animating objects in three dimensions—is billed as the next-generation implementation of VRML. *Exploring Moving Worlds* includes an overview of the Moving Worlds standard, detailed specifications on design and architecture, and software examples to help advanced Web developers create live content, animation and full motion on the Web.

Macromedia Director 5 Power Toolkit

$49.95, 552 pages, illustrated, part #: 289-5

Macromedia Director 5 Power Toolkit views the industry's hottest multimedia authoring environment from the inside out. Features tools, tips and professional tricks for producing power-packed projects for CD-ROM and Internet distribution. Dozens of exercises detail the principles behind successful multimedia presentations and the steps to achieve professional results. The companion CD-ROM includes utilities, sample presentations, animations, scripts and files.

Internet Power Toolkit

$49.95, 800 pages, illustrated, part #: 329-8

Plunge deeper into cyberspace with *Internet Power Toolkit,* the advanced guide to Internet tools, techniques and possibilities. Channel its array of Internet utilities and advice into increased productivity and profitability on the Internet. The CD-ROM features a wide variety of tools and utilities, including Netscape plug-ins, e-mail, searching, file managment, multimedia, online monitoring and more.

The 10 Secrets for Web Success

$19.95, 384 pages, illustrated, part #: 370-0

Create a winning Web site—by discovering what the visionaries behind some of the hottest sites on the Web know instinctively. Meet the people behind Yahoo, IUMA, Word and more, and learn the 10 key principles that set their sites apart from the masses. Discover a whole new way of thinking that will inspire and enhance your own efforts as a Web publisher.

Books marked with this logo include a free Internet *Online Companion*™, featuring archives of free utilities plus a software archive and links to other Internet resources.

To order any Ventana title, complete this order form and mail or fax it to us, with payment, for quick shipment.

TITLE	PART #	QTY	PRICE	TOTAL

SHIPPING

For all standard orders, please ADD $4.50/first book, $1.35/each additional.
For software kit orders, ADD $6.50/first kit, $2.00/each additional.
For "two-day air," ADD $8.25/first book, $2.25/each additional.
For "two-day air" on the kits, ADD $10.50/first kit, $4.00/each additional.
For orders to Canada, ADD $6.50/book.
For orders sent C.O.D., ADD $4.50 to your shipping rate.
North Carolina residents must ADD 6% sales tax.
International orders require additional shipping charges.

SUBTOTAL = $ _____

SHIPPING = $ _____

TAX = $ _____

TOTAL = $ _____

Name _____

E-mail _____ Daytime phone _____

Company _____

Address (No PO Box) _____

City_____ State_____ Zip_____

Payment enclosed ___VISA ___MC ___ Acc't # _____ Exp. date _____

Signature _____ Exact name on card _____

Check your local bookstore or software retailer for these and other bestselling titles, or call toll free: **800/743-5369**